Political Analysis

Series Editors: B. Guy Peters, Jon Pierre and Gerry Stoker

Political science today is a dynamic discipline. Its substance, theory and methods have all changed radically in recent decades. It is much expanded in range and scope and in the variety of new perspectives – and new variants of old ones – that it encompasses. The sheer volume of work being published, and the increasing degree of its specialization, however, make it difficult for political scientists to maintain a clear grasp of the state of debate beyond their own particular subdisciplines.

The *Political Analysis* series is intended to provide a channel for different parts of the discipline to talk to one another and to new generations of students. Our aim is to publish books that provide introductions to, and exemplars of, the best work in various areas of the discipline. Written in an accessible style, they provide a 'launching-pad' for students and others seeking a clear grasp of the key methodological, theoretical and empirical issues, and the main areas of debate, in the complex and fragmented world of political science.

A particular priority is to facilitate intellectual exchange between academic communities in different parts of the world. Although frequently addressing the same intellectual issues, research agendas and literatures in North America, Europe and elsewhere have often tended to develop in relative isolation from one another. This series is designed to provide a framework for dialogue and debate which, rather than advocacy of one regional approach or another, is the key to progress.

The series reflects our view that the core values of political science should be coherent and logically constructed theory, matched by carefully constructed and exhaustive empirical investigation. The key challenge is to ensure quality and integrity in what is produced rather than to constrain diversity in methods and approaches. The series is intended as a showcase for the best of political science in all its variety, and demonstrates how nurturing that variety can further improve the discipline.

Political Analysis Series
Series Standing Order ISBN 978–0–333–78694–9 hardback
Series Standing Order ISBN 978–0–333–94506–3 paperback
(*outside North America only*)

You can receive future titles in this series as they are published by placing a standing order. Please contact your bookseller or, in the case of difficulty, write to us at the address below with your name and address, the title of the series and one of the ISBNs quoted above. Customer Services Department, Macmillan Distribution Ltd, Houndmills, Basingstoke, Hampshire, RG21 6XS, UK

Political
Analysis

Series Editors: B. Guy Peters, Jon Pierre and Gerry Stoker
Editorial Advisory Group: Frank R. Baumgartner, Donatella Della Porta, Scott
Fritzen, Robert E. Goodin, Colin Hay, Alan M. Jacobs, Eliza W.Y. Lee, Jonathon W.
Moses, Craig Parsons, Mitchell A. Seligson and Margit Tavits.

Rational Choice

2nd edition

Andrew Hindmoor

and

Brad Taylor

 macmillan education  palgrave

First edition 2006
Second edition 2015

Published by
PALGRAVE

Palgrave in the UK is an imprint of Macmillan Publishers Limited, registered in England, company number 785998, of 4 Crinan Street, London, N1 9XW.

Palgrave Macmillan in the US is a division of St Martin's Press LLC, 175 Fifth Avenue, New York, NY 10010.

Palgrave is a global imprint of the above companies and is represented throughout the world.

Palgrave® and Macmillan® are registered trademarks in the United States, the United Kingdom, Europe and other countries.

ISBN 978–1–137–42742–7 hardback
ISBN 978–1–137–42741–0 paperback

This book is printed on paper suitable for recycling and made from fully managed and sustained forest sources. Logging, pulping and manufacturing processes are expected to conform to the environmental regulations of the country of origin.

A catalogue record for this book is available from the British Library.

A catalog record for this book is available from the Library of Congress.

Typeset by MPS Limited, Chennai, India.

Printed in China

Contents

List of Boxes, Figures and Tables

Boxes

Figures

Tables

Preface

The first edition of this book was a solo effort by Hindmoor and published in 2006. This second and revised edition is published as an entirely joint effort. Each of the chapters has been updated to reflect the trajectories of recent debates and the contributions of individual scholars. Two new chapters have been included – the first on the theory of the state (Chapter 2) and the second on the economics of information and voter choice (Chapter 8).

The aim of the book remains the same. That aim is to provide a balanced and accessible introduction to rational choice theory. Balance is important here because, as we argue in Chapter 1, rational choice theory continues to polarize political science. Rational choice theorists tend to a view that their approach has revolutionized the study of politics as an academic discipline, whilst rational choice's many and varied opponents argue that it is all mouth and no trousers; that its success marks the triumph of dazzling technical style over explanatory substance. Rational choice theory, this argument runs, makes a series of implausible assumptions about the reasons why people behave in particular ways and so, unsurprisingly, finds itself offering deeply flawed explanations of why particular events occur. Although this argument about the explanatory value of rational choice theory can sometimes make for quite entertaining exchanges in the pages of otherwise rather dry academic journals, it makes the method a difficult one to come to grips with. It is for this reason that we have sought, above all, to write a balanced introductory text. It is probably fair to say that Brad Taylor is a more enthusiastic proponent of rational choice theory than Andrew Hindmoor. It is however also fair to say that the book is better for the collaboration between a sympathetic sceptic and a guarded believer in rational choice theory.

Accessibility is important because the proliferation of mathematical models and quantitative data analysis within rational choice theory deters many students from coming to grips with its underlying assumptions and arguments. This is a shame because no matter how much they are feared and loathed, mathematical modelling and quantitative data analyses are useful techniques which undergraduate programmes in political science ought to be teaching. It is also a shame because, as we try to show in what follows, rational choice theory's assumptions and arguments can be introduced and critically analysed without having to learn these techniques. There is no doubt a strong case to be made for a textbook which provides an introduction to mathematics, data analysis *and* rational choice theory. But this is not that book. Although it contains occasional tables and even the odd diagram, the book assumes no prior knowledge of or particular interest in either rational choice theory or counting.

The book is dedicated to Keith Dowding who is a professor at the Australian National University. Keith suggested that we write this revised edition together. More than that, Keith supervised both of our PhDs – Hindmoor's in the late 1990s at the London School of Economics and Taylor's more recently at the ANU. Keith taught us both a great deal of what we know about rational choice theory and political science. For his work as a generous and steadfast supervisor we both owe him a great deal.

Chapter 1

Introduction

Rational or, as it is sometimes known, public choice theory, is one of the most influential and controversial theories used to study politics. This book aims to provide an accessible account of the origins, assumptions and applications of rational choice theory and a balanced assessment of its strengths, limitations and policy recommendations.

Rational choice can most simply be defined as the application of the methods of economics to the study of politics (Mueller, 2003: 1). More precisely, rational choice theorists, like economists, construct analytical models which assume that individuals are both rational and self-interested. These two assumptions are often thought to constitute the 'hard core' of the rational choice method (Maki, 2002; Vanberg, 2008: 605), though we will see shortly that not all rational choice theorists agree.

In trying to understand the world around us and the people in it we usually proceed on the assumption that people have reasons for behaving in certain ways. When we see someone nodding their head when we are talking we think that they are doing so because they agree with what we are saying and want to show us that this is so. When we are driving and we see a person in the car ahead indicating we assume it is because they are about to turn a corner. Clearly this method is not fool-proof. When we see someone in a lake waving we might conclude that they are greeting us only to find out later that they were in trouble and asking for our assistance. But whilst experience may tell us to be careful about overestimating our ability to understand someone's actions, we nevertheless assume that people *do* have reasons for behaving in particular ways.

Philosophers use the term folk psychology to refer to the conceptual scheme by which we predict and explain people's actions on the basis of the beliefs and desires we attribute to them. Folk psychology assumes that people are rational in the sense that they have reasons to believe what they believe; reasons to act in the way that they act given their beliefs and desires, and that their beliefs and desires

1

actually cause them to act in this way through the creation of an intention (see Davidson, 1980). The 'received' (Satz and Ferejohn, 1994: 71) or even 'ubiquitous' (Lovett, 2006: 268) interpretation of rational choice theory is that it is a variant of folk psychology in which rationality is equated not simply with reason but with optimality (Elster, 1985, 1986). When rational choice theorists assume that people are rational they are not simply assuming that people have reasons to believe what they believe. They are assuming, firstly, that their desires are self-interested and, secondly, that their beliefs are the best possible beliefs they could have given the information available and that this is the reason why they believe what they believe. In a similar way, when rational choice theorists assume that people are rational they are not simply assuming that they have reasons to act in the ways that they act. They are assuming that their actions were the best possible actions they could have taken given their beliefs and desires.

Understood in this way, rational choice theorists employ an instrumental concept of rationality in which actions are judged as being rational to the extent that they constitute the best way of achieving some given self-interested goal. Rational choice theorists use the assumptions of self-interest and rationality to construct models of particular political processes or events. What is a model? People usually think of models as small objects which, in perfect scale, exactly represent some larger object. That is, they think of model aeroplanes and model cities. Models of this sort are 'isomorphic' in the sense of having a high degree of correspondence with the object of which they are a model. Rational choice models are *not* models of this sort. They are, instead, attempts to pick out the *essential* features of some situation. Models are, in this sense, idealizations which, although flawed representations of the world, can nevertheless help us understand something about that world (Cartwright, 1983; Dowding, forthcoming: ch. 2).

Models can be used to explain and predict outcomes by identifying the expected equilibrium which results from the interaction of the component parts of that model. Equilibrium is a stable outcome. Natural scientists conceive of equilibrium as arising when physical forces interact in such a way that a process is either endlessly repeated, as is the case with the movement of the planets around the sun, or comes to a rest, as is the case when a cup of tea eventually cools to room temperature. Economists and rational choice theorists conceive of equilibrium as arising when individuals interact in such a way that no individual has any reason to change their actions. Assume the French government abolishes the legal requirement for drivers to drive on the right-hand side of the road and lets people choose on which side of the road to drive. Would this make any difference to people's actions? The simple answer is that it would probably not. Because once people have learnt to drive on the right and expect others to drive on the right then driving on the right is a stable equilibrium because it is in nobody's interests to unilaterally start driving on the left.

Rational choice models typically result in the claim either that some outcome is a unique equilibrium or, more frequently, that there are multiple equilibria. Rational choice theorists search for and rely upon the notion of equilibrium because the identification of some outcome as equilibrium provides them with an explanation of why that outcome might be expected to arise (Riker, 1990: 175).

The assumptions of self-interest and rationality allow rational choice theorists to construct simple models and identify equilibria which, once applied to actual political processes and events, can be used to generate explanations and predictions. Understood in this way, rational choice is an exercise in *positive* analysis – it attempts to tell us something about how the world *is*. This is not however the end of the story. Rational choice theorists, to paraphrase a line of Karl Marx's subsequently inscribed on his gravestone, are not only intent on interpreting the world but upon changing it. Rational choice theorists want to use their models of how the world works to make recommendations about how it can be made to work better. How is 'better' to be defined? Rational choice theorists, like economists, argue not only that individuals have preferences which they seek to satisfy but that the satisfaction of these preferences ought to be the criteria by which policies and institutions are judged. Rational choice theorists thereby reject a 'truth-judgement' conception of politics in which it is maintained that 'political and political-governmental institutions ... exist as a means through which the unique nature of the "good society" is discovered and/or revealed' (Buchanan, 1975: 15). What counts for rational choice theorists is what people want. The world is to be made better by giving more people more of what they want.

It is worth stating right at the outset that the rational choice method provokes strong passions among political scientists. Its proponents regard it as having developed 'insightful, rigorous, [and] parsimonious' explanations of political outcomes (Monroe, 1991: 2). William Riker (1990) goes so far as to suggest that it is political scientists' past reluctance to embrace rational choice theory which explains why their discipline has lagged so far behind the natural sciences. Rational choice theory's opponents argue that it has, at best, been used to restate what everyone already knows in a language few can understand and, at worst, that it has propagated entirely bogus explanations and legitimized disastrous policy choices.

Robert Grafstein (1992: 259) has likened the debate about rational choice theory to that on abortion rights. What he meant by this is that rational choice is a subject about which any 'self-respecting' social scientist ought to have an opinion. But as a means of characterizing the political science debate about rational choice, the analogy works in a further respect. For discussion about rational choice prompts passionate and sometimes intemperate exchanges exposing fundamental and apparently irreconcilable differences between participants. These include ontological differences concerning the degree to which individuals are compromised 'on high' by aggregate or structural factors; epistemological issues relating to the merits of an instrumentalist theory of knowledge (Box 1.2); methodological issues about formalism and deductive models; and political issues relating to the efficacy of markets and the merits of government intervention.

Some specific criticisms of rational choice theory include the following:

- People are not rational in the sense that they always select the best action to achieve a given goal. People are instead, and at most, boundedly rational (see Box 1.1).
- People do not always act in instrumentally rational ways. In their political activities they often act 'expressively' to demonstrate their commitments to particular projects or values or 'procedurally' to conform with particular norms, conventions and customs (pp. 210–13).
- People are not exclusively self-interested. They are driven both by 'sympathy' with the interests of other people and 'commitments' to particular goals and modes of behaviour that are routinely honoured in the absence of any direct attachments to the people so affected (Sen, 1977, 2002). Rationality is bound up with deliberation and it is through deliberation that people can and do acquire 'desire-independent' and selfless reasons for acting in certain ways (Searle, 2001: 13–14).
- In its focus upon individual agency rational choice ignores the institutional, cultural and social constraints which lead people to behave in predictable and not necessarily instrumentally rational ways. In

particular, rational choice theory ignores the impact of class, ideology and power upon individual action (see Hindess, 1988).

- Although appearing to affirm the importance of individual agency, rational choice theory actually denies the reality of that agency by assuming not only that actors are all rational but that they all reason in the same way. In doing so, rational choice denies the existence of both of freedom of will and individual creativity.

- People do not have a fixed interest in behaving in a particular way. Whether people will come to view a particular course of action as being in their self-interest depends upon how they see and understand the world. It is the 'ideas that actors hold about the context in which they find themselves rather than the context itself which informs the way in which actors behave' (Hay and Rosamond, 2002: 147).

- Rational choice theorists successfully demonstrate that particular actions can be explained as resulting from a particular configuration of interests and an assumption of rationality. This does not however mean that the individuals whose action is being explained *were* self-interested and rational. Rational choice devotes too much time to model-building and not enough time to looking at what people actually want and how they actually reason (Hampsher-Monk and Hindmoor, 2010).

- Through its assumption of self-interested behaviour, rational choice promotes private ownership, competition and incentives. In doing so, rational choice has become a self-fulfilling prophecy. By emphasizing the extent to which people act in self-interested ways it has simply legitimated such behaviour (Hay, 2007).

This is a long list of criticisms and we will spend time in the following chapters developing and discussing them further. This will not only allow us to see how these quite general criticisms play-out in relation to specific rational choice models and arguments but how rational choice theorists have responded to these criticisms and, in doing so, often adjusted their own methods. Before immersing ourselves in this detail we will use the rest of this chapter to provide a general historical sketch of the origins and development of rational choice theory. This historical diversion will provide insight into the methodological underpinnings of rational choice as an application of economic theory, and it also reveals the sustained, and often bitter, debates between critics and defenders of the rational choice approach.

Box 1.1 Bounded rationality

Economists and rational choice theorists tend to assume not simply that people are rational but that they are perfectly rational; that they make faultless calculations about the best means to achieve particular ends. Herbert Simon argues that people are '*intendedly* rational but only *limitedly* so'. People are 'boundedly rational agents [who] experience limits in formulating and solving complex problems and in processing (receiving, storing, retrieving, transmitting) information'. According to Simon (1983: 22) 'there is now a tremendous weight of evidence that this theory describes the way people, in fact, make decisions and solve problems'.

People are boundedly rational in three particular senses: (1) They are not comprehensive decision-makers. They tend to take decisions in isolation from each other without considering the full consequences any one decision might have on other choices they may subsequently face. (2) People do not consider the full range of possible choices. (3) People do not consider all the possible consequences of any one choice. They instead focus upon just a handful of the most prominent and apparently important aspects of any choice. This notion of bounded rationality is closely linked to and is manifested in what Simon (1957) calls 'satisficing' behaviour. Because people are not perfectly rational they do not and cannot attempt to 'maximize' their utility. They instead 'satisfice' in the sense that they take decisions that seem likely to achieve some basic level of utility.

Drawing on and developing the notion of bounded rationality, Amos Tversky and Daniel Kahneman (1974; see Kahneman, 2011 for a recent and accessible overview) identify a number of heuristics humans use in order to simplify complex choices. When asked a difficult question, boundedly rational decision-makers will often answer a *different* question which is a reasonable approximation of the question actually asked (Kahneman and Frederick, 2002). Although psychologists have described numerous heuristics which work in this way, there are two

→

Political economy to economics

Economics and politics are today taught as very different subjects in separate university departments. But theirs has been a relatively recent estrangement. Until the latter part of the nineteenth century, there was, in the place of the separate disciplines of economics and politics, a single subject of political economy generating such classic texts as Adam Smith's (1776) *Wealth of Nations*, David Ricardo's (1817) *Principles of Political Economy and Taxation*, James Mill's (1844) *Elements*

→

which are particularly prominent in the psychological literature and which are relevant to political decision-making: (1) *The availability heuristic*. People estimate the probability of an outcome based on how easy it is to imagine that outcome occurring. One implication of this view is that shocking events covered extensively by the news media will be judged as more likely than more mundane events. Cass Sunstein (2007) has argued that this distorts policy preferences over responses to terrorism and climate change. While climate change is potentially a more serious problem, it is much easier to imagine the problems caused by terrorism – since we have seen them in vivid detail on the news over and over. (2) *The affect heuristic*. People tend to judge a person or thing as having some specific desirable quality when they generally feel positively about it. This means that partisans will often unquestioningly accept positive information about the parties or candidates they support but subject conflicting information to careful scrutiny in an apparent attempt to reject it. This type of 'motivated scepticism' can help reinforce partisan divisions and explains why the same news provokes very different responses from those on different ends of the political spectrum (Lodge and Taber, 2013).

Now it might be argued that research of this sort generates an 'illusion engendered by the fact that these psychologists are trying to produce situations that provoke irrational responses – inducing pathology in a system by putting strain on it' (Dennett, 2002: 52). Experimental economists such as Nobel laureate Vernon Smith (2008) have shown that experimental subjects, despite a significant degree of initial irrationality, normally converge on rational strategies when they are motivated to do so and are given meaningful feedback on their performance. It may be that people normally behave rationally in the real world, but demonstrations in the lab of persistent and predictable irrational behaviour clearly do pose a challenge to standard conceptions of instrumental rationality and should make us hesitant to extend strong rationality assumptions to choices with weak incentives and little feedback. We return to this point in Chapter 8.

of Political Economy, John Stuart Mill's (1863) *Utilitarianism* and Karl Marx's (1867) *Capital.* To have suggested to such 'Classical' political economists that economic decision-making could be studied independently of political decision-making would have been to invite ridicule. The separation between economics and politics can be traced back to the 'marginalist' revolution triggered by the publication of Carl Menger's (1871) *Principles of Economics* and Leon Walras' (1874), *Elements of Political Economy* and the subsequent emergence of a 'neo-classical' school of economics characterized by the use of mathematics to express key arguments and a focus upon the static allocation of resources within markets.

The emergence of rational choice (1950–1970)

The academic discipline of political science first began to attract significant funding during the Second World War when governments funded large-scale research into recruitment, propaganda and decision-making (Almond, 1996). In the immediate postwar years, many of the pioneers in developing the theoretical foundations of the subject were 'behaviourists' who collected and analysed data about, for example, voting behaviour (Campbell *et al.*, 1954, 1960) and the outbreak of war (see Singer, 1963). Behaviourists, many of whom were initially based at the University of Michigan, hoped that by finding recurring patterns in this data they could both predict and explain changes in party support and outbreaks of war. Behaviourism, with its use of quantitative techniques and invocation of behavioural 'laws', certainly promised a more scientific approach to the study of politics. But behaviourism did not constitute an 'economic' approach to the study of politics. It relied upon induction rather than deduction and emphasized limits to rationality. Then, in the 1950s and 1960s, economists began to apply their tried, tested and apparently successful methods to a variety of topics outside the traditional purview of economics. Although this 'economic imperialism' has had a major impact on the academic study of sociology and law, nowhere has the transformational effect been as strong as in political science.

We base each of the chapters which follow around an exposition of one of these classic earlier works in rational choice theory. Chapter 2 which looks at the fundamental positive and normative question of why we organize our political life through states examines James Buchanan and Gordon Tullock's (1962) *The Calculus of Consent*. Chapter 3 which examines the logic of electoral competition takes as its starting-point Anthony Downs' (1957a) *An Economic Theory of Democracy*. Chapter 4 which discusses the process of coalition-building in multi-party democracies begins with William Riker's (1962) *The Theory of Political Coalitions*. Chapter 5 which looks at the more general but fundamental question of whether and how it is possible to aggregate individual preferences to generate a coherent social choice is centred upon Kenneth Arrow's (1951) *Social Choice and Individual Values*. Chapter 6 analyses the circumstances in which individuals will find it in their individual interests to jointly pursue shared collective interests and draws upon Mancur Olson's (1965) *The Logic of Collective Action*. Chapter 7 looks at the way in which organized interest groups engage in 'rent-seeking' and draws upon an early article by Gordon Tullock (1967) on the 'Welfare Costs of Tariffs, Monopolies and Theft'. Chapter 8 looks more closely at the information-gathering and the demands of acting rationally and returns, once again, to Downs' *An Economic Theory*.

Why do we lavish so much attention upon these texts? Rational choice theorists today largely take their method for granted and do not discuss the value or limitations of the assumptions they are making. This is perhaps inevitable but it does make it difficult for outsiders to understand how or why particular assumptions are being made. Precisely because they could not rely upon and cite an earlier body of work, the first practitioners had to proceed more carefully by delineating and defending the assumptions they were making. This is one reason why it is worth looking more closely at these classic texts. Furthermore, these classic texts have set the terms of subsequent debates by identifying key research puzzles and arguments.

The take-off to growth (1970–1994)

In 1965, and following the publication of their book the *Calculus of Consent*, James Buchanan and Gordon Tullock established the Public Choice Society. The following year Tullock edited the first volume of what was soon to become the 'house' journal of rational choice theory, *Public Choice*. Over the following decade, rational choice began to attract more adherents as its basic concepts and techniques were applied to an ever-growing number of subject areas. By the early 1990s, fully 40 per cent of the articles published in the world's most prestigious political science journal, the *American Political Science Review*, used rational choice theory (Green and Shapiro, 1994: 3). In addition to the topics covered in this book, rational choice theorists had also applied their methods, *inter alia*, to the study of dictatorship, Marxism, distributive justice, federalism, campaign contributions and the separation of powers. At this time it was routinely claimed that rational choice had 'fundamentally changed' the study of politics (Lalman *et al.*, 1993: 79). In a review article published to celebrate the twenty-fifth anniversary of *Public Choice*, one leading practitioner, Dennis Mueller (1993: 147), predicted not simply that rational choice would 'dominate political science in a generation or less' but that alternative approaches to the study of politics would eventually wither away and die.

It was during this period of growth that the political as well as methodological commitments of rational choice theory became apparent. One of the great achievements of postwar neo-classical economic theory had been the demonstration that, in conditions of perfect information and perfect competition, markets would clear, allowing profit-maximizing firms and utility-maximizing consumers to achieve a welfare-maximizing equilibrium (Arrow and Debreu, 1954). Perfect markets would generate perfect results, and at a time when America was fighting the early stages of the Cold War this was an obviously significant finding. Yet, as many economists soon recognized, one obvious implication of this is that imperfect markets may generate imperfect results and that market failures provide a *prima facie* justification for state intervention. Take, for example, the case of monopoly. For competition to be perfect there must be a large number of buyers and sellers who are individually unable to influence price. But in the real world many industries are controlled by a handful of firms who can exploit their monopoly position and increase their profits by raising their prices and reducing the quantity they supply to the detriment of consumers. In such conditions a number of welfare economists argued that the state can protect consumer's interests by intervening to either break-up the monopoly or regulate its prices. So whilst the development of neo-classical economics is often associated with and taken to have promoted the development of *laissez-faire* politics, it actually, and unexpectedly, provided a rationale for a more active, interfering government (Hindmoor, 2005a).

Rational choice theorists argued that whilst economists had shown how and why markets might be expected to fail, they had assumed rather than demonstrated the ability and willingness of the state to correct these failures. Economists had, in other words, made an entirely misleading comparison between imperfect markets and a perfect state and so had, unsurprisingly, found in favour of the latter. In actual fact, rational choice theorists argued, the state could be expected to fail for many of the same reasons as markets, rendering government intervention counter-productive. So, for example, William Niskanen (1971) argued that bureaucrats would exploit their monopoly position to inflate their own budget whilst Gordon Tullock (1967) argued that the state would use its monopoly control of economic policy to effectively 'sell' policy favours to firms and pressure groups, so compromising economic efficiency.

During the 1970s and 1980s, these arguments about state failure provided intellectual ammunition and a burgeoning policy agenda for neo-liberal politicians in Britain, America, Australia and New Zealand (see Dunleavy and O'Leary, 1987; King, 1987; Self, 1993; Stretton and Orchard, 1994; Hay, 2007). The influence of rational choice theorists at this time was usually exercised via free-market think-tanks like the Cato Institute in America and the Institute for Economic Affairs in Britain. Starting in the mid-1970s, these groups disseminated and, to an extent, popularized rational choice theory (Cockett, 1995). In other cases, rational choice theorists acquired more direct influence. William Niskanen chaired President Reagan's Council of Economic Advisors whilst Mancur Olson, who founded the Centre for Institutional Reform and the Informal Sector at the University of Maryland, advised the Soviet government on market reform and privatization. As Thomas Christiano (2004) suggests, there is a certain irony in attributing any policy influence to rational choice. If politicians and other actors really are rational and zealously self-interested, they can be expected to engage in rent-seeking and other forms of activity regardless of whether rational choice theorists predict they will do so. Yet there can be little doubt that theorists like Buchanan and Tullock found in rational choice a convenient tool with which to develop a theory of state failure.

This does not mean that rational choice theory is inherently right-wing (see Dowding and Hindmoor, 1997). Indeed, in pointing to the existence of the collective action problem, rational choice theory offers a powerful argument as to why markets might sometimes fail and why state intervention may sometimes be necessary (Barry, 1989) (see Chapter 6). Yet the association between the rise of rational choice theory and neo-liberalism is not entirely coincidental and, if nothing else, accounts for the depth of the hostility toward rational choice theory exhibited by many political scientists.

A difficult decade (1994–2004)

Although rational choice was dominating the pages of the *American Political Science Review* in the early 1990s, its position was, in other respects, a surprisingly precarious one. In America, the majority of political scientists remained, at best, ambivalent about its use. In continental Europe a Public Choice Society had been created in 1972 but largely attracted the interest of economists rather than political scientists. In Britain a detailed textbook survey of this new and apparently all-conquering method was not published until 1987 (McLean, 1987). Outside of a handful of politics departments, British practitioners struggled to acquire institutional footholds let alone strangleholds. If there was a rational choice revolution in political science in the 1970s and 1980s it would appear that it was a Bolshevik one led by an elite and unrepresentative vanguard of the international political science community.

Throughout the 1970s and 1980s, a steady stream of books and articles appeared attacking the scientific pretensions and the implausibility of the assumptions of rational choice theory. More informally, and in the safety of their own studies and seminar rooms, critics argued that rational choice had flourished not because it was better a theory, but because its practitioners had promoted their own interests by appointing each other to vacant lectureships. In Britain the head of one politics department was quoted in a national newspaper as saying of rational choice theorists that they are 'incapable of appointing other than their own: the more vulgar they are the more this is true' (Jacobsen, 2001).

Rational choice theorists initially dealt with criticisms about the plausibility of assuming rationality and self-interest by largely ignoring them. When they did choose to respond, they tended to adopt the instrumentalist defence of arguing that theories ought to be judged in terms of their predictive success rather than the realism of their assumptions (Box 1.2) and that critics had simply failed to take note of rational choice's many and varied empirical achievements in explaining and predicting political behaviour. Then, in 1994, two political scientists at Yale University, Donald Green and Ian Shapiro, published a book, *Pathologies of Rational Choice Theory*, which made it far harder for rational choice theorists to sustain this argument. On the basis of a lengthy review of existing research, they argued that the rational choice emperor had no empirical clothes:

> To date, a large proportion of the theoretical conjectures of rational choice theorists have not been tested empirically. Those tests that have been undertaken have either failed on their own terms or garnered theoretical support for propositions that, on reflection, can only be characterised as banal: they do little more than restate existing knowledge in rational choice terminology. (Green and Shapiro, 1994: 6)

More than this, Green and Shapiro argued that rational choice theory exhibited a number of methodological pathologies which brought into question the overall value of the approach. These included searching for confirming rather than falsifying evidence and *post hoc* theory development. Green and Shapiro did not object to the use of rational choice theory *per se*. What they objected to was rational choice's 'universalism'; to the misconceived attempt to 'construct a unified, deductively-based theory from which propositions about politics – or, indeed, all human behaviour – may be derived' (Green and Shapiro, 1994: 54). Such an approach had, they suggested, encouraged the development of a 'method-' rather than 'problem-driven' approach to the study of politics and to what Shapiro (2005) subsequently termed a 'flight from reality'.

One initial line of defence adopted by rational choice theorists in response to Green and Shapiro's broadside was attack. In a series of essays first published in 1995 and republished as *The Rational Choice Controversy* (Friedman, 2006), a number of practitioners argued that Green and Shapiro had fallen foul of their own methodological standards and unfairly sought-out areas of work such as the paradox of not voting (see pp. 196–9) where rational choice theory was already known to be empirically weak and ignored areas of work like legislative politics and agenda-setting where it was strong. At first, the argument ignited by Green and Shapiro remained a relatively low-key affair conducted in the pages of academic journals. In October 2000 this changed when an anonymous correspondent, Mr Perestroika, widely believed to be a graduate student in political science, circulated a 'flame-mail' denouncing the subservience of the American Political Studies Association (APSA) and its journal the *American Political Science Review* (APSR) to rational choice theory.

> Why are all the articles of APSA from the same methodology – statistics or game theory – with a 'symbolic' article in political theory … where is political history, international history, political sociology, interpretive methodology, constructivists, area studies, critical history, and last but not least post-modernism?

Mr Perestroika's e-mail hit a chord. By January 2001 a petition demanding reforms to APSA and greater methodological pluralism had been signed by around 200 American political scientists (Jacobsen, 2005). Following a series of newspaper articles on the subject, a

---

Box 1.2   Instrumentalism

Instrumentalism is the name given to the view that scientific theories about how the world is are not claims which should be assessed and judged as being literally true or false. Rather, instrumentalists argue, theories ought to be viewed as instruments, that is, as tools which we can use to understand the world (Rosenberg, 2000: 93–6). For this reason, they should be judged in terms of the rigour and accuracy of their *predictions* rather than the realism of their assumptions. Within the natural sciences, instrumentalism is a venerable methodological tradition. Within the social sciences, the instrumentalist position was not clearly articulated until the early 1950s. Milton Friedman's (1953) essay on 'The Methodology of Positive Economics' is, as Daniel Hausman (1992: 162) observes, 'by far the most influential methodological statement [within economics] of the century [and] the only essay on methodology that a large number, perhaps even a majority, of economists have ever read'. This is significant because Friedman actually articulates and defends a particularly extreme version of instrumentalism.

Friedman starts his essay by asserting that 'the only relevant test of the validity of a hypothesis is comparison of its predictions with experience' (1953: 8–9). Only when two theories have equally good predictive records is it appropriate to compare them in terms of other criteria such as 'simplicity' or 'fruitfulness'. Turning to the question of whether it is ever appropriate to judge a theory in terms of the 'realism' or accuracy of its assumptions, Friedman argues that it is not. Indeed at one point he seems to suggest that significant theories, by which he

→

---

notable perestroika-sympathizer, Theda Skocpol, was subsequently appointed APSA president.

Major combat operations are over? (2004–)

Where are we today? Rational choice has not swallowed political science whole. Dennis Mueller's prediction that it would soon do so now seems to serve only as a somewhat ironic reminder of how, *pace* Green and Shapiro, rational choice theorists sometimes struggle to make accurate predictions. But neither has rational choice disappeared. It may no longer have quite the aura of omnipotence it had acquired a few decades ago but rational choice still retains a large number of adherents and continues to shape the political science research agenda.

→

appears to mean those that generate non-obvious predictions, 'must be descriptively false in [their] assumptions' (ibid.: 14). In defending this view he relies upon the following example (ibid.: 19–20). Consider the position of a scientist trying to explain the density of leaves around a tree. Imagine he proceeds by assuming that the leaves are positioned as if they had deliberately sought to maximize the amount of sunlight they received, as if they knew the physical laws determining the amount of sunlight they would receive in various positions, and as if they were capable of instantly and effortlessly moving from one place to another. These assumptions can be used to construct a model capable of accurately predicting how the leaves will fall around the tree. Does it matter that the assumptions are false? Friedman argues that it does not. All that counts is prediction and so the fact that the leaves do not have the properties attributed to them is not 'vitally relevant' (ibid.: 20).

Beyond these headline quotes, Friedman's argument is actually a great deal more subtle. At one point he accepts that scientists are entitled to judge whether a theory is likely to make accurate predictions by assessing the realism of its assumptions prior to formal testing. Elsewhere, he accepts that theories which have more realistic assumptions are more likely to successfully predict a wider variety of phenomena. As far as we can see, the implication of these claims is that the realism of assumptions does matter in important ways. Yet such qualifications tend to get ignored. As he has been interpreted by several generations of economists, Friedman demonstrates that theories ought to be judged in terms of the accuracy of their predictions and not the realism of their assumptions, the assumption of rationality included.

A large number of the articles published in journals like the *American Political Science Review*, the *British Journal of Political Science* and the *American Journal of Political Science* continue to use rational choice theory.

Arguing about rational choice theory remains a 'cause celebre' within political science (Lovett, 2006: 237). The rapturous reception accorded to attempted demolitions of rational choice theory such as Gerry Mackie's (2003) *Democracy Defended*, Michael Taylor's (2006) *Rationality and the Ideology of Disconnection* and Stephen Marglin's (2008) *The Dismal Science: How Thinking Like an Economist Undermines Community* show that rational choice retains its youthful capacity to offend. Neither is this one-way traffic. Rational choice theorists remain more than ready to accuse their critics of failing to understand even the most basic issues in the philosophy of science

(Diermeier, 2006b: 59–60). Yet, at the same time, the intensity of the debate has waned in recent years (Hindmoor, 2010). Why is this?

One answer is that rational choice theorists have developed a number of new arguments in response to their critics – at least some of which imply a more modest and less imperialistic set of ambitions for the approach. One such defence is that of 'partial universalism' (Ferejohn and Satz, 1995). Green and Shapiro, it will be recalled, do not object to the use of rational choice theory and the assumptions of self-interest and rationality *per se*; only to the attempt to use rational choice theory to explain any and every political phenomenon. Confronted with an argument that people are not always self-interested and rational and that this is why rational choice models which assume that they often fail, it is therefore open to proponents to argue that rational choice models ought, in future, only to be applied to situations where the assumptions they make are tolerably accurate. A 'partial universalism' of this sort carries the qualified blessing of Green and Shapiro (2006: 267) who argue that rational choice models may prove effective in situations where the stakes are high and actors are self-conscious optimizers; preferences are well ordered and relatively fixed; actors are presented with a clear range of options and little occasion for strategic opportunity; strategic uncertainty is minimal; and actors have the opportunity to learn from feedback. Looking at the chapters ahead, it is therefore perhaps no surprise that so much rational choice work is now concentrated on the issue of what strategies political elites will adopt to acquire and survive in elected office (Chapters 3, 4 and 7): an area of political life in which it might be argued rational choice assumptions work well.

A second answer offered by its proponents is that rational choice should be judged not in terms of the realism of its assumptions or the extent of its empirical successes but as a heuristic 'aid to thought' (Lane, 2006: 124). One version of this argument can be traced back at least as far as Karl Popper's (1960) defence of the 'zero method' in the *Poverty of Historicism*. Popper argued that it made pragmatic sense to assume perfect rationality and self-interest in the social sciences in order to generate benchmark predictions which can subsequently be refined. On such a reading, rational choice theory serves as a cognitive short-cut; a way of coping with complexity whilst generating falsifiable predictions. Andrew Schotter (2006) similarly suggests that rational choice models can be 'very instructive' in so far as they can be used to inform subsequent research. Hindriks (2008) argues that models ought to be judged not in terms of the realism of their assumptions but their 'explanatory scope'. Rational choice models resting on implausible assumptions are valuable if they can be used to deduce original and interesting conclusions which subsequently encourage other researchers to investigate whether the same conclusions hold when these underlying assumptions are modified and presumably made more realistic. Game theorist Ariel Rubinstein (2012: 16) sees formal models as 'fables' designed to impart some generally useful lesson rather than describe, explain or predict any particular real-world situation. Since a model, like a story, 'hovers between fantasy and reality ... it can be free from irrelevant details and unnecessary diversions'. On this view, we learn from rational choice models in the same sense that we learn from literature: 'We will take the tale's message with us when we return from the world of fantasy to the real world, and apply it judiciously when we encounter situations similar to those portrayed in the tale.'

A third argument open to rational choice theorists is to argue that their approach has been unfairly caricatured (and unfairly defined in the opening part of this chapter) and that there is nothing which requires its practitioners to assume either self-interest or the kind of optimizing rationality outlined previously. Indeed, many rational choice theorists have considered altruistic, moral and spiteful motives while retaining the standard rational choice approach in other respects (for example, Brennan and Hamlin, 2000; Fehr and Fischbacher, 2002; Morgan et al., 2003; Quackenbush, 2004). Herne and Setala (2004) argue that rational choice is a 'research program' constituted by a shared set of epistemic and methodological norms rather than a 'hard core' of assumptions. Looking ahead to some of our later chapters, it should be noted that the assumption of self-interest does not feature heavily in models of coalition-building (Chapter 4) or discussions of preference aggregation (Chapter 5) and that recent work on the economics of information is premised upon relaxing the assumption of complete rationality and perfect information (Chapter 8). This argument about the status of the assumptions within rational choice theory finds methodological support in a much more general and long-standing argument that rational choice theory does not actually seek to provide a psychologically realistic explanation of why people act in certain ways and that criticism about the accuracy of its assumptions are therefore misplaced. On such a view rational choice theory operates with a revealed preference view of utility which absolves it from the need to make any claims about mental states. Choices reveal preferences and rather than thinking about people trying (and often failing) to maximize their utility, the utility function is simply a formal representation of those choices (see Box 1.3).

Box 1.3   The axiomatic approach to rationality

The choices people make can be said not only to reveal their preferences but to be constitutive of them. If a person must make a choice between A and B and chooses A, we can say that their 'revealed preference' was for A. If we look at a *series* of choices a person makes between different bundles of goods and services, their choices constitute their preference-ordering. Assume now that individuals' preference-orderings satisfy four conditions. (1) *Reflexivity*: this requires that any bundle is always as good as itself. (2) *Completeness*: imagine there are just three bundles of goods, A, B and C; a person's preference-ordering is complete if they either prefer one bundle to another (for example A > B) or are indifferent between them (for example A = B). (3) *Transitivity*: a person's preference-ordering is transitive if it is consistent; consistency requires that if a person prefers A to B and B to C that they also prefer A to C. (4) *Continuity*: this requires that, given any two goods in a bundle, it will always be possible to identify another bundle which that person is indifferent to by either fractionally increasing the amount of one good in the bundle or reducing the amount in another.

If and when someone's preference-ordering satisfies these conditions it can be represented by a utility function which assigns a number to each possible bundle of goods such that for any pair of bundles, A and B, when A is preferred to B, the utility associated with A is higher than that of B. In such cases it will be 'as if' the individual, in making their choices, judged different bundles according to the utility they generated and always chose that bundle which maximized their utility. Rational choice theorists using the axiomatic approach do not therefore have to 'peer' inside the minds of the people whose actions they are trying to account for in order to discern their beliefs and desires. Instead, they can follow economists in maintaining that the assumption of rationality is axiomatic in the sense of having 'only to be stated to be recognized as obvious' (Robbins, 1935: 78).

Critics routinely argue that people are not self-interested. Yet once it is assumed that people have reflexive, complete, transitive and continuous preference-orderings, their actions can be analysed and understood *without* having to make any assumptions about whether they are self-interested. Rational choice theorists need to assume that people will consistently choose one bundle of goods over another. They do *not*, however, need to make any assumptions about why people prefer one bundle of goods to another. The reason why people prefer one bundle of goods to another is, in a sense, entirely irrelevant to the practice of rational choice theory and so arguments about self-interest are entirely misplaced.

Yet if rational choice theory has changed and, in some respects, softened over the last decade or so in terms of the way in which it justifies itself, it might also be added that other branches of political science have hardened their approach and, in doing so, further narrowed the gap between rational choice and its critics. Rational choice theorists once argued that it was unfair to judge rational choice theory harshly in terms of the coarseness of its assumptions and the shortfalls in its empirical record when so few other parts of political science even formally stated their assumptions or tested their claims. In his response to Green and Shapiro, Ken Shepsle (2006), a senior professor at Harvard and leading practitioner, invoked what he called the 'first law of wing-walking' in defending rational choice: 'don't let go until you have something else to hold on to'. This argument no longer seems as plausible.

The last decade has seen the rise and rise of 'new institutional' approaches and, in particular, 'historical institutionalism'. Historical institutionalism tends to a view that agents are embedded within and their agency constrained by institutions; that agents' preferences are formed endogenously within institutions (rather than being exogenously fixed); and that embedded agents lack the cognitive resources to always identify the utility-maximizing strategy (Steinmo, 2008; Lowndes, 2010; Bell, 2011; Campbell, 2011). Bell (2002) argues that this approach is very different to that of rational choice theory. Yet unlike much of what passed for political science in the 1980s and 1990s, historical institutionalists are careful to state their assumptions about individual action and the limits of their approach and to test their arguments either quantitatively or through detailed case-studies. Indeed the more formal approach adopted by historical institutionalists has made possible attempts at 'border crossing' (Thelen, 1999).

In a study of the development of vocational training regimes in Germany, the UK, the US and Japan, Thelen (2004: 26) argues that the question, 'Why do institutions take the form they do?' is best answered using historical rather than rational choice institutionalism. Yet from this starting-point she nevertheless shows how the evolution of training regimes can be understood as the product of, amongst other things, self-interested bargaining between unions, employers and the state. Her general argument, that institutional reproduction and institutional change have to be closely studied together and are in some important ways quite closely linked, is presented as a challenge to existing rational choice *and* historical institutionalist literature. Similarly, Rothstein

(2005: 29) argues that the problem of explaining how some countries escape from 'social traps' in which efficient cooperation for common purposes can come about only if people trust that most other people will also choose to cooperate 'cannot be handled solely by either the rationalist or the culturalist approach'. Within his overall argument, an important role is played by the notion of a 'collective memory' which can be manipulated by strategic actors in order to enhance overall levels of trust but 'cannot be reduced to simple utility maximisation' (Rothstein, 2005: 26). Finally, Mayer (2014) draws upon Olson's work on collective action to show how political leaders can manipulate long-standing narratives and stories to construct collective identities and mobilize collective action.

Ken Shepsle, whose first law of wing-walking we have already invoked, described the position rational choice found itself in following Green and Shapiro's assault as amounting to a mid-life crisis. The analogy is an appealing one because the timing is right. If we date the origins of rational choice theory to the 1950s then it was approaching its fortieth birthday when *Pathologies of Rational Choice* was published. Stretching Shepsle's analogy, critics will want to argue that after promising so much, the limitations of rational choice theory were painfully exposed in the early 1990s and that despite incessant protestations to the contrary, there has been no subsequent recovery. But care must be taken here. It is perfectly possible to slide into middle age in the absence of any crisis. Proponents will want to argue that the *enfant terrible* of rational choice theory has grown older gracefully; that it has acquired a greater depth and lost some of the rough edges exposed by earlier critics and that it has settled down and shown that it can work productively with or at least alongside other parts of the political science world.

Chapter 2

James M. Buchanan and Constitutional Political Economy

Overview: The question of why we have a government has preoccupied moral and political philosophers for centuries. The standard liberal answer today is usually based on some version of social contract theory. Such theories are often based implicitly on rational choice theory, though occasionally the debt is much more explicit. In this chapter we consider the framework of constitutional analysis developed by economist James M. Buchanan, which draws on the classic Hobbesian argument for the state while allowing rational and self-interested individuals to bargain over which institutions are to govern society. The other rational choice theories and applications we examine in this book all presuppose the existence of a state and, with this, institutional rules about how political processes are managed. We start the book with Buchanan's work because it can tell us something about the reasons why states develop and the criteria by which we might judge them. Contractarian theories such as Buchanan's are fanciful when interpreted as history or political science, but plausible and enlightening when interpreted as normative political theory. In outlining the position developed in Buchanan's co-authored book *The Calculus of Consent* and in other work, we show how rational choice theory in general and game theory in particular can be used to make normative political arguments.

Setting the stage: the state as an escape from Hobbesian anarchy

Although James M. Buchanan (1919–2013) was an economist by training and profession, the questions motivating his body of work are deeply rooted in normative political theory – what justifies the existence of the state, and what sort of state ought we to have? Over an unusually long and productive career, Buchanan developed, refined and applied a distinctive approach to political theory he called 'constitutional political economy'. The central elements of this approach can be seen in his earliest work published in the late 1940s (Buchanan, 1949) and remained until his death in 2013 at the age of 93 (Buchanan and Yoon, 2014). In 1986 he was awarded the Nobel Prize in economics 'for his development of the contractual and constitutional bases for the theory of economic and political decision-making'.

Buchanan began his doctoral studies at the University of Chicago as a socialist. After six weeks of exposure to Frank Knight's (1885–1972) price theory class, however, Buchanan found himself 'converted into a zealous advocate of the market order' (Buchanan, 2013: 63) but retained a commitment to egalitarianism and held a lasting contempt for hierarchy and privilege. His early work developed a view of political institutions as the voluntarily chosen outcomes of collective choice and provided a normative justification for the extant institutions of American constitutionalism (Buchanan, 1954, 1959; Buchanan and Tullock, 1962). Beginning in the late 1960s, however, Buchanan lost faith in the effectiveness of government as it existed in the United States. He saw significant growth in government spending and regulation during this period as benefiting special interests at the expense of the citizens, and was also concerned with 'behavioural disorder' in civil society, to which government seemed incapable of responding. This prompted him to consider why political institutions might deviate from those which would be unanimously chosen and suggest means of reform (Brennan and Buchanan, 1980; Buchanan, 1975; Buchanan and Congleton, 1998; Buchanan and Wagner, 1977).

A useful analytic starting point in understanding the context and reference points for Buchanan's work is the picture of anarchy presented by Thomas Hobbes (1588–1679) in his book *Leviathan* (1651). Hobbes and Buchanan have a great deal in common: they share an interest in the normative question of political authority and an individualistic standard of evaluation. Furthermore, both were writing during a period of what they regarded as political and civil disorder. Hobbes believed that the bloodshed of the English Civil War arose from the unrealistic desires of reformers and sought to justify absolute monarchy whilst establishing a duty of obedience on the part of subjects. Unlike other monarchists of the time, however, Hobbes sought to establish his conclusion not from the divine right of kings or any other mystical notion, but from the mutual benefit and consent of free and equal human beings.

Hobbes asks us to imagine what life would be like in a world without government. Since individuals have conflicting desires and are roughly equal in their coercive abilities, Hobbes saw the state of nature as characterized by a 'warre of every man against every man'. Hobbes thought that even the strongest inhabitants of the state of nature would be in a poor position. No individual is so strong that they cannot be brought down via stealth or conspiracy. All individuals would constantly fear for their lives and the fruits of their labour. Those raising livestock or building a comfortable home would find themselves vulnerable to attack by their neighbours. With no reasonable chance of benefiting from their investments and living in state of constant fear, inhabitants in the state of nature would have no reason to engage in productive work and every reason to pre-emptively attack their fellows. Life in this condition would be 'solitary, poor, nasty, brutish and short'. The Hobbesian model of anarchy has been extremely influential in contemporary political science, not only being used as a cautionary tale in political philosophy, but also as a description of the situation in which sovereign states find themselves in an anarchical international system in which there is no sovereign power and in which each state must thereby confront an existential 'security dilemma' (see p. 144).

It is worth noting that Hobbes's pessimistic view of life in the state of nature is not, for the most part, driven by a cynical view of human nature. Hobbes's argument is primarily *structural* in the sense that results are driven by the institutional environment in which individuals find themselves rather than the motives of individual actors. Humans are for the most part selfish, but they are not inherently warlike or aggressive. However even those preferring peace are forced to enter the war of all against all, since taking a peaceful stance leaves one open to attack.

Needless to say, those in the state of nature would do whatever it took to escape the state of nature. In particular, they would be willing be give up their own liberty to kill and plunder in exchange for a similar commitment from others. Such an agreement is not however possible because it cannot be enforced. Each person will be tempted to break the agreement and fearful that others will succumb to this temptation. Lacking an effective means of punishment, those in the state of nature find themselves unable to make binding agreements. As Hobbes remarks: 'covenants, without the sword are but words and of no strength to secure a man at all.'

Hobbes was under no illusions that the sovereign would be benevolent – Leviathan is named for a biblical sea monster, and this is no accident. Leviathan will for the most part be selfish and is in no way obliged to respect any individual rights. When there is a conflict between the public interest and the preference of the sovereign, the latter will always prevail. Compared to life in the state of nature, however, those living under Leviathan's rule will be more secure and prosperous. While the interests of ruler and ruled are far from perfectly aligned, the sovereign may, for example, have reason to promote peace and industry in his realm as this will allow them to extract more resources in the form of taxation.

While Hobbes did not have access to the tools of modern rational choice theory, his argument can be interpreted in rational choice terms, and a number of political theorists have used game theory to model the situation faced by individuals in the state of nature (Gauthier, 1969; Hampton, 1986; Kavka, 1983). One popular way of modelling the problem is the widely used prisoner's dilemma game (Box 2.1). Interpreting Hobbesian anarchy as a prisoner's dilemma, we need to make a number of simplifying assumptions. All individuals in the state of nature seek their own survival and material well-being. To this end, they are able to choose between two broad strategies, which we can label as production and predation. Everyone would prefer a world in which they were the only predator: everybody else produces while they murder and steal at will. Everyone would prefer a world in which everybody produces to a world in which everybody predates. The worst option of all, though, is to produce while everybody else preys upon your efforts.

These assumptions are represented in Figure 2.1. This is a game between two players. The results can easily be generalized to larger groups, though the simple visual representation we use here cannot accommodate more than two players. It may be useful to think of the row player as everybody else in society (Hardin, 1982: 26), but it would not quite be accurate to reason game-theoretically in this way since 'everybody else in society' is not an individual actor.

Imagine that you are Alice (A) and your neighbour is Bob (B). How should you behave in the situation represented by this game? Suppose that Bob chooses to produce, leaving you to choose between cells (I) and (III). Production would produce a payoff of 3 (cell I) and predation a payoff of 4 (cell III). If Bob chooses production, your optimal choice is predation. If Bob chooses to predate (cell II or IV), you could produce

Figure 2.1   *Production, predation and the state of nature*

	B Production	Predation
A Production	I 3,3	II 0,4
A Predation	III 4,0	IV 1,1

and earn 0 (cell II) or predate and earn 1 (cell IV). Predation is also preferable here, and since predation produces a higher payoff for Alice regardless of Bob's behaviour, it is a dominant strategy. The payoffs here are symmetrical, and the same logic can be used to demonstrate that predation is a dominant strategy for Bob. The problem with the state of nature is that rational individual action produces an outcome which is worse for everyone. Everybody would be better off if an agreement could be reached that everybody produce rather than predate (so moving from cell IV to I), but each individual has the incentive to break any such agreement. This idea – that individual rationality can produce outcomes which hurt everybody – is common to all prisoner's dilemma games and we will return to it a number of times in this book.

The Hobbesian solution to this problem is to empower a sovereign capable of limiting individual liberty and punishing those who attack others. Life under Leviathan would be preferable to the war of all against all, but Hobbes thought it would still be fairly miserable. Leviathan is constrained by the effect of his actions on production and the threat of revolution, but this leaves very wide scope for exploitation (Mesquita and Smith, 2011; Olson, 1993). As long as life is marginally better than it would be under anarchy, people will continue to submit to the monarch.

Box 2.1   Game theory and the prisoner's dilemma

Game theory examines the way in which actors make choices when the outcomes following from that choice depend not only upon their own choice but the choice made by others. To see what is involved here consider the example of people choosing which side of the road to drive on. When motorists drive towards each other they each have a choice of driving on the left or right. The outcome associated with each choice will however depend upon what the other person does. If one drives on the left and the other on the right then they will pass each other without incident. If they both drive on either the left or the right they will crash. Game theory examines the choice of actions and resulting outcomes in such interdependent situations.

The term game theory stems from the fact that the games played by game theorists share this strategic quality with parlour games like chess, bridge, poker and monopoly. Game theory was initially developed during the Second World War and used to analyse and improve the tactics of fighter pilots. Given its first formal academic airing by John von Neumann and Oskar Morgenstern, game theory remained, for some time, an acquired taste. It was not until the 1950s that an introductory text was first published (Luce and Raiffa, 1957).

In order to model strategic situations, game theorists assume that there are two or more *players* (the individuals in the strategic situation) able to adopt various *strategies* (complete plans of what to do under various conditions) and earning *payoffs* (rewards which are defined in terms of utility) depending on their own strategies and those of other players. Given assumptions about the preferences and strategies of individuals, game theorists assume that each player uses whichever strategy can be expected to maximize payoffs and build models designed to predict real-world outcomes (Mesquita, 2009), or more modestly to provide insight into real-world strategic patterns (Rubinstein, 2012: ch. 2).

Although game theory can be applied to situations in which more than two people choose sequentially and are uncertain about the payoffs of other players, the easiest way to understand how game theory works is to assume two players who each know the strategies and payoffs available to the other (this knowledge is known in game theory as 'complete information') and choose simultaneously.

Perhaps the most well-known game developed by game theorists is the prisoner's dilemma. As it was originally formulated by Albert Tucker (Hargreaves Heap and Varoufakis, 1995: 146), the story behind this game runs as follows. Two hardened criminals, Jake and Keith, are suspected of having committed an armed robbery. They are arrested and placed in separate cells. The hard-bitten, cynical, stands-no-nonsense cop visits each in turn. He tells Jake that if he confesses to the robbery that he'll have a word with the judge and make sure that

→

→ he, Jake, serves no more than one year leaving Keith to serve the maximum four-year sentence. He also tells Jake that he'll put exactly the same deal to Keith and that if neither confess he has enough evidence to send them away for a two-year stretch and that if they both confess they'll each get three years. The cop then tells Jake he has ten minutes to decide what to do, throws his cigarette to the ground and leaves the cell. What should Jake do? He should reason as follows. No matter what Keith does he is better off confessing. If Keith confesses he will be better off confessing because he will get three years instead of four. If Keith does not confess he will be better off confessing because he will get one year instead of two. Jake realizes that Keith will be thinking in exactly the same way and that if they both confess that they'll each get three years and that *each* is therefore better off staying quiet. But this does not make any difference. To repeat, no matter what Keith does, Jake is better off confessing. This is the dilemma. So ten minutes later the cop returns and Jake and Keith both end up confessing and the cop, during the final scene, remarks to a colleague that it is just as well that there is no honour amongst thieves.

Keith

	Does not confess	Confess
Jake — Does Not confess	I 2.2	II 4,1
Jake — Confess	III 1,4	IV 3,3

Prisoner's dilemma

To place this same argument in a more formal setting, consider the matrix above. Each prisoner has the choice of whether or not to confess, and there are four possible outcomes: (I) neither Jake nor Keith confess, (II) Keith confesses and Jake does not confess, (III) Jake confesses and Keith does not confess, (IV) both confess. Each outcome corresponds to one of the four cells of the matrix. The first number in each of these four cells shows the payoff (measured in years) for the player on the left (Jake). The second number shows the payoff for the player on the top

→

→

(Keith). On the assumption that Jake is instrumentally rational and will want to minimize his sentence, he will rank the outcomes as follows:

Jake confesses and Keith does not > neither confess > both confess > Jake does not confess and Keith does.

Keith's preference rankings are symmetrical. He most prefers the outcome in which he confesses and Jake does not, and least prefers the outcome in which he does not confess and Jake does. What should Jake do? If Keith confesses he is better off confessing (three years is a shorter sentence than four years). If Keith does not confess he is still better off confessing (one year is a shorter sentence than two years). Because Keith is also better off confessing no matter what Jake does, confession is the 'dominant' strategy and the equilibrium outcome is 3,3 (cell IV) even though *each* would be better off if they did not confess (two years is a shorter sentence than three years). If the assumptions regarding preferences and the available strategies are correct (i.e. Jake and Keith each care only about their own prison time and there is no strategy available in which they can reach an enforceable agreement to remain silent) and the players are rational, game theory confidently predicts that both Jake and Keith will confess.

Exchange and the constitutional framework

Buchanan's work on constitutions is aimed at answering the same big questions Hobbes grappled with. As Buchanan (2013: 74) says of his own work:

> I am not, and have never been, an 'economist' in any narrowly defined meaning. My interests in understanding how the economic interaction process works has always been instrumental to the more inclusive purpose of understanding how we can learn to live one with another without engaging in Hobbesian war and without subjecting ourselves to the dictates of the state.

The purpose here is clearly normative, but Buchanan uses the tools of positive economics to make his argument. In a series of journal articles and books, Buchanan and various co-authors developed a subtle argument for liberal democracy and a unique framework for normatively evaluating political institutions using the tools of positive economics. While the day-to-day realities of politics involve a great deal of conflict, Buchanan saw politics as an essentially cooperative exercise at a deeper level. Agreement on concrete policies or actions is unlikely given differences of opinion and interest, but agreement on a set of durable rules structuring political interaction and fostering cooperation and compromise are in everybody's interest and can be agreed upon by all reasonable people. Rather than asking what government should do, Buchanan insists that we step back a level and ask how collective decisions should be made.

Buchanan sees politics as a complex form of exchange. Legitimate political action is a bargaining process through which individuals reach mutually beneficial agreements. The explicit normative assumption underlying this contractarian enterprise is individualism. Individuals are taken as the sole source of value and their interests are to be judged by their subjective preferences. But how can we compare different outcomes? The classic utilitarian answer to this question is that we can measure the utility individuals have in different situations and choose the one in which the total utility is highest. Buchanan rejects this idea as unscientific nonsense. Since we cannot objectively compare one person's well-being against another's (Box 5.1), we have no way of knowing whether a change which benefits some at the expense of others is a net improvement.

Yet Buchanan does want to use positive economic science for normative purposes. To do this, he uses the notion of Pareto efficiency (Box 2.2). If the change from one situation to another is preferred by at least one person and opposed by nobody, Buchanan takes it to be desirable in an objective sense. It should be emphasized, however, that the Pareto criterion as Buchanan understands it is a sufficient but not necessary condition of desirability. Economics can tell us that proposals favoured by some and opposed by none are desirable, but not whether proposals supported by some and opposed by others are, on balance, desirable. The economist as value-free scientist 'is simply silent on such matters' (Buchanan and Tullock, 1962: 92). Moves which are not Pareto improvements are *not objectively good*, but this does not make them *objectively not good*.

At a first glance, it might appear that the Pareto criterion is very restrictive since there will be very few policy changes which will make nobody worse off. Unanimous consent does not however require a perfect harmony of interests, since compromise through bargaining is possible. Suppose we have some policy which benefits a small number of firms in a particular industry and harms all consumers. We cannot evaluate the efficiency of removing such a policy on Pareto grounds. If political bargaining is possible and if the gains of the winners are

Box 2.2   Pareto superiority and Pareto optimality

If we cannot make interpersonal comparisons of utility can we say anything about the potential welfare attractiveness of different distributions? The Italian economist Vilfredo Pareto (1909) argues that we can. Suppose we compare two distributions and find that at least one person regards him- or herself as being better off in the second distribution and none regard themselves as being worse off. Without having to make any interpersonal comparison of utility, we can say that the second state is preferable, or Pareto-superior, to the first.

In the diagram below Alice's utility from the consumption of x is measured along the horizontal axis and Ben's on the vertical axis. The line M–M' shows the maximum possible utility levels each can achieve given a fixed supply of the good. M shows that point where Ben consumes all of the good and M' that point at which Alice consumes all of the good. (1) The move from A to B is Pareto-superior because Alice and Ben are both better off in B. (2) The move from A to C is also Pareto-superior because Alice is better off in C, and Ben no worse off. (3) The move from A to D is Pareto-inferior because both are worse off in D. (4) The move from A to E is Pareto-incomparable because Alice is better off, and Ben worse off. It may well be that total utility at E is higher than it is at A, but because we cannot make interpersonal comparisons of utility we cannot know whether this is the case. We simply cannot say anything about the relative attractiveness of A and B using the Pareto criterion. We can also identify a set of Pareto-optimal points running from M to M' from which it is not possible to make any Pareto-superior moves.

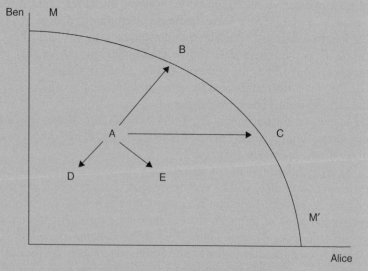

Pareto superiority and Pareto optimality

greater than the losses of the losers, it ought to be possible to negotiate a level of compensation such that everyone will be better off and unanimous consent can be achieved. If there are no transaction costs (Box 4.4), all welfare-enhancing political bargains will be struck and the Pareto criterion becomes a much stronger normative tool, allowing us to say not only that consent demonstrates desirability but also that a lack of consent demonstrates a lack of desirability. The assumption of zero transaction costs is, of course, an unrealistic one. Recognition that not all mutually beneficial bargains can be struck weakens the normative force of unanimity. Indeed whilst Buchanan retains unanimity as a conceptual starting point for efficiency analysis, decision-making costs play an important role in relaxing the strict requirement of unanimous consent, as we will see in our discussion of *The Calculus of Consent* below (Buchanan and Tullock, 1962: 90–91).

Choice within rules versus choice among rules

When interpreted in terms of day-to-day politics, the Pareto criterion may seem to be of only limited value. Buchanan accepts that conflict is an unavoidable part of politics but nevertheless suggests that unanimity is conceptually, if not practically, possible if we shift our focus from choices within a given set of rules to choice among alternative sets of rules. Constitutional rules – rules which structure the political system and thus determine how other rules are made – are durable and applicable to a broad range of concrete decisions, and Buchanan argues that people's interests are more closely aligned at this level.

There is a useful analogy to which Buchanan often returns. Suppose you sit down with a group of friends and deal a hand of cards with the intention of playing a friendly but competitive game of poker. If the cards are dealt before the rules are agreed upon, there will be little hope of agreement: those drawing a flush will be happy to play by conventional rules while others will want to make deuces wild or propose a new rule in which any hand containing the four of clubs automatically wins the pot. The luck of the draw has produced conflict between the players, and it is clear that impartial agreement on a set of rules is unlikely here. If rules are agreed upon before the cards are dealt, however, the interests of the players are for the most part aligned and it is much more likely that everyone will be able to agree on the rules.

Impartiality and agreement on rules are possible when individuals are uncertain whether any unfairness will be to their advantage or detriment. This is also the central premise of the hypothetical contractarian position imagined by John Rawls (1921–2002) in his classic work in political theory *A Theory of Justice*. Rawls (1971) asks his readers to consider what kind of a society a rational individual would choose if denied knowledge of their identity and, in particular, knowledge of the social and economic position they will be born into. This 'veil of ignorance' forces hypothetical contractors to consider everyone's interests. Ignorance forces impartiality. Buchanan's answer to the Rawlsian veil of ignorance is the veil of *uncertainty*. While individuals agreeing to constitutional rules retain knowledge of their place in society, the generality and durability of constitutional rules means that they will be uncertain of the effects such rules will have on them. A constitutional structure which enables the majority to have its way on all matters will be beneficial for an individual when they form part of the majority, but this will not generally be true of all issues and the shifting of political alliances over time may erode any predicted benefits.

Buchanan's constitutional contractors need not imagine themselves in some idealized original position; they simply need to step back from the perspective of everyday politics and consider instead the rules which define what individuals can do through political institutions. The veil of ignorance is for Rawls a useful analytic fiction, but the veil of uncertainty is for Buchanan a real force in the actual world. Recognizing that there are mutually beneficial bargains to be struck at the constitutional level, rational and self-interested individuals should be willing to step back and engage in constitutional bargaining. Since the veil of uncertainty goes some way towards aligning interests, unanimous consent on the choice among rules is much more likely than unanimous consent to any choice within rules.

Buchanan accepts the Hobbesian rationale for the state but rejects Hobbes's binary choice between anarchy and Leviathan by attributing to contractors a greater range of meaningful institutional options. Once reasonable individuals have agreed in principle to form a government, they will consider alternative rule systems which could govern the behaviour of government. Buchanan sees a broadly democratic system of equal decision-making power and equal treatment under the law as essential and rejects outright the Hobbesian idea of empowering a single sovereign.

The Calculus of Consent

Buchanan and Tullock's *The Calculus of Consent* is the book which first developed the constitutional framework outlined above, and it also applied this framework to the choice of voting rule. In rational choice terms, there are some reasons to think majority rule – the decision rule which allows 50%+1 of voters to have their way – is desirable. American mathematician Kenneth May (1915–1977) proved that simple majority rule is the only way to choose between two options which is decisive, responsive, impartial between individuals, and neutral between options (May, 1952). The decisiveness and responsiveness conditions here are straightforward and reasonable, requiring only that the rule always gives us an answer and that ties can be broken by a single individual changing their vote. The impartiality and neutrality conditions are stronger, but on the face of things they seem quite reasonable. Impartiality requires that all individuals are treated equally, with their say in the collective decision being determined solely by their ranking of the alternatives. If any two individuals were to 'switch' votes – I change my vote from X to Y and you change from Y to X – the decision will always remain unchanged. This implies that we do not distinguish between individuals on the basis of their personal characteristics, but also requires us to ignore the intensity of preferences. Neutrality means that both options are treated the same. If all voters were to switch their votes, the result would reverse. This means that we cannot privilege the status quo. May proves mathematically that the only voting system capable of satisfying all of these criteria is simple majority rule. If we think all of these criteria are essential features of democracy, majority rule is our only option (this type of argument is associated with social choice theory, which we discuss in Chapter 5).

Buchanan and Tullock, however, see nothing special about simple majority rule and ask what majority requirements rational people behind the veil of uncertainty would prefer. As May's theorem shows, this means that they must reject at least one of decisiveness, responsiveness, impartiality and neutrality. Buchanan and Tullock relax the neutrality condition by giving the status quo a privileged position and treating unanimity as a conceptual starting point. In a straightforward sense, a unanimity requirement for voting choices would ensure that nobody could be tyrannized by others. If we allow bargaining and compensation and assume away the existence of transaction costs, a constitutional rule requiring unanimity would be unambiguously desirable as it would protect everybody's interests. In the real world, of course, political bargaining is costly in time and effort and not all mutually beneficial political bargains will be made. There is thus a trade-off between the 'external costs' of inefficient political action and the 'decision costs' of missed political opportunities which is the central element of Buchanan and Tullock's model of the optimal majority.

Return yourself to the position of a single individual deciding on general and durable rules for collective action, and in particular, the level of support needed in order to agree to a proposed policy change. You are interested in protecting yourself from the tyranny of the majority, but you also want to be able to engage in collective action when required. Your former concern is over external costs. Collective action with less than perfect unanimity imposes costs on some unwilling parties. The level of external costs depends on various features of the particular collective action, and also on the proportion of the population required to agree for an action to be taken. The external cost function as used by Buchanan and Tullock is shown in Figure 2.2 (only the general shape is

Figure 2.2 *External costs*

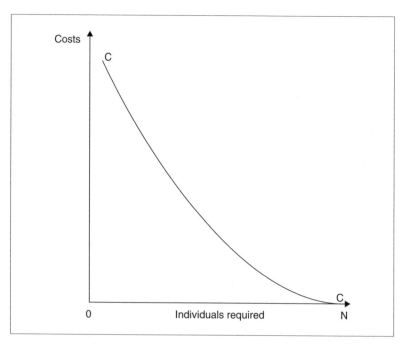

Source: Slightly adapted from Buchanan and Tullock, The Calculus of Consent (University of Michigan Press, 1962), p. 65.

relevant). The horizontal axis represents the number of individuals out of a population of N required to initiate collective action and the vertical axis the expected level of external costs entailed for each decision-making rule. At the very right of the graph at N is unanimity. Here there are no external costs of collective action, since each individual holds a veto right. As we move leftward by relaxing the unanimity requirement, external costs increase. At the extreme left-hand side of the horizontal axis, any individual could initiate government action unilaterally and external costs are very high. This is anarchy in the sense that there is no central control, but presumably worse than Hobbesian anarchy in the sense that the power of the state can be used in support of the slightest individual whim.

It is important to take note of not only the external cost function's slope, but also its curvature. It is concave, which means that as we move away from the extreme case of any individual being able to initiate collective action, external costs decrease at a decreasing rate. A simple move from allowing unilateral action to one requiring that two people agree would prevent the most egregious acts of predation. Requiring the agreement of three individuals would make things better still, but the marginal effect would be slightly less than it was for the move from one to two. Once we get close to unanimity, external costs will be so close to zero that the final move to a full unanimity requirement will barely be noticeable.

If our only goal were avoiding the external costs of collective action we would choose unanimity every time. We also want to use the government to advance our own ends, however, and this requires that we consider the decision cost function. The decision cost function includes the time and effort it takes for political agreements to be reached and the opportunity costs of collective actions not taken. Remember, we are considering such costs from an individual perspective so we need not think about which political bargains *should* be struck all things considered, only those policy changes which the individual *wants* to happen.

Like external costs, decision costs depend crucially on the threshold for collective action. With a unilateral action rule, there are no decision costs whatsoever: individuals can take whatever collective actions they damn well please. With a unanimity rule, decision costs will be extremely high, since any attempt to secure agreement will involve a great deal of bargaining and a good number of potentially desirable bargains would presumably be left unmade. The decision cost curve D is shown in Figure 2.3. Again, it is important to note the slope and the curvature. Decision costs increase as we raise the threshold for

Figure 2.3   *Decision costs*

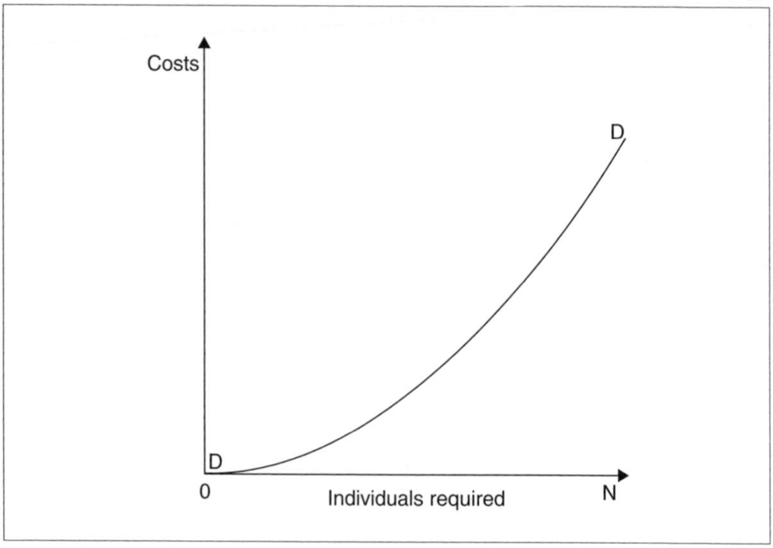

Source: Slightly adapted from Buchanan and Tullock, The Calculus of Consent (University of Michigan Press, 1962), p. 70.

collective action at an increasing rate. Convincing one other fool to support your plans for world domination would be trivial, but the second would be harder, and the third harder still. As we approach the unanimity requirement, the cost of convincing the last holdout will be extremely high. Buchanan and Tullock do not offer any mathematical proof as to why the external and decision cost curves will have the curvature shown in Figures 2.2 and 2.3; these are simply assumptions of their model which are common and intuitively plausible but also informal and as such, open to empirical or theoretical challenge.

An individual behind a veil of uncertainty asked to specify the appropriate threshold for collective action will need to weigh decision costs against external costs in order to minimize the sum of these two costs. We can consider this trade-off graphically by vertically summing the two cost curves into one curve. At any point along the horizontal axis, we simply add the height of the external cost curve and the decision cost curve, and this shows the total costs of collective action at any level of collective action. As we have drawn Figures 2.2 and 2.3, the resulting cost function would look something like that in Figure 2.4. At the extreme left we have only external costs and at the extreme right we have only decision costs. Since both functions are concave, we know that moving slightly from either extreme will result in a reduction in

Figure 2.4 *The optimal majority*

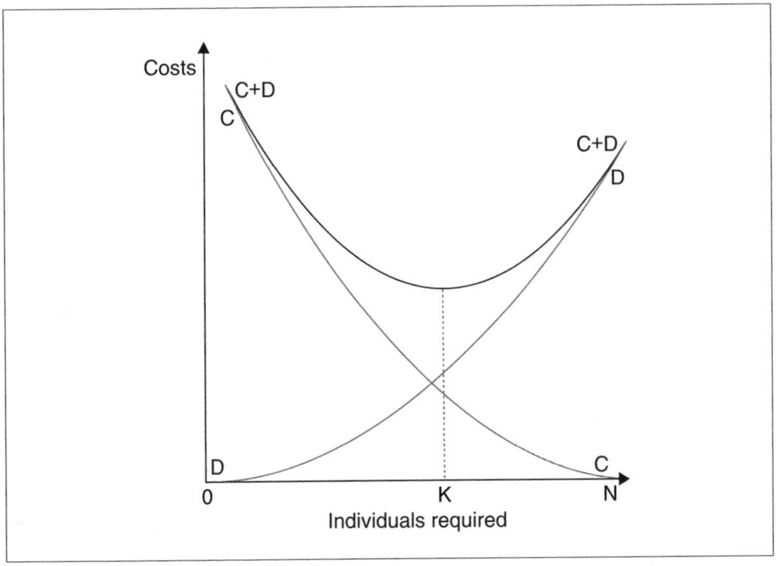

Source: Slightly adapted from Buchanan and Tullock, The Calculus of Consent (University of Michigan Press, 1962), p. 71.

total costs. Moving from a threshold of one to two people will increase decision costs, but it will decrease external costs by a much greater amount. As we increase the threshold further the gap will narrow until the effect on decision costs become greater. There will be some unique point, labelled K in Figure 2.4, where total costs are minimized. A rational constitutional contractor behind the veil of uncertainty would prefer this point, and thus for Buchanan and Tullock K/N is the optimal majority threshold in this case.

The precise value of K in relation to N is determined by the shape of the external and decision cost curves. If the external cost curve is relatively low and flat, the decision cost curve will tend to dominate the total cost curve and K would have a low value. Intuitively, this makes sense. If there are few external costs regardless of the collective action threshold, it is more acceptable to allow a small number of people to initiate collective action. If, on the other hand, external costs are very high relative to decision costs it will be preferable to set the threshold higher. A simple majority requirement is one possible outcome of this framework, but it enjoys no privileged position. For some types of decision we will want a strong supermajority requirement; for others we will want only a submajority requirement (i.e. a supermajority needs to be opposed to prevent policy change).

This depiction of the costs of decision-making rules, like Buchanan's constitutional project more broadly, should be seen as a framework for institutional design and evaluation rather than attempt to reach concrete policy conclusions. Nevertheless, it is not difficult to see how this abstract framework can be applied to real-world political issues. Most obviously, there will be certain spheres of life where external costs are likely to be extremely high relative to decision costs, and the model presented above suggests it would be wise to set majority requirements higher in such areas and perhaps isolate them from democratic choice altogether. This is the reasoning behind constitutional bills of rights which protect the freedom of expression and religion, among other things, from democratic abrogation: there are few, if any, legitimate reasons to restrict speech or religious practice and illegitimate restriction could cause a great deal of harm. It also suggests that the ability to change constitutional rules should be protected from majorities, since constitutional restrictions are only effective when entrenched (though it should be noted that such entrenchment might happen informally via convention) and modification of a well-designed constitution will have high external costs in a variety of areas. For constitutional rules to be robustly effective, the rules for changing rules need to be protected by something akin to a supermajority requirement, and this is indeed what we see in a variety of constitutions.

Returning to the contractarian-constitutional framework more broadly, Buchanan has made a number of suggestions for constitutional reform in the American context, including devolution of authority to the states (Brennan and Buchanan, 1980: 9; Buchanan, 1995b) and a balanced budget requirement (Buchanan, 1985, 1995a; Buchanan and Wagner, 1977). One particularly interesting proposal relates to the idea of generality. Buchanan's concern with majority rule is that it can allow the majority to exploit the minority by using the political system to unfairly redistribute resources to itself through discriminatory policy. In the American context, this can be seen in various regulations and tariffs which grant specific industries or firms advantage over others and in complex tax systems which favour some sections of society over others – married couples with children over the single and childless, for example. It might also be seen in the designation of certain banks above a certain size as being 'too big to fail' (Bell and Hindmoor, 2015, 188–9). In a co-authored book, Buchanan and Roger Congleton (1998) argue on constitutional grounds for 'nondiscriminatory democracy' which prevents such redistribution from one group to another. Generality in taxation would require a uniform system which did not distinguish between people based on features such as marital status, income level or income source. In practical terms, this would imply something like a proportional tax on all income or expenditure. Redistribution as a form of social insurance would remain possible under the generality restriction, but it would need to take the form of a uniform 'demogrant' available to all individuals, such as that embodied in the idea of a universal basic income (Van Parijs, 2004). When it comes to trade protection, tariffs would be permitted, but only if they treated all industries and products equally, meaning that current trade supports for corn farmers and the steel industry, for example, would not be allowed under a generality rule.

Covenants without the sword

Buchanan follows Hobbes in thinking about the state in terms of contract and considering centralized coercion as unavoidable if we want to avoid the chaos of the Hobbesian jungle. Various rational choice analyses building on and critiquing Buchanan's work have taken a different approach, seeing constitutions as self-enforcing codifications of spontaneously emerging customs or suggesting that cooperation is possible without government. Though we cannot offer a comprehensive review of such ideas, in this section we outline some important contributions.

As we saw above, Buchanan sees constitutions as a way of solving the prisoner's dilemma game of in-period politics. Russell Hardin (1989, 1999) offers an alternative view of constitutions as conventions. To understand his argument, we need to distinguish between the three broad classes of strategic situation studied by game theorists: pure conflict games, mixed-motive games and pure coordination games. If players have strictly opposing rankings of outcomes, the situation is one of pure conflict. In such zero-sum situations, one player's gain is necessarily another's loss and there is no scope for mutually beneficial agreement. If the players' rankings of the outcomes are perfectly aligned, on the other hand, we have a pure coordination game. There is no conflict here and the only challenge is in letting each player know what the others will do in order to ensure the best outcome. In between these two extremes are mixed-motive games such as the prisoner's dilemma. Here, players' rankings are neither perfectly aligned nor perfectly opposed. In such situations there may be conflict, but there are also possible mutually beneficial agreements which could be made (Box 6.2). Hardin views constitutional agreements in these terms. Citizens may disagree over the best constitutional rules, but their differences in opinion are much less serious than their shared desire that some constitutional rule be established.

An agreement to follow rule X or Y in this case is not a contract, but a convention. Contracts are designed to secure cooperation when there would otherwise be an individual incentive to defect; conventions are self-enforcing rules which set expectations. The quintessential example of a convention is the rule of driving on the left- or right-hand side of the road. Neither option is intrinsically any better than the other, but it is very important that one or the other is chosen by everyone. There are two important features of a convention as opposed to a contract. First, there will be only weak disagreement over the substance of a convention. Second, a convention, once established, provides its own incentives for obedience. Such conventions often arise spontaneously and are never explicitly codified, though such spontaneous norms are sometimes later codified in law (as the rule about driving on the left-hand side of the road was in England) or explicitly created by government fiat (as was Samoa's shift from driving on the right to driving on the left in 2009 in order to enable cheaper car imports). The rules of the road are not contracts in any meaningful sense, since they are effective without external enforcement.

If constitutions are conventions in Hardin's sense, their normative force derives not from the consent of the governed but from the fact that they are practically effective at coordinating social life. American political theorists do not spend any time worrying about whether the convention of driving on the right is justified or if individuals are obliged to drive on the right, and British political theorists are similarly inattentive to the justification for driving on the left. There may be minor conflicts of interest, but the very existence of a stable convention is a powerful normative argument in its favour and a very strong prudential reason for everyone in society to follow the convention. Political legitimacy is, for Hardin, just not an issue when it comes to conventions and Buchanan's normative focus on consent is ill placed.

Other rational choice theorists have rejected the idea – shared by Buchanan and Hobbes – that the state of nature is characterized by disorder and instead argued from a variety of perspectives that rational individuals in the state of nature have a variety of means at their disposal to avoid conflict without resorting to the state (for a review, see Powell and Stringham, 2009).

One influential early argument to this effect is made by Michael Taylor in his 1976 book *Anarchy and Cooperation* (revised and reissued as Taylor, 1987, which is the version we reference here). Though he considers a variety of game-theoretic models of anarchy which can produce cooperation, the most influential and interesting is his use of the *iterated* prisoner's dilemma. In the game-theoretic interpretation of Hobbes's argument for the state, the state of nature is modelled as a series of one-shot prisoner's dilemma games. Players are interested only in the payoffs they receive from this particular game, and the possibility that their actions in this game might affect others' behaviour towards them in the future is not considered. Taylor makes the obvious but important point that inhabitants of the state of nature will often be dealing with each other repeatedly. In addition to the isolated prisoner's dilemma game, players are engaged in a *supergame* of many prisoner's dilemma games, with behaviour in any particular subgame (individual round of play) affecting the behaviour of other players in future subgames.

Taylor (1987: 3) shows that even in a world of rational egoists, repeated interaction can produce cooperation in an iterated prisoner's dilemma. Assume that the state of nature consists of two people and that each distinct interaction they have with one another is characterized by a prisoner's dilemma, but they expect these interactions to repeat an indefinite number of times. Are there any incentives for cooperation? If we think of cooperation here as meaning unconditional cooperation – cooperating whatever the other player has done in the past – it remains irrational, since the other player will be able to defect with impunity. On the other hand, *conditional* cooperation will be a viable strategy in some cases. If we cooperate only on the condition that the other player has cooperated in the past, our partner will need to consider not only their payoff in this round of play but the effect their current choice has on their future prospects. If I know that you will cooperate in the future only if I cooperate now, this gives me some incentive to cooperate now in order to secure higher payoffs in the future, even though in the short term cooperation is dominated by defection.

It is important to note that Taylor does not show that anarchy *will* be peaceful and productive or that iterated prisoner's dilemmas will always elicit cooperation. Taylor's game theoretic analysis simply shows that orderly anarchy is a *possibility* under some conditions. For a two-player prisoner's dilemma, Taylor (1987: 66–9) shows that the determining factor in cooperation is the 'discount rate' of the players in relation to the payoffs of cooperation and defection. Revealed preference tells us that people generally prefer to have things sooner rather than later – $100 now is worth more to people than $100 in a year's time, even after controlling for inflation. The degree of impatience an individual demonstrates is known by economists as their inter-temporal discount rate or less formally their level of time preference. A high discount rate means that future payoffs are discounted by a large factor and thus have less sway over current decisions. In an iter-ated prisoner's dilemma, conditional cooperation requires that players find it in their interest to resist the temptation of higher payoffs in the current round (remember, defection is always the dominant strategy in each round considered in isolation) in order to secure long-term bene-fits. High discount rates are a barrier to cooperation.

When extending the analysis to more than two players and mod-elling the state of nature as an iterated N-person prisoner's dilemma, the situation becomes a little more complicated. Taylor (1987: ch. 4) assumes that each player's payoff in each round depends on whether they cooperate or defect and on the proportion of other players in the population choosing to cooperate. Since each round of play is an N-person prisoner's dilemma, by assumption it must be the case that each player gets a higher payoff in a given round and for any given level of cooperation among others by defecting rather than cooperating – defection remains a dominant strategy in a one-shot sense. Further, it must be the case that everyone prefers the situation in which they along with everyone else cooperate to one in which they along with everyone else defect. That is, the cooperative outcome is Pareto superior to the non-cooperative one. As in the two-person case, the N-person super-game does allow for the possibility of cooperation. The likelihood here depends not only on the players' discount rate but also on the number of other cooperators involved in the game. If players used a strict con-ditional strategy of cooperating only if *all* other players cooperated in the previous round, one bad apple would spoil the bunch and the Hobbesian equilibrium would prevail. If players took the less stringent approach of only defecting if some proportion of other players pre-viously defected, the cooperative equilibrium could withstand a few bad apples, but not too many. The latter rule would, of course, provide scope for a few to exploit the rest of the population by defecting. If too many people do this, however, cooperation falls apart completely and everyone is worse off. As Taylor (1987: 92–3) shows, this results in an N-person game of chicken (see Box 6.2) within the prisoner's dilemma supergame. Each person wants to be a defector in a broadly coopera-tive game, but in defecting they increase the chance that cooperation will break down. This is a game of impure coordination. Players have opposing interests over who gets to be in the defecting group but a shared interest in making sure the defecting group is not too big. It is difficult to know whether coordination will succeed here, but Taylor's point is simply that high levels of cooperation is a possible outcome and the 'chickens nesting in the prisoner's dilemma supergame' is another possible way this could happen.

Though Taylor's formal analysis is quite unrealistic, it does provide insight into the factors likely to promote or inhibit cooperation without external enforcement. We have already mentioned discount rates, and they do indeed seem important. Another point which emerges from Taylor's (1987: 105) N-person analysis is the importance of group size. The temptation to defect will be lower when an individual's action has a greater effect on aggregate outcomes and small groups will find it easier to monitor the behaviour of members, an essential component of conditional cooperation. Group size is a crucial factor in cooperation and we will have much more to say about it in Chapter 6, which can be thought of as a more general version of the argument presented here.

Robert Axelrod (1984) draws on Taylor's work in his book *The Evolution of Cooperation*, which provides an ingenious demonstration of how cooperation can be a successful strategy even for rational egoists. Axelrod invited a number of game theorists to submit strategies for a computer tournament in which the submitted programmes would compete with one another in iterated two-person prisoner's dilemma games. Of the 14 strategies submitted, the simplest won. TIT FOR TAT, submitted by Anatol Rapoport, cooperated on the first move and then cooperates if its partner cooperated on the previous move and defects if its partner defected on the previous move.

What should we make of such theoretical arguments? Empirically, there are a number of cases in which cooperation has been sustained without a centralized sate. Most obviously, many pre-modern societies were governed by polycentric and customary systems of law (Benson, 1990; Berman, 1983). Additional examples include trade networks (Bernstein, 2000; Greif, 2006), settlers on the American frontier (Anderson and Hill, 2004) and criminal groups (Gambetta, 1993; Kostelnik and Skarbek, 2012; Leeson, 2009; Leeson and Skarbek, 2010; Skarbek, 2011, 2014) These examples by no means prove that a large-scale stateless society is viable, but they do suggest that the Hobbesian argument for the state – which Buchanan more or less accepts – is problematic. If the state of nature turns out to be a reasonably nice or at least tolerable place, it is unclear whether rational people would want to escape it. Historically speaking, the modern state emerged as a highly predatory institution (Tilly, 1985). Though modern constitutional democracies are benign in comparison, citizens have in no sense revealed a preference for them over statelessness and it is not entirely self-evident that a unanimous preference for the state would be forthcoming if the choice were somehow made available.

Assessment

An assessment of Buchanan's contractarian approach to constitutionalism needs to carefully distinguish between Buchanan's normative and positive projects. In terms of normative theory, Buchanan's constitutionalism is an important supplement to the more popular contractarian political theory of Rawls.

Buchanan's work makes a significant contribution to normative political theory, but there are a number of grounds on which the approach might be criticized. One common criticism is that Buchanan's use of Pareto efficiency is excessively conservative (Barry, 1980). While some such criticisms are based on a misunderstanding of Buchanan's position as implying that policy moves which are not Pareto improvements are objectively *un*desirable, there is an argument to be made that the Pareto criterion as advocated by Buchanan is biased towards the status quo in practical terms and so legitimates and perpetuates potentially unfair inequalities.

Buchanan recognizes that there might sometimes be good reasons to think a particular distribution is unjust. His view of politics as a cooperative and practical exercise, however, leads him to treat the status quo as an inescapable starting point for positive analysis and normative evaluation:

> History itself dictates the distribution of rights and claims in the *status quo*. We cannot choose an alternative history that might have been. We can, however, engage in constructive dialogue concerning ways and means through which that which is might be changed to the benefit of all participants. (Buchanan, 2004: 142)

Buchanan's emphasis upon unanimity is deeply connected to his assumptions of normative individualism and subjectivism. Outcomes are valuable to the extent that individuals value them. Moreover, value can only be established by choice. Preferences cannot be aggregated or compared, and the only way we can say that one outcome is better than another is if everyone agrees to it.

The positive aspects of Buchanan's constitutionalism which have received the most criticism are his claims that constitutional choice is relatively impartial and that constitutions are binding. Central to Buchanan's normative project is his claim that choices are impartial when agents step back from choice within rules and focus on choice among rules. While Buchanan never claims the veil of uncertainty is complete, he does think that it is capable of generating a good deal of impartiality.

Buchanan and Tullock admit that the veil of uncertainty can be undermined by the existence of sufficiently dominant, stable and homogenous faction (Buchanan and Tullock, 1962: 80–81). Consider, for example, a situation in which 51 per cent of the population belonged to a particular religion so comprehensive that it perfectly aligned the preferences of its adherents and prevented exit. In such a case, the representative member of this group would have no problem with the tyranny of the majority, since he knows he will always be in the majority. More realistically, those in a majority group with highly correlated preferences across a wide range of important economic and social policy issues will tend to be biased towards majoritarian institutions, while those in minority groups across many issues will tend to be biased towards high thresholds for collective action. Neither individual is fully uncertain of their position in the decisions which will be made using the constitutional rule and thus each does have a conflicting and idiosyncratic interest at the constitutional level.

Even if individuals are completely uncertain of their place in the future chain of decisions made on the basis of a constitutional rule, people still vary in terms of their tolerance of risk. If people trade-off risk and reward in idiosyncratic ways and alternative constitutional rules have different risk profiles, individual judgement will be biased by risk preference (Witt and Schubert, 2008). More generally, we need to consider moral commitments and other 'expressive' factors in addition to material incentives. Difference is likely to remain on these matters, and this might produce bias and prevent consensus (Brennan and Hamlin, 2002).

These objections are by no means decisive. Buchanan admits that the veil of uncertainty can only ever be partially successful in its role in promoting impartiality. Still, in a comparative sense it remains plausible that impartiality is increased and the range of disagreement reduced as we move up the ladder of generality. Nevertheless, debates in America over the status of the constitution show that agreement at the constitutional level is far from complete. In broad terms, many conservatives see the constitution as a sacred document to be followed literally while many liberals see it as a useful guide which needs to be updated as conditions change. In other democracies there are debates over the merits of proportional and plurality systems, with minor parties and their constituents pushing for proportional representation, which would give them greater policy influence than a majoritarian rule. Although these debates seldom reach the same level of partisan disagreement as do debates over abortion in America, choice among rules does not exhibit anything like unanimity.

The other point on which the contractarian approach to constitutions is criticized is the issue of enforceability. If we view a constitution as a contract, we need to consider how it is enforced. The contracts we make in everyday life are enforced by government, but since constitutions are intended as a constraint on government this is obviously not a possibility. For some, the idea that government power can be limited is pure fantasy. Since constitutional rules are interpreted and enforced by the very government it is intended to constrain, constitutions have no effect at all (de Jasay, 1989). While this is an extreme view, the challenge of enforceable constitutional constraints is widely regarded as an important factor. Even the co-author of *The Calculus of Consent* is uncertain of the prospects for a self-enforcing constitution, seeing it as a problem which has 'so far evaded solution' (Tullock, 1987: 318).

Constitutional rules are only rules in a meaningful sense if enforced. The problem of constitutional enforceability is essentially that constitutions limiting government power are, to borrow Hobbes's phrase, 'covenants without the sword'. If agreement between individuals is not possible in anarchy because there is no external enforcer, the same problem arises when we try to constrain government. If we want government to enter into a binding agreement, there needs to be some external enforcer able to ensure performance of this agreement, but then this second-level government is granted a great deal of power which ought to be limited and we end up in an infinite regress. For constitutionalism to work, we need to assume that government is benevolent in its respect for constitutional rules, and this is exactly the type of romanticism that Buchanan's constitutionalism attempts to avoid (Farrant, 2004: 449).

There are a number of ways through which constitutional rules might be undermined. Most obviously, the rules can simply be ignored.

As Aristotle (*Politics*, Book 7, Part IX) says, 'those who carry arms can always determine the fate of the constitution'. If an electoral majority desires some constitutionally proscribed policy strongly enough it may be willing to ignore the constitution and there will be little a victimized minority is able to do about it (de Jasay, 1989). Second, the constitution may be interpreted in ways which change its meaning. This may be an intentional and disingenuous attempt to get around constitutional rules (Higgs, 1988), or it may simply be that the meaning of constitutions 'drift' over time as various interpretations gain precedence (Voigt, 1999). Institutional features such as judicial review may mitigate these problems to a greater or lesser extent, but the point remains that constitutional rules cannot simply be assumed to be effective when they are interpreted and enforced by the same body they are meant to constrain.

There is an important distinction here between substantive and structural constitutional rules. Substantive constitutional rules such as those enacted in bills of rights attempt to prohibit or place limits on certain collective choices, such as those involving the media or religion. For this type of constitutional rule the enforceability critique is a serious and unresolved challenge: such rules do seem to be little more than words on paper and some governments do seem to violate them with some regularity. Many structural rules, as the theorists cited above with reference to constitutions as commitment devices have emphasized, are self-enforcing. Federalism, electoral systems and the separation of powers are structural in this sense. Such structural rules are, however, subject to implicit change over time. A good example of this is the centralization of power in American federalism. Regardless of one's view of the relative merits of political centralization, it is clear that power has flowed from the states to the federal government to a much greater extent than was allowed for in the original interpretation of the constitution.

Buchanan does see structural rules as important, as demonstrated by the analysis of the optimal majority in the *Calculus* and his support for federalism, but the constitutional provisions he supports most strongly, such as balanced budget and generality requirements, are substantive rules which present only parchment barriers to dominant factions wishing to violate them. Such parchment barriers may be effective in setting expectations, but in this case Buchanan would be forced to admit that such rules are conventions rather than contracts in Hardin's sense.

Chapter 3

Anthony Downs and the Spatial Theory of Party Competition

Overview: In this chapter we examine the behaviour of political parties in two-party representative democracies such as the United States and the United Kingdom. The central question to be addressed is the following: In what circumstances will competition force parties to converge upon the electoral centre ground? The initial answer to this question is provided by Anthony Downs's (1957a) *An Economic Theory of Democracy*. Within political science the argument that parties will move to the electoral centre in an effort to maximize their vote has acquired the formal title of the median voter theorem. It is a theorem routinely linked to Downs; when textbooks offer an account of the median voter theorem, it is Downs's name that appears in the first paragraph; and when theorists provide criticisms of and alternatives to the theorem it is Downs's name that appears in the first footnote. We shall set out the basic terms of Downs's argument and identify its intellectual precursors. Downs's argument rests upon a particular set of assumptions. Alternatives to these assumptions and explanations as to why parties might sometimes retain distinctive policy positions are explored. This exercise takes up the single largest part of the chapter and offers an introduction to more recent rational choice scholarship. In terms of the broader political science context, we start by looking at the way in which our understanding of democracy has changed over the last few centuries, and shall conclude the chapter by contrasting accounts of democratic legitimacy developed by political theorists with the model of democracy analysed by Downs.

Setting the stage: the demands of democracy

We are used to describing as democratic regimes in which decisions are taken by elected representatives (Pitkin, 1967). Yet at the time of its inception following the English, French and American revolutions, the founders of what we now call representative democracy presented their preferred method of decision-making as an alternative to, rather than as a particular form of democracy (Dupuis-Deri, 2004; Manin, 1997). At that time democracy was equated with direct democracy and direct democracy with anarchy. Ordinary citizens would, it was argued, be too easily swayed by populist rhetoric. For proponents like James Madison, one of the authors of the *Federalist* (1751–1836), representation would

> refine and enlarge the public views by passing them through the medium of a chosen body of citizens, whose wisdom may best discern the true interest of their country and whose patriotism and love of justice will be least likely to sacrifice it to temporary or partial interests. (*Federalist*, 10)

Although this distinction between republicanism, as it was known, and democracy lives on in the names of America's two largest political parties, it has, in other respects, been largely forgotten. We tend nowadays to judge the credentials of a democratic system, representative or not, in terms of the tightness of the fit it provides between public opinion and policy outputs. The idea that representation is to be favoured because it loosens this fit seems increasingly alien.

It was in the later part of the nineteenth and early part of the twentieth century that theorists first began to argue that the practice of representative democracy was flawed because elected agents did *not* pursue the interests of their voting principals. Marxists argued that representative or bourgeois democracy was a sham and that policy outputs reflected the interests of business. Elitists like Pareto suggested that 'we need not linger on the fiction of "popular representation" – poppycock grinds no flour' (quoted in Dunleavy and O'Leary, 1987: 140). Such arguments have contributed to a more general loss of faith in democracy and to the rise of parties openly extolling alternatives to it. This disillusionment can be seen in the rise of 'anti-parties' and non-electoral political movements spanning the political spectrum. On the left, the Occupy Wall Street movement has seen the US government as being controlled by the finance industry. In the UK, actor Russell Brand generated a great deal of controversy by claiming that '[a]s long as the priorities of those in government remain the interests of big business, rather than the people they were elected to serve, the impact of voting is negligible and it is our responsibility to be more active if we want real change' (Brand, 2013). Meanwhile the Tea Party movement in US and the UK Independence Party in the UK have expressed similar concerns about the motives of politicians, and organizations such as WikiLeaks have sought to expose government corruption in order to make leaders accountable to citizens.

In the postwar years, the academic task of defending democracy's credentials initially fell to pluralists like David Truman (1951) and John Kenneth Galbraith (1953). Though diverse, pluralists generally argued against Marxists and elitists that ordinary citizens could and did influence government policy but that they did so primarily through their membership of pressure groups. Policy outputs, they argued, broadly reflected the inputs of competing pressure groups and because pressure group membership was broadly representative of public opinion, this meant that policy-making could be described as being democratic (see the further discussion of pluralism in Chapter 6). Pluralists accepted that some groups, most notably business groups, would dominate policy-making in particular sectors. But they denied either that the state was structurally predisposed to favour business interests or that business held a dominant position in every policy sector. But notice what is missing from this account: elections. Pluralists did not altogether ignore elections. The single most influential pluralist, Robert Dahl (1956: 131), argued that the prospect of having to fight elections forced political leaders to anticipate and so respond to public opinion. But pluralists tended not to dwell very long on elections. With the publication of *An Economic Theory*, this was to change.

The precursors of party competition

Downs's argument can be approached and best understood in terms of two earlier pieces of work. The first is Joseph Schumpeter's (1942) *Capitalism, Socialism and Democracy*. Schumpeter (1883–1950) was an economist who, shortly before presiding over a period of disastrous hyper-inflation as Austria's finance minister, proclaimed himself to be the greatest horseman in Austria, the greatest lover in Europe and the greatest economist in the world. Most of Schumpeter's work revolved around the subjects of economic development, entrepreneurship and the business cycle. But his writing on democracy, although amounting to no more than a few thousand words, has proven to be one of his most lasting contributions to the social sciences.

Schumpeter's vision of democratic competition emerges from his argument that public opinion is ill informed, fickle and easily manipulated, an argument we will return to in Chapter 8. Schumpeter argued that people make rational choices on matters of practical concern and experience. Though we have myriad irrational impulses, many of our choices are 'subject to the salutary and rationalizing influence of favorable and unfavorable experience' (Schumpeter, 1942: 262). Political choices are not like this, however. Since we are not individually decisive over electoral outcomes and elections happen only infrequently, learning opportunities are weak and political choices remain guided by irrational impulses. The notion of there being a settled and reasonable public will which it is the duty of politicians to discern and respect is, Schumpeter argues, nonsense. The popular will is 'the product and not the motive power for the political process' (1942: 263). Elitists like Pareto, Michels and Mosca, who made a number of similar observations, thereby concluded that representative democracy was a sham. Schumpeter did not. Democracy was that 'arrangement for arriving at political decisions in which individuals acquire the power to decide by means of a competitive struggle for the people's vote' (Schumpeter, 1942: 269). Parties have to compete with each other to get elected, and competition forces them to select policies they believe voters will find attractive. Downs (1995: 197) credits Schumpeter with providing 'the inspiration and foundation for my entire thesis' and is, in particular, much taken with Schumpeter's argument that policy emerges as the by-product of the competitive struggle for votes. But whilst Schumpeter waxes lyrical about the nature and meaning of democracy he is remarkably vague about the tactics parties will adopt in order to get elected. Using a military metaphor he at one point suggests that parties will fight to gain control of 'hills' that afford them 'strategic advantage'. But it was another and very different metaphor which Downs eventually employed to analyse party competition.

The use of left and right as general analytical contrasts is long standing. In the Pythagorean table of opposites, left is associated with darkness and evil and right with light and goodness (Lloyd, 1962). Yet as a term of political description the origins of the spatial metaphor are more recent. At the very start of the French Revolution delegates to the Estates-General broke away to form a National Assembly. Because voting within this Assembly was conducted by physically standing at required moments, representatives started to sit themselves next to like-minded colleagues on, literally, the left- and right-hand sides of the Assembly floor. Because Assembly rules prevented representatives from describing each other as belonging to named political factions such as the Girondists, 'left' and 'right' were soon being used as terms of description and abuse.

Out of this simple and exclusive contrast between left and right there soon developed a conception of political space as a continuum with a centre, centre-left, centre-right and so on (Hindmoor, 2004: 3–4). Within a few months, Mounier, for example, emerged as the leader of a faction sitting at the physical centre of the Assembly and advocating a kind of English constitutionalism as an alternative to both the absolute monarchism of those on the right and the republicanism of those on the left. Propelled first by the Revolutionary and then Napoleonic wars, the use of the spatial metaphor spread first to Scandinavia and the low countries, then to Southern Europe, and, eventually, to Britain. By the start of the twentieth century the spatial metaphor offered voters, politicians and commentators a kind of political Esperanto, a universal language of politics which could be used to describe political processes and outcomes in seemingly very different countries.

The first attempt to understand political competition in spatial terms is generally credited to another economist, Harold Hotelling. The question Hotelling addressed himself to might, initially, seem incredibly obscure. Imagine there is a one-dimensional space, perhaps the 'main street' of a town, across which customers are equally arranged (Hotelling, 1929: 46). Where will two profit-maximizing shops locate? Most people's intuition is that one will locate to the left-of-centre and the other to the right so minimizing the average distance customers have to travel to the nearest shop. But Hotelling shows that this is not so if customers always choose the closest shop. Each shop will actually move to the centre of the street. For it is only then that each will be able to prevent its rival from gaining a larger share of the market. Consider, for example, the position of a shop which moves to the left of the centre. Its rival could locate immediately to its right and in doing so acquire the business of the majority of those customers who live to the right. A key assumption driving this result is that all consumers go to their closest shop – that is, nobody stays home because the trip is too long. As we will see below, this is an important consideration in spatial theories of party competition. The crucial point in Hotelling's argument then comes at the very end of the article. Extending his discussion from economics to politics he suggests that

> so general is this tendency [to converge upon the centre] that it appears in the most diverse fields of competitive activity, even quite apart from what is called economic life. In politics, it is strikingly

exemplified. The competition for voters between the Republican and Democratic parties does not lead to a clear drawing of issues, an adoption of two strikingly contrasted positions between which the voter may choose. Instead each party strives to make its platform as much like the other's as possible. (Hotelling, 1929: 54)

Hotelling did not actually use the terms left and right to describe the position of parties in political space, did not seek to represent the position of parties using a linear scale and did not use the nomenclature of the median voter. Nevertheless, it is his spatial analysis which Downs (1957a: 115) sees himself as 'borrowing and elaborating' upon. Political parties will, as Schumpeter suggests, compete to attract the support of voters. This competition, as Hotelling argues, pushes the parties toward the centre ground.

The median voter theorem

Stated more formally, the median voter theorem rests upon the set of assumptions listed below. Whilst these all obviously call for elaboration and perhaps qualification, we want, for the moment, to concentrate on their implications.

1 There are only two parties.
2 Political space is one-dimensional.
3 Parties can move to and occupy any point in this one-dimensional space.
4 Parties are vote-maximizers.
5 Voters vote for the party closest to them in political space.
6 There is perfect information.
7 Voters' preferences are fixed.

In Figure 3.1 the horizontal axis shows a series of positions in political space running from left to right. Voters' preferences can be mapped on to this one-dimensional scale (assumption 2) and are fixed (assumption 7). The vertical axis shows support for these alternative positions. In Figure 3.1(a) the aggregate distribution of preferences shows a situation in which most voters are clustered at or near the centre of the horizontal axis and in which there are relatively few voters on the far left or far right. Figure 3.1(b), on the other hand, shows a very different distribution in which there are a large number of left-wing voters, very few voters at the centre and a cluster of voters at the far right. The important point to note here is that *whatever* the distribution of voters, there will always be a median voter, a person whose preferences are such that there are exactly as many voters to their right as to their left. In Figure 3.1(a) the median voter is located at the very centre of the horizontal axis, whilst in Figure 3.1(b) the median voter is located further to the left.

For the same reason Hotelling argued that competition forces businesses to locate at the centre of a street, the median voter theorem

Figure 3.1 *Two-party competition with standard and bimodal distributions*

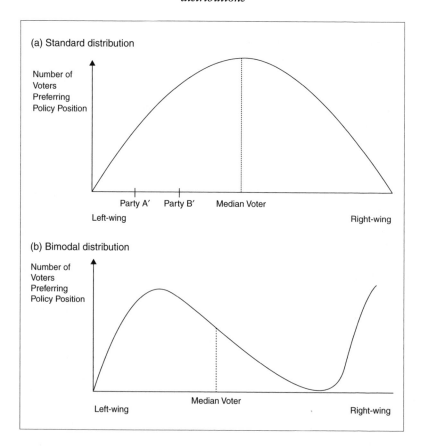

holds that competition forces parties to move to the position of the median voter. We know that there are only two parties (assumption 1) and that these parties will seek to maximize their vote (assumption 4). Consider now what would happen if party A were, in Figure 3.1(a), to locate to the left of the median voter at A'. We know that the second party, B, can move anywhere in political space (assumption 3) and that it knows the distribution of voters' preferences (assumption 6). If it were to move immediately to the right of A', to B', it would attract the votes of the majority of voters to its right (by virtue of assumption 5). So B would win the election. This would give A an incentive to move immediately to the right of B so regaining majority support. But B could then move to the right of A and so on. This process of competitive 'leapfrogging' would, however, come to an end when both parties straddled the position of the median voter, for neither would then be able to increase its share of the vote by moving to either the left or right. Convergence upon the position of the median voter is in this way a stable equilibrium (for a more detailed discussion of the median voter theorem turn to the discussion of Duncan Black's work on voting cycles in Chapter 5).

It is not unusual to find political commentators willing to attribute the triumph or failings of a particular party or candidate in terms of its ability to move toward and occupy the political centre ground. Politicians routinely describe themselves as occupying the political centre whilst deriding their opponents as extremists who are out of touch with public opinion (Hindmoor, 2005b). In 2006 the newly elected leader of the Conservative Party in the UK, David Cameron (2006), defended his 'modern conservatism' by arguing that 'the alternative to fighting for the centre ground is irrelevance, defeat and failure'. Following the conclusion of negotiations with the Liberal Democrats to form a Coalition government in 2010, Cameron vowed that under his leadership the Conservatives would 'never vacate the centre ground' (Hennessy, 2010).

Precisely because the electoral significance of the centre ground is and always has been so widely recognized, it is open to critics to argue that the median voter theorem is 'banal' (Green and Shapiro, 1994: 6). But Downs is not simply arguing, as political journalists routinely argue, that parties can gain an advantage by moving to the centre. Downs can be understood as attempting to specify the reasons why and the necessary and sufficient conditions in which parties find it in their interests to converge upon the centre ground.

Qualifying the argument: accounting for divergence

Critics routinely argue that rational choice models have little or no explanatory value because they are constructed from a series of implausibly heroic assumptions, most notably that individuals are rational. One possible defence against this argument is the instrumentalist one that theories ought to be judged in terms of the accuracy of their predictions rather than the realism of their assumptions (see Box 1.2). To this end, we might re-cast the median voter theorem as a prediction about the way in which parties will behave. There is plenty of evidence that the members and leaders of political parties in Britain and America believe that something like the median voter theorem holds. Members often choose party leaders on the basis of judgements about which candidate will prove most appealing to the wider electorate; newly elected leaders routinely talk about the need to appeal to voters at the centre ground and berate activists who want to return the party to its ideological roots; and party leaders use opinion polls and focus groups to road-test policies. Indeed and to this extent, the median voter theorem is a self-fulfilling prophecy. Politicians move to the centre ground because they believe that they need to move to the centre ground to win elections. That said, politicians' faith in the veracity of the median voter theorem is not without foundation. There is plenty of evidence that candidates can increase their share of the vote by moving closer to the position of the median voter (see, for example, Gelman, 2009: 153–8).

The problem here is, however, that the theorem does not simply predict that parties will converge *towards* the position of the median voter. It predicts that parties will move *to* the position of the median voter and so adopt *identical* policy positions. Now parties do sometimes signal a change in position by adopting some of their opponents' policies. Prior to the 2010 general election, David Cameron signalled the Conservative's move toward the centre ground by promising to protect the NHS and the overseas aid budget from real spending cuts. But no matter how intent upon outflanking their opponents they are, parties do *not* simply adopt other parties' policies wholesale. Detailed surveys of manifesto commitments (Budge, 1999) and policy outputs (Chappell and Keech, 1986) show that political parties retain distinctive characteristics. Left-wing parties tend, for example, to pursue more expansionary monetary policies, run-up larger budget deficits, spend more on welfare and preside over falling unemployment. Conversely, right-wing parties tend to pursue more restrictive monetary policies, cut budget deficits, spend more on defence and preside over falling inflation (see Mueller, 2003: 447–50 for a review of the evidence).

Instrumentalists maintain that theories ought to be judged in terms of the accuracy of their predictions rather than the realism of their assumptions. Yet the obvious rejoinder to this is that bad assumptions lead to poor predictions. Given that political parties do not converge upon the position of the median voter and adopt identical policy positions, do we therefore need to abandon Downs's assumptions in order to understand the process of party competition? The simple answer to this question might be that we do. But this does not mean that Downs's theory is a poor starting-point for a discussion of party competition. The assumptions employed by Downs are valuable not necessarily because they are accurate, they are often not, but because they serve as explanatory prompts which we can use to account for the behaviour of actual parties. Downs's model of party competition specifies the necessary and sufficient conditions in which parties will find it in their interests to converge upon the position of the median voter. Having identified these conditions we can therefore start to explain why parties in the 'real world' do not always converge upon the position of the median voter in terms of variations in these conditions. Recall, in this context, the defence of rational choice theory offered by Schotter and Hindriks in Chapter 1 (see pp. 16–17). Rational choice is valuable because it can be used to generate interesting and powerful findings which stimulate further research.

Over the following pages we will look at and consider the plausibility of each of the assumptions Downs makes and show how alternative assumptions can be used to account for policy divergence.

Assumption 1: there are only two parties

In a now classic study of the impact of voting systems upon the number of parties, Maurice Duverger (1951) first formulated what has since become known as 'Duverger's law' and 'Duverger's hypothesis' (Riker, 1982b). Duverger's law holds that plurality (or first-past-the-post) voting systems tend to lead to two-party competition. Duverger's hypothesis holds that proportional voting systems tend to be associated with multi-party competition. This argument rests upon the identification of 'mechanical' and 'psychological' effects associated with the use of plurality systems. The mechanical effect refers to the way in which plurality systems discriminate against third parties or candidates whose vote is evenly divided across a number of constituencies. In the 1992 and 1996 US presidential elections, for example, Ross Perot acquired 19 and 9 per cent of the national vote respectively. Yet because he came in third in most states, Perot did not acquire a single vote in the Electoral College. The psychological effect refers to the tendency of voters, knowing that third parties are discriminated against in this way, to avoid 'wasting their vote'. Ralph Nader's presidential bids in 2000, 2004 and 2008 provide a good example. Though he never received more than 3 per cent of the popular vote, Nader received a great deal of media attention. Arguably, this was because many voters considered Nader the best candidate but realized that splitting the left-wing vote between him and the Democrats would benefit the Republicans.

Does Duverger's law hold? The answer to this question depends upon the way in which the number of parties in any one country is counted, and there are a number of possibilities here. At one extreme we could count any party which put forward any candidate in any election. In this case there would be no two-party systems. Indeed judging by the number of parties officially registered with, for example, the British Electoral Commission, Britain would be a 393-party system with the Don't Cook Party led by Richard Murfitt and campaigning for the social acceptability of takeaway food counting equally with the Conservatives and Labour. At the other extreme, and following the suggestion of Giovanni Sartori (1976), we might only count a party if it has a realistic chance of governing alone. But realistic is a term obviously open to interpretation and this method would have the unfortunate consequence of rendering some stable democracies as one-party states. The compromise suggested by Rein Taagepera and Matthew Shugart (1989) is therefore to count the 'effective' number of parties (Box 3.1). Using this method, parties are counted in proportion to their size in such a way that small parties, although counted, do not count to the same extent as larger ones.

By the usual standards found within the social sciences, the evidence for the existence of Duverger's law and hypothesis is quite strong (Benoit, 2006; Grofman et al., 2009; Riker, 1982b). As Table 3.1 shows for the case of both votes cast and seats taken, the effective number of parties in plurality voting systems is significantly lower than it is in proportional voting systems. This is not necessarily to say that Duverger is beyond reproach. For it may be that countries in which there is only one salient political cleavage, and which therefore naturally lend themselves to two-party competition, choose plurality voting systems for this reason. Conversely, it may be that countries with multiple cleavages – socio-economic, religious, linguistic and territorial – which

Box 3.1   The effective number of parties

The following account is drawn from Taagepera and Shugart (1989: 77–80). Imagine four possible party systems in each of which there are five parties attracting the following vote shares:

Party	A	B	C	D	E
System 1	51%	42%	5%	1%	1%
System 2	51%	26%	11%	11%	1%
System 3	40%	37%	11%	11%	1%
System 4	40%	37%	9%	9%	5%

Intuitively, we might describe system 1 as a two-party system. But it is far less clear how we might describe systems 2, 3 and 4. In each of these, the two largest parties, A and B, account for more than two-thirds of the total votes cast. Yet in each case the smaller parties attract some support. In order to resolve this problem we could establish a 'cut-off' point below which a party would not be 'counted'. But any such number would clearly be arbitrary. If, for example, we set this cut-off at 10 per cent then system 3 would be a four-party system and system 4 a two-party system even though there is very little actual difference between them.

The best way of calculating the effective number of parties is to let the vote shares determine their own weights in the following manner:

1 Multiply the fractional share of each party against itself. So in the case of system 1, the fractional share of party A is 0.51 and 0.51 × 0.51 = 0.2601.
2 Add together the resulting figures for each party in this system: 0.2601 + 0.176 + 0.0025 + 0.0001 + 0.0001 = 0.4388.
3 Divide 1 by this number = 2.278.

So restricting ourselves to one decimal place system 1 has 2.3 effective parties, system 2 has 2.8 effective parties, system 3 has 3.1 and D has 3.2. Note that the effective number of parties can be calculated in terms of the votes cast (as it is here) or in terms of the number of seats each party holds within the legislature following the election.

naturally lend themselves to multi-party competition choose proportional voting systems. The number of parties in a country may, in other words, cause the voting system rather than the voting system causing the number of parties (Bogdanor, 1984; Colomer, 2005). But we do not need to resolve this issue here. What matters is that Downs's assumption of two-party competition is, in those countries using the plurality voting system, a reasonably plausible one.

Table 3.1   *The effective number of parties*

Country	Year	Effective number of parties by vote	Effective number of parties by seats
Countries using plurality voting			
Canada	2011	3.4	2.4
United Kingdom	2010	3.7	2.6
United States	2010	2.2	2.0
Average		3.1	2.3
Countries using proportional voting			
Belgium	2010	10.0	8.4
Costa Rica	2010	4.8	3.9
Czech Republic	2010	6.8	4.5
Denmark	2011	6.5	5.8
Finland	2011	6.5	5.8
Netherlands	2010	7.0	6.7
Portugal	2011	4.0	3.0
Sweden	2010	4.8	4.5
Switzerland	2011	6.4	5.6
Average		6.3	5.3

Source: Data from the Democratic Electoral Systems data-set, described in Bormann and Golder (2013). The table lists 'full democracies' as classified by Economist Intelligence Unit's democracy index who held a lower house legislative election in 2010–2011 and used either a first-past-the-post or plurality list system.

Assumption 2: political space is one-dimensional

Downs (1957a: 115) assumes that 'political preferences can be ordered from left to right'. There are clearly some issues which split opinion *within* the left and right. There are those on both the left and right of politics favouring the liberalization of drug laws, for example, and there is no obvious sense in which this is a left–right issue. Some social scientists (Giddens, 1994) and occasional politicians have argued that, in a post-industrial, post-communist, post-modern society, the 'terms left and right no longer have any relevance'. These arguments are, we think, overdone (see Bobbio, 1996). Left and right continue to form a staple part of political discourse, but it is clear that political competition in Britain and America is no longer, if it ever were, exclusively one-dimensional (Albright, 2010).

Before proceeding any further we need to be clear about the terminology being used here. Dimensions refer to policy issues over which voters or politicians have connected beliefs. Empirically, we would say that two issues are on the same dimension when we can predict individual preferences on one issue on the basis of the other – that is, highly correlated beliefs can be collapsed into a single dimension. The economic left–right and environmental dimensions might seem quite different, for example, but if positions on the left–right spectrum are closely related to those on the environmental spectrum, we are dealing with a single underlying dimension when it comes to party competition. Another factor to consider is the salience of a dimension. If politicians and voters are aligned on a single axis on all-important issues with another axis emerging for only unimportant issues which almost never change voters' minds, we would generally want to say that party competition is one-dimensional, since all the *electorally relevant* variation in party position can be represented along a single dimension.

Bakker et al. (2012) look at party platforms in European countries and find three dimensions – economic left–right, social libertarian-authoritarian and EU integration – which are present in all but which vary in their salience and independence from one another. In some countries, such as Spain, the correlation between these three dimensions is so strong that political space is almost entirely one-dimensional. In others, such as Finland, each dimension is relatively distinct. The UK provides an intermediate case, with the left–right dimension being the most salient by far and the other two dimensions being somewhat but far from perfectly correlated (see also Benoit and Laver, 2006).

What happens to the dynamics of party competition when there is more than one dimension? Figure 3.2 shows a situation in which there are three voters (A–C) whose preferred positions (marked as A, B and C) are mapped against a socio-economic and libertarian – authoritarian dimension. Voter A is extremely left-wing and authoritarian, voter B is moderately right-wing and libertarian and voter C is extremely right-wing and moderately authoritarian. Assume that there are two parties, X and Y, and that X has initially located itself at point X_1. Where could Y position itself in order to attract more votes? To answer this we need to construct a set of indifference curves (a_1a_1, b_1b_1, c_1c_1) intersecting at X_1 and showing points in political space between which each voter is indifferent (Box 3.2). Look at, for example, the circular arc a_1a_1.

Box 3.2   Indifference curves

Indifference curves are one of the core building blocks of modern micro-economics. By constructing a series of curves representing bundles of goods a consumer is indifferent among, indifference curves provide a visual representation of preference relations. Economists normally assume that more goods are always preferable to less but political scientists are generally interested in situations where an individual or party has a particular ideal position in mind, thus the visual presentation of indifference curves we provide here is somewhat different to that found in economics texts (e.g. Mankiw, 2014: 437–41), though the underlying logic is the same.

Assuming that policy space is two dimensional, each individual voter or party has an 'ideal' or 'bliss' point – the point that they would choose if completely unconstrained. In the figure below, a voter's bliss point is labelled as point A. At point A, the voter is completely satisfied with policy and would not change a thing. When evaluating party platforms, however, voters will generally be forced to choose between alternatives which diverge from their bliss point. The voter generally agrees with party X's position on the authoritarian–libertarian dimension, but is much closer to party Y on the left–right dimension. How does the voter choose between these two parties? In an intuitive sense, it is obvious that the voter needs to ask which difference is larger. To make things simpler, we will assume for the moment 'simple Euclidean preferences' – preferences which depend straightforwardly on the distance in policy space between an alternative and the individual's ideal point. If we assume that each policy dimension is given equal importance and preference satisfaction decreases steadily as we move away in either direction from the bliss point, the voter will be indifferent between all points on any particular circle with their bliss point at the centre, since all such points will be an equal distance from the bliss point. These circles are an individual's indifference curve in two-dimension policy space, and it is possible to draw an infinite number of them. Two such indifference curves are shown below as the circles labelled a_1 and a_2. Individuals are indifferent between all points on a given indifference curve, but prefer to be on the innermost curve possible. Thus, we can see that the voter in this case would choose party Y over party X, since Y is on the inner indifference curve a_1 and X is on the outer curve a_2. If X had instead chosen position X_1 and Y had chosen Y_1, however, the voter would prefer party X to Y.

Of course, not everybody considers each issue dimension equally important. Some voters may be relatively uninterested in the authoritarian–libertarian dimension and base their decision primarily on the left–right dimension. That is, individuals may differ in terms of the salience they give on various issues. If this is the case, the concentric circles of the upper graph are not an accurate representation of preferences, and we need to abandon the simple Euclidean assumption. If the left–right dimension is more salient, the voter might prefer point X over point Y, despite the closer spatial proximity of the latter. Graphically,

→

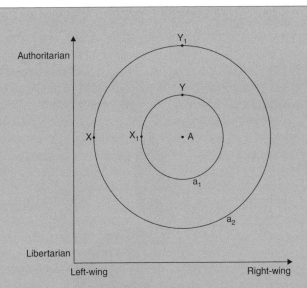

Simple Euclidian preferences

this can be represented by 'stretching' the indifference curves along the salient dimension, so that they are elliptical rather than circular, as in the figure below. Now, point X is on a more inward indifference curve than point Y and is thus preferred despite its greater linear distance from the ideal point A. More complex forms of preference relations can also be represented on indifference curves, though we do not pursue these avenues here (See instead Hinich and Munger, 1997: 52–61). For simplicity, we will generally assume simple Euclidean preferences in this book.

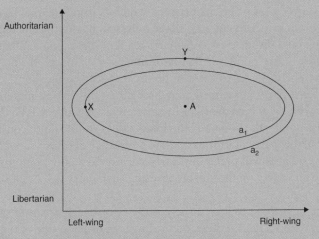

Weighted Euclidian preferences

Figure 3.2   *Party competition in two dimensions (i)*

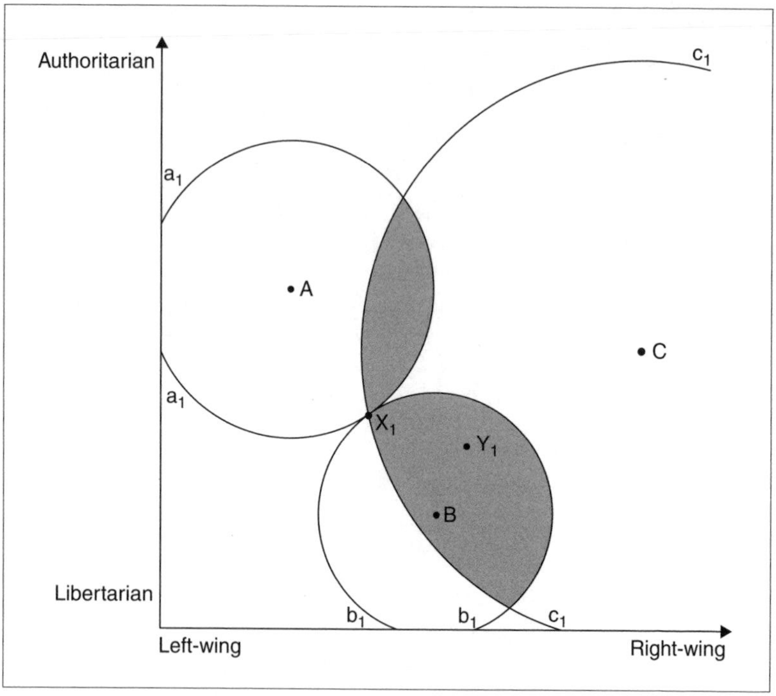

This shows a set of points between which A is indifferent. To put the same point in a different way, all the points along this line, including X_1, are an equal distance away from A's ideal or 'bliss' point. What about all those other points in this two-dimensional space? If voters vote for the party closest to them in political space (assumption 5), A will vote for a party positioned anywhere along this line in preference to any beyond it and to the right because any such party will be closer to its bliss point – the point an individual would choose if not constrained by available party platforms and the preference of other voters. We can also say that A will prefer any party positioned at any point inside the line to any party on the line because any such party will be closer to its bliss point.

The next thing to look at here is the two shaded areas or 'winsets'. The first and larger of these, on the lower right-hand side of the figure, shows those points voters C and B prefer to X_1. We know that B prefers any point in this area to X_1 because these points are closer to its bliss

Figure 3.3   *Party competition in two dimensions (ii)*

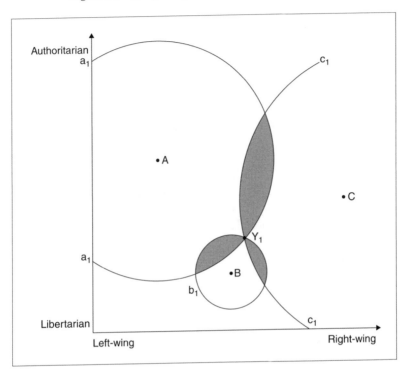

point. We know that C prefers any point in this area to X_1 for the same reason. The second and smaller winset at the top shows those points voters A and C prefer to X_1. We can now return to the question with which we started. Where could Y position itself in order to attract more votes? By moving to *anywhere* within *either* winset it could attract the support of two of the three voters.

Assume that Y actually positions itself at Y_1 in Figure 3.2. Where could X now position itself to attract more votes? Figure 3.3 shows a set of indifference curves (a_1a_1, b_1b_1, c_1c_1) this time intersecting at Y_1. There are now three shaded winsets. The largest, running towards the top of the diagram, shows those points that both A and C prefer to Y_1. The smaller winset on the lower right shows those points preferred by B and C, and the one on the lower left shows those preferred by A and B. So X could move anywhere within these areas and attract the support of two of the three voters and so win the election. The important point to note here is that we could repeat this exercise indefinitely.

With this particular distribution of preferences no matter where one party positions itself the other party could always attract more votes by moving to a different location.

Richard McKelvey (1976, 1979) proved that without some means of agenda control, or very restrictive assumptions about voter preferences (which we discuss in Chapter 5), there would be no stable equilibrium in majority voting. Moreover, he showed that whoever controlled the agenda would be able, through a complex but finite chain of pairwise votes, to shift the outcome to *any* point in policy space. This result, which has come to be called the 'chaos theorem', came as something of a shock to rational choice theorists. It had been recognized for some time that this sort of instability was possible (see Chapter 5), but the general assumption had been that it would be unlikely in the real world and that any instability would be confined to a relatively small and central area of policy space (Tullock, 1967). McKelvey showed that the types of preference giving rise to instability are omnipresent with two issue dimensions and instability was not necessarily restricted to any central region (see also Riker, 1980).

In recent years the argument has, however, swung back. Theorists accept that there will not usually be a stable equilibrium when there is more than one dimension, but they maintain that for most plausible distributions of preferences, parties will find it in their interests to adopt positions within a relatively small region known as the 'uncovered set'. What is the uncovered set? A position P_1 is said to cover position P_2 if P_1 is majority-preferred to P_2 and if all the alternatives which are majority-preferred to P_1 are also majority-preferred to P_2. There will usually be a set of positions that P_1 does *not* cover and to which it is therefore particularly vulnerable. These positions are the uncovered set of P_1. Assume now that the uncovered set of each and every position has been identified. By looking at the intersection of all these points (the set of points they have in common) it will be possible to identify the uncovered set for the whole policy space. Parties will find it in their interests to adopt positions within this space because, though such positions can be beaten, they will always be within one step of beating any other position. Whilst parties may, in the short term, adopt positions outside of the uncovered set, in the longer term competition will usually lead parties to return to it (McKelvey, 1986; N. Miller, 1980; Mueller, 2003: 236–41). Because voters' preferences can be arranged in countless ways, rational choice theorists have found it difficult to reach any firm general conclusions about the size, location or attractive force of the uncovered set. The general assumption was that it would normally be centrally located, would be reasonably small for large numbers of voters and that most collective outcomes would fall within it (Feld et al., 1988; N. Miller, 2007). Recently, software allowing for the simulation of elections under a variety of assumptions has shed light on these questions and suggested that the earlier conjectures were basically right: for most distributions of preferences (an important exception being the highly polarized), outcomes normally fall within a reasonably small and central uncovered set (Bianco et al., 2004; Bianco et al., 2008; N. Miller, 2007, 2014).

We will have much more to say about the type of instability described by McKelvey in Chapter 5. For now, we simply note that the median voter theorem does not hold when there is more than one issue dimension. Attempting to straightforwardly extend the Downsian model to two-dimensional space produces a chaotic result, but if we allow parties and voters to be forward-looking and tactical, instability might well be constrained to relatively small and central portion of policy space.

Assumption 3: parties can move to and occupy any point in this one-dimensional space

The median voter theorem requires that parties can move anywhere in political space. What might prevent them from doing so? One possible answer is internal party dynamics. Downs (1957a: 24–5) defines a political party as a 'team of men seeking to control the governing apparatus by gaining office in a duly constituted election'. He then goes on to assume that 'members agree on all their goals' and that each party can therefore be treated as if 'it was a single person'. But this is simply implausible. Intra-party conflict can frequently be as intense as inter-party conflict – consider the highly competitive nature of American primary elections and the secretive political manoeuvring involved in leadership challenges in parliamentary parties. Such conflicts arise because ordinary party members tend to have different political views from party leaders and ordinary voters (May, 1973). That the beliefs of party members should differ from those of ordinary voters is hardly surprising; people will presumably only join the Labour or Democratic Parties if they regard themselves as being to the left of the Conservatives or Republicans. So given this self-selection filter, the median Labour or Democratic Party activist is bound to be to the left of the median voter in the country as a whole.

The constraints imposed by intra-party conflict can be seen in the effect of presidential primary elections in the United States. The existence of primaries means that candidates are faced with a two-stage competition, with a distinct constituency in each stage. At the primary stage, candidates need to appeal to members of the party, and the logic of the median voter theorem applies here too, meaning that leadership candidates will be forced to converge on the platform preferred by the median party member. Since the median Democrat is to the left of the median Republican, this can result in party divergence and possibly a very polarized political system.

Upon winning a primary election, however, vote-maximizing candidates will have an incentive to move towards the centre in order to appeal to the median voter. Although this seems likely to happen to some extent, there may be factors which limit the ideological mobility of candidates over an electoral cycle. Anecdotally, it seems that voters punish candidates for 'flip-flopping'. Party leaders may find promises they made during a leadership election thrown back at them by a rival during a subsequent national election campaign, and voters might see them as insincere or unreliable, a point we will return to later in this chapter. If voters have a preference for candidates who maintain the same position over the electoral cycle, movement towards the median will be limited by the prospect of losing the votes of disillusioned party members. The attraction of the median may produce some convergence in the second stage of a two-stage race, but under reasonable assumptions it seems that this convergence will be less than perfect (Hummel, 2010).

Similar dynamics might limit ideological mobility in systems without primary elections. Party activists might be able to influence the platform away from the median voter position. Candidates rely on donations of time and effort from supporters in order to run a campaign. If these supporters make their decisions on the basis of candidates' ideological distance from their own ideal point, moving towards the centre will indirectly cost the party votes by decreasing the campaign resources available (Moon, 2004). If candidates also rely on financial donations from interest groups such as business associations or trade unions, the responses of these groups will need to be taken into consideration when attempting to woo the median voter (Grossman and Helpman, 2002). In general, we need to think about the diverse groups candidates need to satisfy in order to run a successful campaign. Voters are obviously one crucially important audience, but they are not the only one.

Assumption 4: parties are vote-maximizers

Downs (1957a: 27) maintains, rather gruesomely, that politicians, all politicians, 'act solely in order to attain the income, prestige and power which come from being in office'. Because they have no preferences over policy they 'formulate policies in order to win elections rather than win elections in order to formulate policies' (ibid.). Now it is certainly the case that voters have an overwhelmingly poor view of their elected representatives and to this extent Downs's assumption may ring true, but judging by the lengths they go to champion their favoured policies in internal party debates, the assumption of vote-maximizing nevertheless looks like a caricature.

Representative democracy is a principal–agent relationship between voters and representatives (see Box 7.2). We know that representatives are unlikely to have preferences which exactly match those of the median voter, but electoral competition can generally be expected to force politicians to act as faithful representatives of the voting public. As in other principal–agent relationships, however, oversight and control are less than perfect. Voters are often unaware of what their representatives are up to and may forgive minor transgressions. Knowing this, representatives will find that they have some slack to pursue their own interests at the expense of the median voter. This slack can be used to pursue selfish interests – engaging in minor corruption or pursuing pet projects (see Chapter 7) – or ideological preferences (Kalt and Zupan, 1990; Kau and Rubin, 1979, 1993).

It is, with sufficient ingenuity, always possible to account for any pattern of behaviour in terms of the assumption of self-interest. So it might, for example, be argued that politicians argue about policies because doing so allows them to publicly express their allegiance to factions within a party they believe can further their career. But it is incumbent upon social scientists not simply to find explanations which are consistent with the facts but which best explain those facts. As rational choice theorists have subsequently come to accept (Laver and Hunt, 1992; Wittman, 1977), the most plausible explanation of most politicians' behaviour is that they care about both policy and votes; that they have both policy-seeking and office-seeking motives. Politicians have principles. They will not say or do anything in order to be elected, but their principles are not cast in stone. Politicians will formulate their policies with at least one eye upon the prevailing public mood. From this point it is of course easy to see how we might account for the fact that parties adopt differing policy positions in terms of their distinctive policy preferences. But such an argument obviously risks looking entirely *ad hoc*. In recent years the argument that preferences over policy can be used to explain policy divergence has, however, been given greater empirical and analytical bite through a challenge to another of Downs's assumptions.

Assumption 5: voters vote for the party closest to them in political space

Downs maintains that the position a party occupies depends solely upon the policies it has adopted and that voters only care about policies. Consequently voters will always select the party closest to them in political space. Empirical research has shown that voters are, statistically, far more likely to vote for the party closest to them in political space; but they have also shown that the relationship between position and vote is an imperfect one (e.g. Singh, 2010). Voters, it would appear, care about policy but they do not only care about policy. At this point, rational choice theory rubs up against an older, behaviourist, political science tradition which emphasizes the extent to which many voters identify with and vote for parties that, in policy terms, they may not actually be closest to (see Butler and Stokes, 1969; Campbell et al., 1954, 1960). Voters, it is argued, do not step back and look at the policy position of each party and then rationally choose between them. Because they are rationally ignorant (see Chapter 8) they usually vote for the party they have always voted for. It would appear that the strength of such partisan identifications has waned in recent decades. In Britain, for example, the proportion of voters who 'strongly identified' with a political party fell from around 44 per cent in the early 1960s to around 10 per cent by 2005 (Dunleavy and Gilson, 2010). In other words, it may be that voters are becoming more Downsian in their behaviour. But the relationship between policy position and vote nevertheless remains a probabilistic rather than deterministic one.

What difference does this make to party competition? If party leaders only care about getting elected it makes no difference. If voting is probabilistic, parties can still increase their *chances* of getting extra votes by moving towards the position of the median voter. But, as James Enelow and Melvin Hinich (1982, 1989) have shown, if candidates have both office-seeking and policy-seeking motives, parties will be more reluctant to sacrifice preferred policy positions for the uncertain prospect of acquiring more votes. Probabilistic voting sustains equilibria in which parties converge towards the median voter but do not adopt identical policy positions.

Another problem with assumption 5 is that, at least in countries without compulsory voting, voters may become 'alienated' if there is no party close to them in political space and choose not to vote at all (Mueller, 2003: 232–3). A common refrain of the extremist is that the major parties are indistinguishable on important matters or simply too divergent to deserve support. This will not always make a difference to party behaviour. If voter preferences are unimodal and symmetric, as in Figure 3.1(a), the number of votes lost due to alienation will be outweighed by those gained by moving towards the median, as we can see from the relative height of the preference map at various points. Suppose that both parties are currently at the median point. If one party tries to move slightly to the left in order to reclaim alienated leftist voters, they will lose the centre ground which contains a greater number of voters. The median voter result holds, even though those at the extremes are alienated and choose to abstain.

If preferences are unimodal but asymmetric, as in Figure 3.4(a), the possibility of alienation does make some difference. Suppose that both parties are initially located at the median and that the left-wing voters around the mode are currently alienated and so abstain. By moving leftward, a party would lose voters to the right and around the median, but pick up a larger number of left voters around the mode. In practice, however, the difference between median and mode is likely to be too small to have any noticeable impact on party platforms (Comanor, 1976).

If preferences are bimodal as in Figure 3.4(b), however, alienation has a greater possibility of producing divergence from the median voter equilibrium. As in the unimodal asymmetric case discussed above, with a sufficient number of alienated voters near one or both of the modes, parties may gain votes by giving up centrist votes and reclaiming alienated partisans. If both parties take this strategy, we would see divergence towards each mode, with neither party claiming the centre ground. Here, a large difference between the median and modes is more realistic than in the asymmetry case, since partisan loyalties may push people one way or the other. There is a great deal of debate over the unimodality or bimodality of political preferences in the United States and whether this leads to an unhealthily polarized political

Figure 3.4   *Voter alienation*

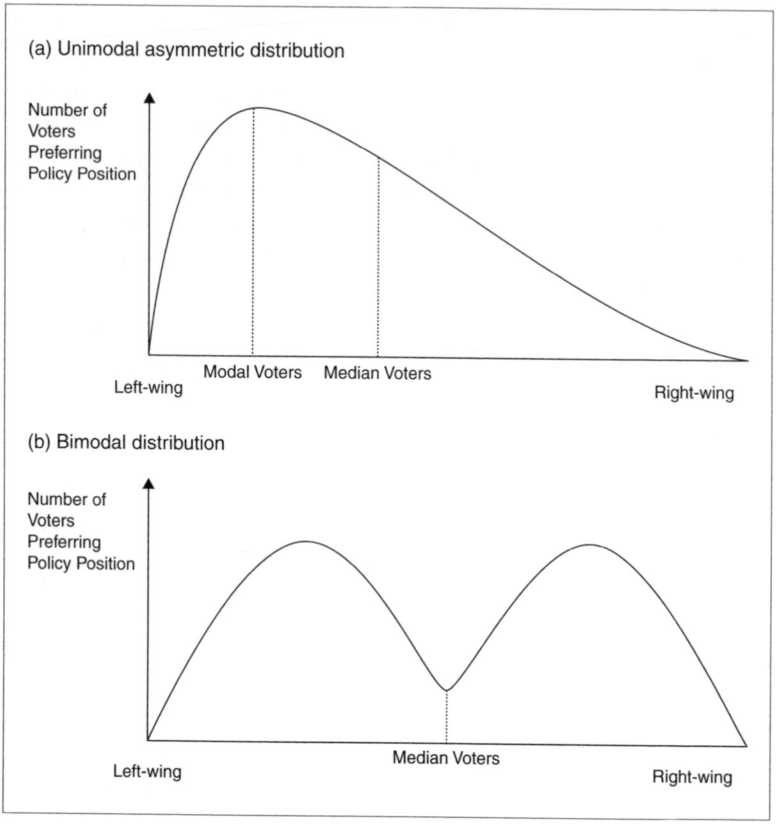

culture (Abramowitz and Saunders, 2008; Fiorina et al., 2005). In France, bimodality seems to be a reality which has a genuine impact on politics insofar as it benefits extreme rather than moderate parties (Lemennicier et al., 2010).

Assumption 6: there is perfect information

As we will discuss more generally in Chapter 8, information is an important factor in politics and rational choice analyses thereof. The median voter theorem is no exception. Parties can only move to the position of the median voter if they know where that voter is located. Equally, voters can only vote for the party closest to them if they know where the parties are located. Perfect information is the lubricant that keeps the median voter theorem running smoothly and predictably. It is therefore not difficult to see what difference a little bit of uncertainty – which Downs (1957a: 77) defines as 'lack of sure knowledge about the course of past, present, future or hypothetical events' – might make. If, for example, parties disagree about where the median voter is located, they will obviously end up adopting different positions. This much seems obvious. But uncertainty also matters in a more interesting way. In committing themselves to particular policy positions, parties are making promises. They are promising, if elected, to implement one set of policies rather than another. But voters cannot know with absolute certainty whether a party intends to or will be able to fulfil its policy promises (Hinich and Munger, 1996), and for this reason in an uncertain world it matters a great deal whether voters regard a party as being trustworthy.

Downs recognizes this and suggests that competition leads parties to act reliably and responsibly. A party is reliable if 'its policy statements at the beginning of an election period – including those of its preelection campaign – can be used to make accurate predictions of its behaviour during the [subsequent] period' (Downs, 1957a: 104–5). The easiest way for parties to acquire a reputation for acting reliably is to keep their policy promises. Because 'rational men will vote for an unreliable opposition party only if the [alternative] parties have such abysmal proposals that random policy selection is preferable to them' (Downs, 1957a: 107), the desire to be re-elected gives parties an incentive to act reliably. What then of responsibility? A party is responsible if 'its policies in one period are consistent with its actions (or statements) in the preceding period, i.e. if it does not repudiate its former views in formulating its new programme' (Downs, 1957a: 105). A responsible party retains faith with its policy position over a long period of time; an irresponsible party constantly changes its position. But if voters value responsibility parties may not always be able to maximize their vote by moving to the position of the median voter – particularly if the position of the median voter is itself changing (i.e. if assumption 7 does not hold). Consider the position of a party which has, wittingly or unwittingly, strayed to the left of the median and so lost an election. On the one hand it can gain votes by moving to the right and toward the median voter. This much we already know. But if voters value responsibility it will risk losing votes by changing its position. What its vote-maximizing strategy is will depend upon the precise number of votes it risks losing. But it is not hard to see why the need to appear responsible might lead parties to retain distinctive policy positions.

It is easy to see why voters might care about whether a party has a reputation for acting reliably. But what is unclear here is why they should care about whether a party has acted responsibly. Why does it matter what a party has said or done in the distant past? The best answer to this question is, we think, one which draws us back to the earlier discussion of politicians' motives. If a party has retained its policy position over a long period, voters may infer that it has a genuine, policy-seeking, commitment to its position and that the party can, if elected, be trusted to do what it says it is going to do. If, on the other hand, a party has only recently adopted a policy position and only done so when that position became popular, voters might worry that its commitment is purely instrumental and vote-seeking and that the party might, at the first sign of trouble, renege upon its promises. Responsibility matters because reliability matters. This suggests a striking and seemingly paradoxical conclusion. Parties which attempt to maximize their vote by constantly changing their policies to suit the message of the latest opinion poll or focus group, might actually risk losing support. Parties which adopt policy positions because they genuinely believe in them may end up attracting more votes. The dichotomy previously posited between vote-maximizing and policy-seeking may therefore be a false one. The attempt to vote-maximize might be self-defeating.

Assumption 7: voters' preferences are fixed

Downs (1957a: 55) assumes that the preferences voters have over policy positions derive from their underlying 'fixed conceptions of the good society'. But Downs simply does not say where these conceptions come from or why they should be considered as fixed. Some voters, it would appear, are simply right-wing and others are simply left-wing. The blame here does not simply lie either with Downs or, more generally, rational choice theory. Although psychologists have done a great deal of work on preference formation, much remains unknown. Social scientists now know a great deal about what people want. They know far less about why they want it. We do know, however, that preferences often change in response to persuasion and changing circumstances (for example, Bowles, 1998; Weingast, 2005). If parties are able to discern the factors which change political preferences, they may be able to pull public opinion towards their own platform, rather than altering their platform in response to public opinion.

There are two broad ways through which such endogenous preference change could occur. Most obviously, parties may be able to convince voters to adopt their own positions through rhetoric. This is what Schumpeter had in mind when he argued that public opinion was a product of democratic competition rather than a precondition for it. Politicians do not simply adopt their positions to suit voters; they also seek to adopt voters to suit their positions through persuasion. This is the day-to-day 'stuff' of politics and, by focusing on external circumstances at the expense of internal values and beliefs, rational choice theorists are in danger of missing it. Moreover, there is evidence that voters tend to adapt their preferences to party platforms independent of rhetoric (Sanders et al., 2008). This may seem irrational, but, as we suggest in Chapter 8, if voters have limited information and cognitive capacity, relying on a trusted party 'brand' may be a low-cost way of evaluating policy alternatives. Reasonable decisions need not be based on vast amounts of information if voters know that parties or other groups or individuals are informed about the issues and share their interests and values. The fact that a trusted party which has generally proved itself a good protector of your interests takes some policy position might be reasonable evidence that you should also adopt that position (Lupia and McCubbins, 1998). If this is the case, parties may be able to alter the preference distribution simply by taking a position.

A second broad strategy is available to incumbents: using policy to alter the nature of the electorate. At the crudest of statistical levels we know that people from similar socio-economic backgrounds are more likely to have similar political stances. From mass surveys of voting behaviour we know, for example, that people who went to state schools, have manual jobs, belong to a trade union, work in the public sector and live in council houses are more likely to regard themselves as being on the left than people who went to public schools, have professional jobs and so on. As Patrick Dunleavy (1991) argues, knowledge of such relationships, whether simply intuitive or confirmed by polling data, gives incumbent parties the opportunity to pursue policies that will increase their vote. By giving larger tax breaks to public schools, reducing the powers and so attractiveness of trade unions, privatizing firms and selling council houses, right-wing parties can increase the number of people going to private schools, owning their own homes and so forth and, by doing so, lead some people to change their conceptions of the good society (see Stubager, 2003 for a detailed empirical analysis). Left-wing parties may be able to shape the electorate by encouraging immigration or changing naturalization laws, since in many cases immigrants are more supportive of redistributive policies than the native population (Benhabib, 1996; Mayr, 2007). The preferences voters have and, by extension, the location of the median voter is not, it must be concluded, fixed. Parties have a choice. They can either accommodate themselves to the preferences voters have or they can try to 'shape' those preferences to suit their policy preferences.

Assessment

In some subsequent chapters, principally but not exclusively those on social choice theory (Chapter 5) and rent-seeking (Chapter 7), we express a number of reservations about the trajectory of rational choice theory. *An Economic Theory of Democracy* is, however, a book we believe students of politics can all learn from. In the first place, the issue the book addresses is an important one. It obviously matters a great deal whether competition leads parties to move towards or away from the median voter. In the second place, Downs's demonstration that parties will, when a particular set of circumstances hold, converge upon the position of the median voter remains a compelling one. Finally, Downs's argument is an attractive one because it is presented so simply. The literature on party competition that *An Economic Theory* has inspired is also interesting and valuable. An increasing level of technical sophistication has made some of this material less accessible to outsiders. But technical sophistication has not in this case become an end in itself. Research in this area is 'problem' rather than 'method-driven' (Shapiro, 2005). The issues rational choice theorists are continuing to address, about the dynamics of multi-dimensional competition, about the extent and impact of uncertainty and so on, retain an obvious relevance to politics in the 'real world'. In the final part of this chapter we do, however, want to briefly identify one way in which developments within the political science discipline have robbed *An Economic Theory* of at least a part of its significance.

The distinction between positive and normative, between is and ought, is a long-standing and important cornerstone of the way in which we think about the world. Within political science departments, the distinction is usually manifested in the work of political theorists, who think about the way the world ought to be, and others, public policy analysts, area specialists and comparative politics experts, who look at and try to understand the world as it is. Clearly this is a crude division. To the extent that 'ought implies can', political theorists have an obvious responsibility to consider whether their proposals are feasible (Brennan and Hamlin, 2009, Gilabert and Lawford-Smith, 2012). But in terms of the way most political scientists approach their task, the division is nevertheless a recognizable one. It is tempting to regard Downs's work and the literature on party competition it has inspired in exclusively positive terms as being about the way parties behave. In the introduction to his book Downs certainly encourages such a reading. Casting an envious eye towards the rigour and status of general equilibrium theory within economics he writes that

> little progress has been made toward a generalised yet realistic behaviour rule for a rational government similar to the rules traditionally used for rational consumers and producers. As a result, government has not been successfully integrated with private decision-makers in a general equilibrium theory ... *this thesis is an attempt to provide such a behaviour rule for democratic government.* (Downs, 1957a: 3; emphasis added)

Yet, as we argued in the introduction to this chapter, *An Economic Theory* can also be understood as offering a normative defence of representative democracy. For if what we require of democracy is a 'tightness of fit' between public opinion and policy outputs, the median voter theorem shows that competition gives parties an incentive to formulate policies in order to please the voters rather than to please themselves. That said, the normative appeal of the median voter theorem might be challenged in another respect. The Downsian framework is fundamentally majoritarian, ignoring preference intensity and potentially threatening the interests of minorities. A quip widely misattributed to Benjamin Franklin gets at the heart of the problem: 'Democracy is two wolves and a lamb voting on what to have for lunch.' If majorities favour the repression of minorities, democratic competition will force candidates to provide such repression. Most people would want to say that the preferences of the lamb in some sense outweigh those of the wolves, but the 'one man, one vote' logic of majoritarian democracy throws preference intensity out the window and forces us to side with the wolves. As we saw in Chapter 2, this provides a compelling reason to think carefully about the scope of democratic authority and the appropriate thresholds for collective choice.

Chapter 4

William Riker and the Theory of Coalitions

Overview: In this chapter we examine the behaviour of parties in multi-party representative democracies such as Germany, Holland and Belgium, in which governments are routinely formed by coalitions of parties. The central question addressed is this: What kind of coalitions will emerge from the post-election negotiations between party leaders? Rational choice theorists have offered a number of answers to this question. We do not provide a general review of them here (see Diermeier, 2006a; Nyblade, 2013), instead we distinguish between two broad approaches within coalition theory. The first, exemplified by William Riker's (1962) theory of the minimal winning coalition, assumes that politicians are self-interested office-seekers. The second, exemplified by Michael Laver and Kenneth Shepsle's (1996) portfolio-allocation model, assumes that politicians are policy-seekers who care, above all else, about seeing their preferred policies implemented. In examining and assessing these accounts, we show how rational choice theory has been informed by and can be used to account for the findings of other political scientists working in this area.

Setting the stage: choosing a voting system

In the previous chapter we examined the behaviour of political parties in countries using plurality or 'first-past-the-post' voting systems. Electoral competition will then usually be between two major parties one of which will acquire a legislative majority and form a government (see the discussion of Duverger's law, pp. 57–8). The obvious point we want to start by emphasizing here is that the use of plurality voting systems is a matter of political choice. In Britain, the third party, the Liberal Democrats, have campaigned for some form of proportional representation for a number of years. In 2011 they managed to secure a referendum on the introduction of the Alternative Vote system as part of their coalition agreement with the Conservatives, but the proposal was decisively rejected by the electorate. In Canada, dissatisfaction with plurality voting led to a Law Commission report in 2004 recommending the use of a mixed member system of proportional representation, and since that time referenda have been held in British Columbia, Prince Edward Island and Ontario. Because the only parties that either have or are likely to acquire power in these countries are the ones that benefit from the maintenance of the status quo, it is tempting to view demands for electoral reform as being somehow utopian. Although major parties do have a clear incentive to maintain plurality systems, the experience in the Canadian provinces and the fact that New Zealand abandoned plurality voting in favour of a form of proportional representation as recently as 1993 (Karp and Bowler, 2001) show that voting systems are not set in stone.

Proponents and opponents of electoral reform seem broadly to agree that proportional representation will increase the effective number of parties, significantly reduce the chances of any one party gaining enough seats to form a majority government, and so increase the chances of coalition government (Box 4.1). What they disagree about is whether coalition government is a good or a bad thing. Proponents of electoral reform argue it is only fair that parties which receive a minority of the popular vote should have to share power. They also argue that coalition government forces parties to compromise and that compromise leads to better and more effective public policies. Opponents argue that coalitions undermine electoral accountability by giving politicians rather than voters the power to decide which party or parties should form a part of the government. Accountability is further diminished in coalition government if voters are unable to tell which coalition partner is to blame for bad policy or poor outcomes. They also argue that coalitions give extremist parties an opportunity to enter government and that they give a disproportionate and unfair influence to often very small centrist parties. Finally, they suggest that coalitions are prone to instability (Hermens, 1951; Schumpeter, 1942: 268–71) (for a more detailed review of all these arguments, see Reynolds et al., 2005).

One way in which political scientists have contributed to this debate about electoral reform is by assessing the normative claims being made by participants in it. Consider, for example, the claim that power sharing is a fairer method of governance. Political theorists are well placed to identify the possible meanings and requirements of fairness and to determine whether plurality systems which give winning parties a larger proportion of the legislative seats than of the popular vote are inherently unfair (see Blau, 2004; McGann, 2013). Alternatively,

Box 4.1   Proportional representation and multi-party competition

In this chapter we tend to talk, rather loosely, about 'proportional' voting systems. It must, however, be emphasized that there are a number of different methods of proportional voting including open and closed 'list' systems, mixed-member systems and the single transferable vote (for detailed accounts of the differences involved see Farrell, 2001). A key concept within the study of electoral systems is the 'break-even' point. This is the point at which a party's proportional share of legislative seats can be expected to equal or exceed its share of votes. The more proportional a voting system is, the lower this break-even point will be. In countries using proportional voting systems, the break-even point ranges from around 2 per cent in Denmark, Belgium and Holland to around 8 per cent in Germany where parties must receive at least 5 per cent of the vote before they are entitled to any seats (Taagepera and Shugart, 1989: 88–91). But whilst there is a considerable variation of break-even points within countries using proportional voting systems, it is nevertheless the case that break-even points in countries using plurality voting systems are consistently higher. In the case of, for example, elections to the American House of Representatives, the break-even point is around 45 per cent. To this extent, the simple contrast drawn here between proportional and plurality voting systems is defensible.

In the previous chapter we spoke about Duverger's 'Law': the claim that the use of plurality voting leads to two-party competition. The corollary of this is Duverger's 'hypothesis', the claim that 'the simple-majority system with second ballot and proportional representation favours multi-partyism' (Duverger, 1951: 239). As Table 3.1 indicates, the effective number of parties in countries using proportional voting systems is indeed generally higher than it is in those using plurality ones. The relationship between proportional representation and multi-party competition is, however, an imperfect one and this is why political scientists continue to talk about a hypothesis rather than a law (Riker, 1982a). Liechtenstein and Sri Lanka both use a list PR system but have fewer than two and a half 'effective' parties. This has led many sociologists to argue that the key issue in determining the number of parties is not the electoral system but the number of cleavages in that society (Cox, 1997: 14–17; Lipset and Rokkan, 1967 and references therein). In countries where there is only one, salient, socio-economic cleavage, including Liechtenstein and Sri Lanka, there will, it is argued, usually only be two parties whatever the voting system employed. In recent years political scientists have however shown that the number of effective parties in a country will depend upon both the number of cleavages and the electoral system (Ordeshook and Shvetsova, 1994).

consider the argument about extremist parties. Is it a good thing that extreme parties are routinely excluded from office? Might it not be argued that democracy itself is compromised when this happens?

Political scientists have also evaluated some of the empirical claims made by participants about the consequences of coalition government. A number of their conclusions are listed below:

1 The use of proportional voting systems does indeed seem to be associated with an increase both in the effective number of parties and the incidence of coalition government. Of 216 governments formed between 1945 and 1987 in 12 West European countries using various types of proportional representation, only 14 were formed by single parties holding a majority of the legislative seats (Schofield, 1993: 3).

2 Coalition governments are somewhat less durable than governments formed by single parties. Using an extensive data-set, Kaare Strøm (1990: 116) reports that single-party majority governments survived for, on average, 30 months whilst majority coalition parties only survived for 17 months. Such figures should, however, be treated with caution, for instability at the cabinet level may mask a great deal of stability in the distribution of particular cabinet posts (Fischer et al., 2012). For when one governing coalition is replaced by another, many of the same politicians remain in post. Italian governments are, for example, notorious for their fragility. Yet during the postwar period Italy actually had one of the lowest turnovers in cabinet membership because the Christian Democrats dominated almost every government (Mershon, 1996).

3 On the basis of a statistical comparison between the performance of 36 democracies, Arend Lijphart (2012) argues that countries in which executive power is shared between parties have higher voter turnout, more liberal criminal justice systems and better equal opportunity records (but see Armingeon, 2002 for a contrary analysis). Others have found that closed-list proportional representation systems are more susceptible to corruption than open-list or plurality systems (Kunicova and Rose-Ackerman, 2005; Persson et al., 2003).

4 There is little evidence that coalition government gives extremist parties – conventionally defined as fascist and communist parties – much opportunity to participate in government (Budge and Laver, 1992: 9–10).

5 Coalition government does, however, seem to give a great deal of political influence to often quite small centrist parties (Laver and

Schofield, 1990). Despite only ever acquiring around 10 per cent of the vote, the German Free Democratic Party was, for example, continuously in government between 1969 and 1998, first in a coalition with the Social Democrats (1969–1982) and then with the Christian Democrats (1982–1998).

Political scientists have arrived at these findings on the basis of detailed surveys about the composition, durability and policy outputs of West European governments over a period of time. As such, their findings offer a good example of the possibilities of an inductive approach to political science. What can rational choice theorists with their deductive models and heroic assumptions add to these findings? What is it they can tell us about coalition government that inductive political scientists cannot? The answer rational choice theorists would want to give is that they can add explanatory bite in the sense of not only telling us what happened, but why it happened.

Riker and the theory of the minimal-winning coalition

William Riker (1920–1993) has almost certainly been the single most influential exponent of rational choice theory in political science. Riker, who studied politics at Harvard University, first acquired an interest in rational choice theory in 1954 after reading a short paper on political power by two mathematical economists, Martin Shapley and Lloyd Shubick (Box 4.2). Within a few years, he had started to apply game theory to the study of politics and had written a short paper on the methodology of social science (Riker, 1957). In 1962 Riker moved to the University of Rochester, and over the next twenty or so years he went on to create America's first political science department devoted almost exclusively to the study of rational choice theory (see Amadae and Bueno de Mesquita, 1999 for historical discussion).

In contrast to much of Riker's later work on democracy and party competition, a small part of which we will touch upon in the following chapter, *The Theory of Political Coalitions* (1962) is a rather dry book for which it is difficult to develop any great affection. It does, however, contain an important argument about the nature of political competition. In *An Economic Theory of Democracy*, Downs, as we have seen, argues that politicians seek to maximize the total number of

Box 4.2   The Shapley–Shubik power index

Martin Shapley and Lloyd Shubick (1954) sought to devise a way of measuring the power of individuals on a committee. Assume for the sake of argument that you have a committee with three members, A, B and C, all of whom cast their vote in the same way. Assume further that they vote in turn, one after the other. If issues are decided by majority voting then the second person who votes will always be pivotal in the sense of creating a majority.

The Shapley–Shubik power index can be calculated as follows. (1) Identify all the possible orders in which the members can vote either for or against a proposition. With three members there are six such orders: a (followed by) b (followed by) c, acb, bac, bca, cab, cba. (2) Identify that person whose vote is decisive or pivotal for each decision. In this case because each member of the committee has one vote, the person who votes second is always pivotal. In other words, B will be pivotal in the first instance, C in the second, A in the third and so on. (3) Determine the total number of times each person is pivotal. In this case A is pivotal on the third and fifth vote, B is pivotal on the first and sixth vote, and C is pivotal on the second and fourth vote. (4) Divide the total number of times any one person is pivotal by the total number of times everyone is pivotal. This number is that person's power index. Here, each person is pivotal on two occasions out of a total of six so each person's power index is 1/3.

To see why the index is so interesting consider a legislature in which there are 100 seats and in which party A has 50 members, party B 49 members and party C 1 member. In order to pass a measure, assume that the support of 51 members is needed. (1) There are, once again, six possible orders in which the parties can vote. (2) If each person in each party votes the same way and each party votes the same way, the pivotal party is the one underlined in the following sequence: a<u>b</u>c, a<u>c</u>b, <u>b</u>ac, bc<u>a</u>, c<u>a</u>b, cb<u>a</u>. (3) Party A is pivotal on four occasions, party B on one occasion and party C on one occasion. (4) The power index of A is 4/6. Despite having a very different number of seats, B and C each have a power index of 1/6. In the previous section we noted that opponents of proportional representation and coalition government argue that it gives too much power to small parties. We can use the Shapley–Shubik power index to help us understand why this might be so.

The Shapley–Shubik index has been used to calculate the distribution of power of various institutions within the European Union (see Aleskerov et al., 2002; Algaba, E. et al., 2007; Turnovec, 2008). But remember that the index depends upon the crucial assumption that everyone votes in the same way. The index cannot therefore account for the way in which a person's preferences might constitute a source of power. In a committee in which four people always voted in one way and four other people always voted in another, the ninth person would be pivotal and possess a great deal of 'outcome' power (see Barry, 1980; Dowding, 1991: 59–63).

votes that they receive. For this reason, politicians will, he argues, seek to forge as broad an electoral coalition as possible composed of voters with potentially very different views. Riker echoes Downs in arguing that politicians are office-seekers who 'act solely in order to attain the income, prestige and power which come from being in office'. But he also argues that politicians regard the business of acquiring votes as a costly one taking time and effort and requiring them to make policy promises that, once elected, limit their freedom. Starting from this premise and drawing on the work of economist Oskar Morgenstern and mathematician John von Neumann (1944), Riker (1962: 32–3) argues that politicians will therefore seek to 'create coalitions just as large as they believe will ensure winning and no larger'. Such coalitions will be minimal-winning in the sense that the ejection of just one person or party from that coalition will render it no longer winning.

The Theory of Political Coalitions makes a case for understanding politics, all politics, as entailing the construction of minimal-winning coalitions. As such, the examples Riker uses to illustrate his argument range from nineteenth-century American domestic politics to the break-up of the Napoleonic Empire. Yet, since its publication, Riker's theory has been applied almost exclusively to the study of government coalition formation. There are some good reasons for this. The question of why one coalition might form rather than another is, as we have seen, an important one. Furthermore, this is a subject area in which there is no shortage of empirical data against which the claims of various models can be tested. But at the same time this narrow range of application does risk obscuring the significance of Riker's argument and the extent of his disagreement with Downs. The difference between these two is not, as the lay-out of the chapters in this book might imply, that the one is examining two-party competition and the other multi-party competition. It is rather that they are making very different assumptions about the ways in which politicians behave.

In order to see how the theory of the minimal-winning coalition might be applied to the study of coalition formation, we need to make the following formal assumptions. (1) A winning coalition is one whose membership constitutes at least one-half plus one of the legislature. (2) Politicians are purely office-seeking and derive utility from occupying cabinet posts. The total amount of utility to be gained from being in office is fixed. Parties can bargain about the number of cabinet posts they receive but the total number of posts is fixed. Coalition bargaining is zero-sum. (3) Coalitions control their membership. Parties can only join and remain within coalitions with the approval of the other members of that coalition. (4) Each instance of government formation is a purely isolated event. (5) There is perfect information. Parties know the rules and payoff structure of the game and know that other parties know the rules and payoff structure as well.

Given these assumptions, it follows that parties will form minimal-winning coalitions. For if parties derive utility from their possession of cabinet seats and believe that the total number of such seats is fixed (assumption 2), they will try to maximize the number of seats they hold. If all a winning coalition needs is a bare majority in the legislature (assumption 1) and they know precisely how many seats each party has (assumption 5), then the parties in any proto-coalition will have a strong incentive to eject from that coalition any parties whose votes are not needed to sustain its majority. Forming long-term political alliances by including unnecessary parties won't work since by assumption each instance of coalition bargaining has no effect on future behaviour (assumption 4). Coalitions control their own membership and can eject any party from that coalition (assumption 3). For this reason, only minimal-winning coalitions will form.

Consider, for example, a situation in which seven parties hold the following number of legislative seats: A (15), B (28), C (5), D (4), E (33), F (9) and G (6) (= 100) and in which any coalition must therefore secure 51 seats in order to form the government (Mueller, 2003: 280–81). Imagine that parties B (28 seats), E (33 seats) and G (6 seats) are considering whether to form a coalition. Between them, these three parties control a clear majority of 67 seats. But because B and E alone control 61 seats they can eject G from this coalition without compromising their winning status and by doing so can acquire for themselves whatever cabinet seats G had been offered in order to form a part of the coalition. The coalition between B, E and G is not, in other words, minimal-winning and so will not form. What are the minimal-winning coalitions? Given this configuration of seats there are 11: BE (61 seats), ABF (52 seats), ACE (53 seats), ADE (52 seats), AEF (57 seats), AEG (54 seats), ABCD (52 seats), ABCG (54 seats), ABDG (53 seats), CDEF (51 seats) and DEFG (52 seats).

Which of these minimal-winning coalitions will actually form? Riker's argument is that the winning coalition will be not only *minimal*-winning in the sense that the ejection of any partner would render the coalition non-winning but also of *minimum*-winning size in terms of legislative seats (Riker, 1962: 257–70). If the rewards the members of a coalition receive depend upon the number of seats they take in that coalition, forming an unnecessarily large coalition will reduce the potential number of seats available. Suppose, for example, that the possible coalition DEFG is about to be formed. This coalition is minimal-winning with 52 seats: no member can be removed without the coalition falling below majority threshold. Can the members of this coalition do better for themselves by removing one party and inviting another to join? The coalition has one more seat than it needs for victory, so if it could kick out a partner and replace it with a smaller party demanding a smaller share of the cabinet posts, the other members would be able to share the extra rewards among themselves. Since party C has five seats to party G's six, the members of DEF would prefer to invite C rather than G into the coalition. Among the 11 minimal-winning coalitions of parties A–G, there is only one minimum-winning coalition, CDEF (51 seats).

One curious implication of Riker's analysis is that it's not always good to be a large party (Riker, 1962: 138–43). Party G has one more seat than C and we would normally see this as an unambiguous advantage in politics. As we saw above, however, C benefited by having fewer seats than G and thus being better placed to push an otherwise losing coalition just barely above the majority threshold. An obvious objection to this view is that party G will recognize its weak bargaining position and demand a less than proportionate share of the political spoils. Riker (1962: 139) admits that this is possible but thinks it 'psychologically difficult' for individuals to break with the idea that large parties deserve a greater share of the cabinet posts. Party C can avoid this psychological difficulty and will more readily agree to a viable coalition bargain. Moreover, it should be remembered that Riker sees all politics as being about the formation of coalitions. Political parties are not unitary actors but coalitions of voters united in order to seek office. Smaller parties have fewer voters, and minimizing the size of the winning coalition would provide more reward per person.

Policy-seeking parties

Rational choice theory is founded on the assumption that actors are self-interested. The assumption of self-interest has a particularly curious status. On the one hand it is consistent with and may indeed have contributed to the growth of tabloid political culture which maintains that politicians will say or do anything to get re-elected, that bureaucrats are lazy and self-serving and that local government officials are all on the make. At the same time, most people have little sympathy with the view that people, politicians included, are exclusively self-interested. Rational choice theorists have nevertheless been able to retain and defend this assumption for two principal reasons. Firstly, because it is so flexible that it can be used to account for almost any kind of behaviour. Consider the assumption made within Riker's theory that politicians are self-interested office-seekers. How might we reconcile this assumption with the apparently abundant evidence that politicians argue with each other about policy, sometimes resign from office following policy disputes and retain consistent policy positions over a long period of time? The simple answer is that we can do so quite easily. Politicians who argue about policy can be interpreted as investing in reputations for reliability and responsibility which will enhance their long-term electoral appeal. How can this explanation be reconciled with politicians' own and very different accounts of their actions? It can be done so by recognizing that self-interested politicians will frequently have good self-interested reasons for not wanting to reveal their true motives.

Rational choice theorists have also defended the assumption of self-interested behaviour by arguing that their work ought to be judged in terms of the accuracy of its predictions rather than the realism of its assumptions (Box 1.2). Now in the case of two-party competition, the assumption that politicians 'formulate policies in order to win elections rather than win elections in order to formulate policies' has survived at least in part because there is plenty of evidence that parties *do* often converge upon the position of the median voter and plenty of scope to account for their failures to do so in terms of the absence of particular conditions (Ahmed and Green, 2000). We do not necessarily mean to suggest that this evidence is overwhelming or that rational choice theorists have sought carefully to falsify their theories. The point we are making is more of a sociological one. For better or for worse, there has been enough supporting evidence to sustain rational choice theorists working in this area in their assumption that politicians are entirely self-interested.

Starting with the work of Robert Axelrod (1970) and Abram De Swaan (1973), rational choice theorists working on coalition theory first qualified and then gradually abandoned the assumption of office-seeking behaviour in favour of one of policy-seeking. To consider the implications of a policy-seeking model of coalition formation, assume that we have three equally sized parties A–C aligned along a single left–right policy dimension as in the Downsian model of the previous chapter.

Since each party has one-third of the total seats, no single party can form a majority government but any two parties can. Whereas Riker's theory provides no basis for choosing between any of the possible two-party coalitions (AB, AC and BC), the policy-seeking assumption makes it clear that the coalition AC is unlikely and that B has an awful lot of power in deciding policy.

Suppose that parties A and C had struck a potential policy bargain somewhere between their ideal points. This agreement will either be exactly on the centrist party B's ideal point or to its left or right. If the agreement is at B's ideal point, B will be perfectly content staying out of government (remember, we have assumed that parties are motivated entirely by policy). If the agreement is to B's right, B could propose an alternative coalition with A at any point to the left of the AC's proposed agreement. If A demanded an agreement to the left of B's ideal point, however, B could refuse to deal with A and instead propose a deal with C. Since B is the median legislative party, there is no point in policy space which is majority preferred to its ideal point. Since neither A nor C have any bargaining power, they will be indifferent between being on the inside or the outside of a majority coalition or having B rule alone. The median party, like the median voter, gets whatever it wants in one-dimensional policy space, and this will be so regardless of whether it governs alone, in a grand coalition, or not at all (Laver and Schofield, 1990: 110–13). This provides a possible explanation for some of the empirical findings outlined in the introductory section, including the strength of small centrist parties, the weakness of extreme parties and the occurrence of minority governments and grand coalitions.

The median party result is precisely analogous to the median voter theorem introduced in the previous chapter, and like the median voter theorem, the stability of the median party collapses into instability if we introduce another policy dimension. Figure 4.1 shows the same three parties A–C but now with a libertarian–authoritarian dimension in addition to the left–right economic one. Continue to assume that any two parties can form a majority and that no single party has enough seats to do so. Which coalition will form? The problem here is that for any possible policy outcome a coalition may adopt, it will *always* be possible to find another policy which is majority-preferred to it. Assume, for example, that A and B form a coalition at X. By drawing a set of indifference curves (a1a1, b1b1, c1c1) (Box 3.2) intersecting at this point, we can identify those points any two of the three parties prefer to X. In this case, we can, for example, see that A and B prefer policies which are more left-wing and libertarian than X (those

Figure 4.1   *Coalition instability in two dimensions*

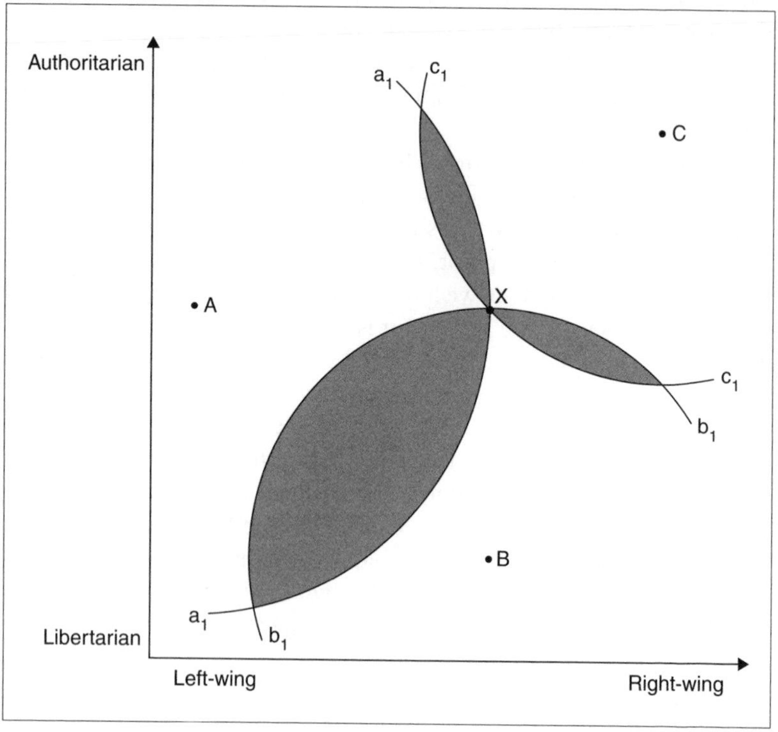

points in the large winset to the left of X), that A and C prefer policies which are more left-wing and authoritarian than X (those points in the winset above X) and that B and C prefer policies which are more right-wing and libertarian than X (those points in the winset to the right of X). By selecting any point within either of these areas we could then repeat this exercise and identify further points which were majority-preferred to this new status quo.

If parties are policy-seeking and there are multiple-dimensions we would expect the resulting process of coalition formation to possess a number of characteristics. Firstly, it should be highly unstable; as one governing coalition formed we would expect it to be immediately replaced with another. Secondly, we would expect centrist parties to play no more influential a role in the coalition-building process than any other type of party. Thirdly, and as an extension of this point, we would expect to see extremist parties regularly, albeit only temporarily, forming a part of winning coalitions. Yet this is of course precisely what political scientists studying the coalition process have *not* found. Centre parties do play an important role in the coalition formation process and extreme parties are usually excluded from winning coalitions. Coalition governments are slightly less durable than those formed by single parties, but they are far from being chaotic. The problem with assuming that politicians are policy-seeking and that competition takes place across multiple dimensions is that whilst each assumption seems individually plausible, they combine to generate a set of findings entirely at odds with what we actually know about coalitions.

The portfolio-allocation model

In recent years rational choice theorists have sought to develop models of the coalition formation process which can be used to explain why, for example, centre parties play such an influential role in the coalition process, but in which it is assumed not only that politicians are policy-seekers but that there are multiple dimensions of competition. One important contribution has been Michael Laver and Kenneth Shepsle's (1996, 1998) portfolio-allocation model, which has provided the inspiration for more recent work on the ways in which specific institutional arrangements can affect the outcome of coalition negotiations.

The single most important assumption Laver and Shepsle make in their model is that of ministerial discretion. Coalition theorists have usually assumed that parties bargain over and reach a compromise about each of the policies they pursue in office. Laver and Shepsle argue that this is a mistake. The process of government formation is not one in which parties bargain directly about policy within a particular area, but is instead one in which they bargain about which ministry is to be allocated to which party. This is not to say that policy is unimportant. Parties negotiate about control of ministries precisely *because* they recognize that control of particular ministries will provide them with control over the formulation and implementation of policy in that area. This is for a number of reasons. (1) Ministers have considerable agenda-setting powers; policy changes may have to be approved jointly by a cabinet but will usually be initiated by particular ministers. (2) Cabinet ministers do not usually have the expertise necessary to question proposals made by other ministers. Policy decisions may normally be taken at cabinet level but cabinet decision-making is usually a formality. (3) Ministries are responsible for the implementation of policy; policies are agreed by cabinets but ministers are usually given discretion in implementing them.

> The cabinet is not simply a *collection* of coalition partners, but instead is a *distribution* of specific powers over policy formulation and implementation among those partners. Thus, the very same set of parties in a cabinet comprises quite different effective governments if cabinet portfolios are reallocated between parties. (Laver and Shepsle, 1996: 282; original emphasis)

To see why the assumption of ministerial discretion is such an important one, assume, once again, that there are three parties (A–C) with the same policy positions as those shown in Figure 4.1. But assume now that policy on the left–right dimension is controlled by the finance office and that policy on the authoritarian–populist dimension is controlled by the interior office. In Figure 4.1 it was assumed that *any* point in this two-dimensional space was a possible policy outcome. But if policy is controlled by departments there are, as Figure 4.2 indicates, only nine possible policy outcomes: AA in which party A holds both the finance and interior offices, AB in which A controls the finance office and B the interior office, BA in which B controls the finance office and A the interior office, AC, CA, BB, BC, CB and CC.

This reduction in the available political space can, firstly, be used to account for the relative stability of the cabinet-formation process. Assume that a governing coalition in which B controls the finance office and A the interior office is in place (that is, at point X in Figure 4.1). In Figure 4.2 the lines a1a1, b1b1 and c1c1 once again show those points each party prefers to this status quo. But notice that whilst there are plenty of points which are majority-preferred to the status quo, none of the feasible cabinets falls within them. Because there are no feasible majority-preferred alternatives to it, the coalition between B and A will therefore survive. In this way, ministerial discretion generates stability.

Secondly, the assumption of ministerial discretion can be used to account for the existence of single-party minority governments. Figure 4.3 shows another situation in which there are three equally sized parties and nine possible policy outcomes. Assume that B has formed a minority administration and taken control of both the finance and interior offices. The large winset contained within the indifference curves a1a1 and c1c1 shows those outcomes A and C prefer to BB. Notice that of all the possible alternative cabinets, two fall within this area. The first is BA in which B holds the finance and A holds the

Figure 4.2 *Coalition stability with portfolio allocation*

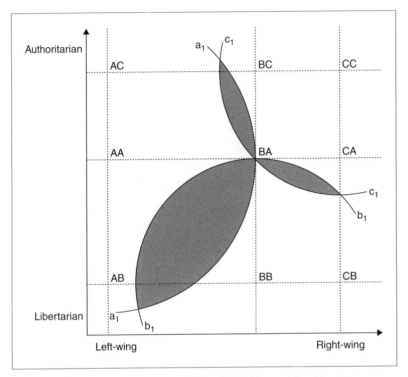

Source: Slightly adapted from Laver and Shepsle, Making and Breaking Governments (Cambridge University Press, 1996), p. 64.

interior office. The second is BC in which B holds the finance and C holds the interior office. But this means that B forms a part of each of the alternative coalitions which are majority-preferred to BB. Such are the ideological differences between A and C that they cannot form a coalition they each prefer to BB. In this sense B is a 'strong party' (Laver and Shepsle, 1996: 69). If it can hold its nerve and face down any implausible threats from A and C to form a joint administration it will be able to govern alone by vetoing a move from BB to BA or BC.

Thirdly, the assumption of ministerial discretion can be used to account for both the preponderance of centre parties and the exclusion of extreme parties from coalition government. For reasons already outlined, the only coalitions which will form following an election are those which are majority-preferred to the status quo and to which there are no feasible majority-preferred alternatives. Laver and Shepsle demonstrate that such coalitions are far more likely to be at or near the position of the dimension-by-dimension median. This is why centre

Figure 4.3 *Coalition stability with 'strong' parties*

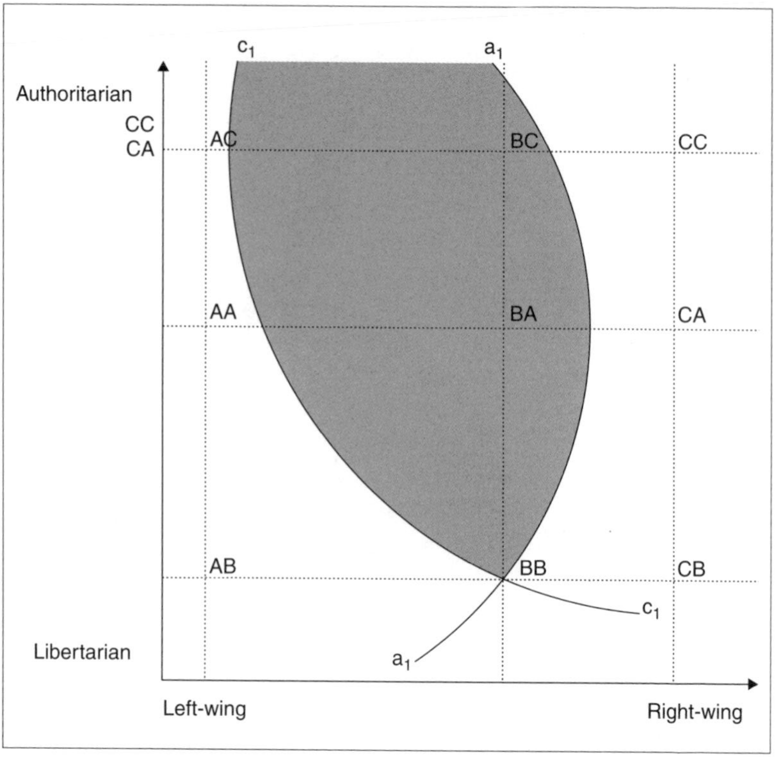

Source: Slightly adapted from Laver and Shepsle, Making and Breaking Governments (Cambridge University Press, 1996), p. 64.

parties can be expected to play such an influential role in the cabinet formation process whilst extreme parties – those located the furthest from this point – are routinely excluded from government. The basic logic of this argument is not difficult to follow. For any given distribution of parties and any given set of ministerial portfolios, the winsets of those possible cabinets located a significant distance away from the position of the dimension-by-dimension median will be larger than those located near it. All things being equal it is therefore more likely that these winsets will contain at least one of the feasible coalition alternatives. To see this notice that the dimension-by-dimension median is actually located at BA (B is the median on the left–right dimension with A to its left and C to its right. A is the median on the authoritarian–libertarian dimension. B is a more libertarian party and C is a less libertarian party). As we have already seen, there are *no*

Figure 4.4   *Coalition stability and the dimension-by-dimension median*

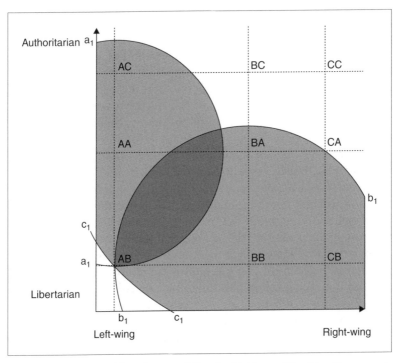

Source: Slightly adapted from Laver and Shepsle, Making and Breaking Governments (Cambridge University Press, 1996), p. 64.

feasible majority-preferred coalitions to this status quo. Figure 4.4 shows the winsets of the cabinet, AB, located furthest from this point (the darker region shows those points unanimously preferred by A, B and C). Notice here the size of this coalition's winsets and the existence of six feasible majority-preferred alternatives to it (AC, AA, BA, CA, BB, CB).

The transaction costs of policy agreements

The most important and controversial assumption Laver and Shepsle make in their model is of course that of ministerial discretion. In this section we want to show how critical debate about it has stimulated research into the ways in which institutions and reputations affect coalition negotiations. Before looking at these criticisms, it is worth briefly noting that Laver and Shepsle themselves are quite defensive about the assumption of ministerial discretion. On the one hand, they are prepared to affirm that if their model is to 'say something of relevance about the world', that the assumptions it rests upon 'must derive in some way from the real world' (Laver and Shepsle, 1999: 395). Because they clearly do believe that their model can tell us something about the real world, the implication of this seems to be that the assumption of ministerial discretion is a defensible one. Yet, at other times, they suggest that this assumption is a 'provisional and convenient fiction' which 'scholarly advances over our initial efforts' will refine and develop (1999: 414).

The problem with the assumption of ministerial discretion is that it would seem to deny to politicians the capacity for deal-making and compromise which animates politics in general and coalition negotiations in particular. For the sake of argument, let us start here by assuming that ministerial autonomy is the commonly recognized default position within coalition negotiations; that parties will, in the absence of any negotiated agreement to the contrary, give other parties absolute and unqualified control over one ministry in return for their control of another. But even given this starting-point we still need to show why parties will be unable to agree on policy compromises that will leave *each* of them better off. To see what is at stake here consider Figure 4.5. We will start here by assuming that the default position is a coalition between A and B in which A controls the interior office and B the finance office. Rather than look at the 'winsets' of coalitions containing alternative parties, consider, instead, the set of outcomes that A and B *themselves* prefer to this point.

On the assumption that both parties care equally about the two issues, the winset below and to the left of BA shows those points A *and* B prefer to BA. That there are such a set of mutually preferred positions should come as no surprise. It is a cornerstone of economic theory that individuals can enhance their welfare through trade and this is all that is happening here. The winset shows those points in which A has traded some policy ground to B on interior affairs and in which B has, in return, traded some ground to A on finance matters and in which both, as a result, are better off.

So even if ministerial discretion is a default position, A and B still have an incentive to reach a policy deal. Can we say precisely what kind of a deal they will reach? Without making additional and quite specific assumptions about, for example, bargaining tactics, this is not a question that can be easily answered. On the assumption that A and B are rational and that each will seek to maximize their gains from

Figure 4.5   *Policy compromises and portfolio allocations*

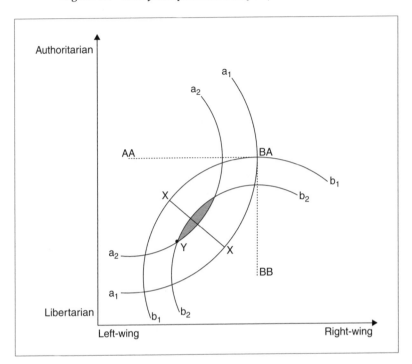

trade, what we can however say is that the eventual outcome of their policy negotiations is likely to fall somewhere on the 'contract' line XX. This line shows all those points in which the possible gains from policy compromise between A and B have been exhausted (see Box 4.3). Consider, for example, a position like Y which falls within the winset of BA but off the contract line. At this point, the possible gains from policy compromise have not been exhausted because it would be possible for A *and* B to move closer to their respective 'bliss' points at AA and BB by agreeing to any compromise within the shaded winset. Only at those points along the contract line will the policy relationship between A and B take on a zero-sum form in which the gains of one party will be the losses of another.

So if there are potential mutual gains from policy compromise, can we assume that these gains will necessarily be realized? At this point, it is open to Laver and Shepsle to defend the assumption of ministerial discretion by arguing that the 'transaction costs' (Box 4.4) of

Box 4.3   The Edgeworth box and the contract line

The contract line, also known as 'the contract curve' or 'the core', is a key concept in bargaining theory. Put simply, the contract curve is the set of alternatives where all gains from trade or compromise have been exhausted. In order to introduce this concept as generally as possible, we will use the graphical device known as the Edgeworth box, named after the Irish philosopher-economist Francis Ysidro Edgeworth (1845–1926), which provides a way of showing the distribution of a fixed amount of two goods between two individuals and those individuals' preferences over such distributions. Although the context here is economic rather than political, the basic idea of the contract line can easily be extended to two-dimensional policy space as in Figure 4.5.

The figure below describes the distribution of goods 1 and 2 between Alice and Bob. If we ignore Bob for the moment, we can think of the graph as showing a normal indifference map between two goods for Alice (see Box 3.2). If Alice always prefers more of each good, her ideal point will be in the upper right corner, where she has all of both goods. Assuming that she has diminishing marginal utility from consuming each of the goods, here indifference curves will be convex to the origin (0_A in the bottom left corner, where Alice consumes none of either good) like $a_1 a_1$ and $a_2 a_2$. Alice always prefers to be on the highest (or rightmost) of her indifference curves but is indifferent among all points on a particular curve.

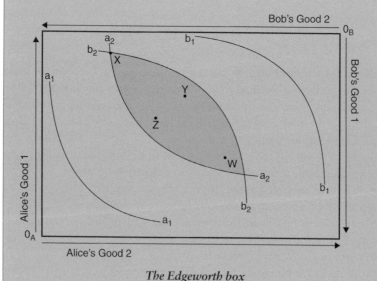

The Edgeworth box

→

→

Since we have assumed a fixed quantity of both goods, the quantities of goods enjoyed by Bob can be represented in the same space by effectively rotating Alice's graph 180 degrees. Every unit of good 1 consumed by Alice is one fewer consumed by Bob. Moving downwards on the vertical axis takes away some quantity of good 1 from Alice and gives it to Bob. Similarly, moving leftward on the horizontal axis gives Bob more of good 2 and Alice less. Just as Alice wants to be as close as possible to the upper right extreme of the Edgeworth box, Bob would like to be as close as possible to the lower left extreme. Assuming that Bob experiences diminishing marginal utility from each good, his indifference curves will be convex to the origin of his indifference map at 0_B in the upper right corner, as are b_1b_1 and b_2b_2.

In an obvious sense, Alice and Bob's interests are completely opposed. Since they are struggling over a fixed quantity of resources, any gain to Alice is a loss to Bob. Bob's most preferred outcome is Alice's least preferred, and vice versa. Since preferences are convex, however, there will often be potential gains from trade. If Alice has most of good 1 and Bob has most of good 2 (putting us near the upper left corner), both could gain (i.e. move to a better indifference curve) if Alice gave up some good 1 in exchange for some of Bob's good 2. Any trades mutually agreed to must result in a Pareto improvement (see Box 2.2). Suppose the current distribution is at point X. As we can see, this puts Alice on indifference curve a_2a_2 and Bob on b_2b_2. Since Alice would like to move to an indifference curve above and to the right of the one she is currently on and Bob would like to move down to the left, any point within the lens-shaped area between a_2a_2 and b_2b_2, such as points W, Y or Z. This is a winset as introduced in the previous chapter, though here we have only two players and the winset is the area mutually preferred to the status quo. The move from X to Y involves Alice giving Bob some good 1 (the downward shift on the vertical axis) and Bob giving Alice some good 2 (the rightward shift on the horizontal axis). The curvature of the indifference curves makes this move a Pareto improvement. Assuming that transaction costs are not too high, we should expect Alice and Bob to mutually agree to some trade resulting in a distribution like W, Y or Z.

Any point within the winset Pareto dominates the status quo, but most of these points will themselves be dominated by others. If a distribution is dominated, there remain gains from trade and we should expect bargaining away from this point. How do we tell whether a point within the winset is itself dominated? For any point in the Edgeworth box it is possible to draw an indifference curve for each person which crosses that point, as a_2a_2 and b_2b_2 cross at point X. The vast majority of possible points will, like point X, intersect and thus produce a corresponding lens-shaped winset. The graph below shows W's winset – the dark shaded region between a_3a_3 and b_3b_3. Moving from X to W is a

→

→
Pareto improvement, but it is not Pareto optimal, since there are gains from trade remaining unrealized. At some points (such as Y and Z), however, the indifference curves of each player will tangent rather than intersect. These points have no winsets – all gains from trade have been exhausted and the distribution is Pareto optimal.

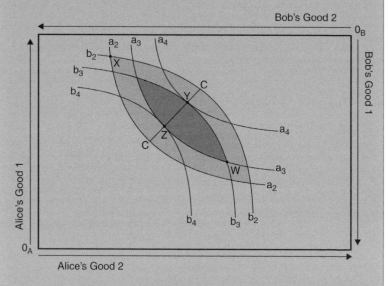

The contract line

Within X's winset there will be an infinite number of tangential pairs of indifference curves, and if we draw a line connecting them, we have the contract line (which may be straight or curved depending on the relative shapes of the players' indifference curves). This is shown in the figure above as the line CC. Each point on this line is Pareto superior to X and is not itself dominated by any other point. If Alice and Bob start at point X and transaction costs are low, we should expect them to reach some point on the contract line, and once they reach such a point we should expect them to stay there as long as their preferences and constraints remain unchanged. What point on the contract line they reach is, however, another matter entirely. Alice would prefer an alternative like Y while Bob would prefer Z, and the struggle for ground along the line is zero-sum. Where we end up will depend on such factors as fall-back positions and the negotiating skill of each player.

reaching and enforcing policy deals will be greater than the potential benefits to be derived from them and that parties will therefore revert to the default position of ministerial discretion. Given that ministers have, according to Laver and Shepsle, considerable autonomy over the implementation of policy within their departments, why should any party trust its coalition partner to abide by the terms of any policy trade? The deals made between parties are not, after all, like the contractual agreements made between private individuals or firms which can, in principle at least, be enforced through the courts. Political deals are above and beyond the law. But such a conclusion seems unduly pessimistic. There are good reasons for thinking that parties will be able to reduce the potential transaction costs involved in the formulation and enforcement of policy deals and that policy deals will indeed be made.

Coalition partners, once they have agreed to make policy trades, will need to reach agreements about what kind of policies to pursue in various issue areas. The time spent negotiating such agreements represent one possible source of transaction costs. These costs may be quite high because politicians will not only have to settle existing policy differences, but anticipate possible future differences relating to issues that have not yet even arisen. Yet the available evidence here suggests that politicians actually invest relatively little time in coalition negotiations and that they have therefore managed to minimize this transaction cost (see Mueller and Strøm, 2005). One way in which they seem to have done so is by using initial negotiations to agree *ways* in which future policy disputes will be settled. The Coalition agreement between the Conservatives and the Liberal Democrats negotiated in May 2010, for example, specifies a clear procedure for resolving inter-party disputes via a Cabinet Coalition Committee co-chaired by the Prime Minister and Deputy Prime Minister and supported by the Cabinet Secretariat. Furthermore, a 'quad' group composed of the Prime Minister and the Chancellor on the Conservative side and the Deputy Prime Minister and the Chief Secretary to the Treasury on the Liberal Democrat side meets prior to cabinet meetings to try to resolve differences.

Once policy agreements have been reached, they need to be monitored and enforced and this represents another potential source of transaction costs. Yet parties can usually rely upon a number of institutional devices to minimize the extent of these costs and so make deals possible (see generally Strøm et al., 2010). Parties can, for example, appoint junior 'watch dog' ministers to departments controlled by one of their coalition partners to ensure that policy promises are being kept

---

Box 4.4   Transaction costs

Transaction costs are the costs of exchanging rather than producing goods and services. More formally, they are

> the costs of deciding, planning, arranging and negotiating the action to be taken and the terms of exchange when two or more parties do business; the costs of changing plans, renegotiating terms, and resolving disputes as changing circumstances require; and the costs of ensuring that parties perform as agreed. (Milgrom and Roberts 1990: 60)

Transaction costs arise from a number of different sources:

(1) *Complexity*: A proposed exchange can be described as being complex when a large number of contingencies have to be considered by both parties to that exchange. Consider the position of a government department negotiating with a large software firm to deliver a new way of processing welfare benefits. The transaction costs of such an exchange are likely to be high because the government will struggle to specify what, precisely, constitutes satisfactory performance.

(2) *Thinness*: By signing a contract with a particular agent to undertake a particular piece of work, an organization may be leaving itself with little alternative but to work with that firm in the future. Think, once again, of a software firm bidding for a contract. Once a system has been installed it will be very costly to change supplier. In such a situation, the government may hesitate about signing a potentially beneficial contract in the short term for fear of being exploited in the long term.

$\rightarrow$

(Thies, 2001). Consistent with this hypothesis, recent empirical work suggests that junior ministers are more likely in coalition governments with large policy disagreements, when other oversight mechanisms are unavailable, and when the policy dimension is salient (Falcó-Gimeno, 2012; Lipsmeyer and Pierce, 2011).

In formulating the theory of the minimal-winning coalition, Riker, it will be recalled, assumed that each instance of government formation is a purely isolated event. On the one hand, and as we might expect, Laver and Shepsle offer a far more sophisticated analysis. The portfolio-allocation model assumes that each instance of cabinet formation begins with an incumbent caretaker government in place and that this government will only be replaced if there is a feasible majority-preferred alternative to it. On the other hand, Laver and Shepsle, like

→

(3) *Information asymmetries*: If a person is unsure about the quality of the product they are buying, they may have to invest resources in order to try and find out what they know they do not know about that product. A potential car buyer may, for example, have to pay for an independent inspection by a mechanic in order to find out whether they are being sold a 'lemon' by an unscrupulous dealer (Akerlof, 1970). The problem here is that costs of acquiring this information may be greater than the potential benefits to be derived from the exchange. In a similar way, a person who knows that they do not know whether their partner is fulfilling the terms of an agreement may have to pay someone to collect that information for them. The costs involved in monitoring compliance within an agreement may, once again, be greater than the potential benefits of the trade.

If we assume that transaction costs are zero then every possible mutually beneficial exchange will take place. This is the so-called Coase theorem (Coase, 1960) (see Box 4.5). If transaction costs are positive then potentially beneficial exchanges may be threatened. In such cases, actors will design and use institutions that minimize transaction costs and so make exchange possible. Transaction cost analysis is one of the more prominent strands of the 'new institutionalism' that has swept through the social sciences. Whether the theory is of the firm (Williamson, 1975), bureaucracy (Horn, 1995), state (North, 1990) or legislature (Weingest and Marshall, 1988), the transaction cost story is that institutions evolve to economize on transaction costs and that different levels of transaction costs lead to the development of different types of governance structures (Hindmoor, 1998).

Riker, ignore the potential importance of reputation in the coalition formation process. Parties will certainly be tempted to renege upon policy agreements, but they may well be forced to recognize that the short-term benefits of doing so are likely to be outweighed by the long-term costs of acquiring a reputation for being untrustworthy. For such a reputation is likely to make them unattractive coalition partners in future years (see Axelrod, 1984; Frank, 1988). The incentive parties have to acquire good reputations may also explain why coalition government is characterized by relative stability. If parties are, as we have suggested, able to negotiate policy deals at any point in political space, then, as we have seen, it is likely, given the existence of multiple dimensions, that there will always be some majority-preferred coalition to the status quo. Yet parties may have to set the potential policy gains from

---

Box 4.5   The Coase theorem

The so-called Coase theorem, named after the American economist Ronald Coase (1910–2013) is concerned with situations in which the 'actions of business firms have harmful effects on others' (Coase, 1960: 1) and offers a critique of the conventional argument that such 'negative externalities' can only be resolved through coercive government intervention and careful regulation.

Imagine a situation in which a cattle rancher and a farmer own adjoining plots of land between which there is no fence. The rancher's cattle can be expected to roam on to the farmer's land damaging his crops. Assume that the rancher must, however, compensate the farmer for any damage. It would then only be in the rancher's interests to allow their cattle to graze if either the profits they could make from doing so would be greater than the costs of the compensation they would have to pay, or the profits they could make from doing so would be greater than the costs of building a fence to stop their cattle from roaming. Either way, it is in the farmer's self-interest to make an economically efficient decision. What, however, if the rancher is not obliged to make any compensation payments? In this case it would appear that the rancher has no incentive to take account of the externalities generated by their action and that the market will fail. But this is not the case. The farmer will have an incentive to either pay the rancher to reduce the number of cattle they have or to build a fence if the profits they expect to make from their crops are greater than the profits the rancher expects to make or the cost of building the fence.

The result here may be judged unfair. Why should the farmer have to pay the rancher to stop damaging their crops? But it would be

→

leaving one coalition and joining another against the long-term costs of acquiring a reputation for being untrustworthy and abandoning their partners.

Assessment

By what criteria ought we to evaluate coalition theory? The instrumentalist answer routinely offered by rational choice theorists themselves is that we ought to do so in terms of its predictive capacity. Of all of the areas of rational choice theory examined in this book, coalition theory, blessed as it is with a strong data-set against which models can be tested, is perhaps the most stridently empirical. Laver and Shepsle seem, for example, in no doubt that their model ought to be judged in economically efficient. So long as property rights are demarcated and responsibility for externalities assigned, there is no need for government intervention. Self-interested actors will be able to bargain their way towards an efficient solution and will be able to do so whatever the initial allocation of property rights is:

> It is necessary to know whether the damaging business is liable or not for damage caused since without the establishment of this initial delimitation of rights there can be no market transactions ... but the ultimate result (which maximizes the value of production) is independent of the legal position if the pricing system is assumed to work without cost. (Coase, 1960: 8)

The Coase theorem only holds when there are zero transaction costs, an assumption Coase (1960: 15) recognizes is 'very unrealistic'. When there are positive transaction costs actors may be unable to reach potentially mutually beneficial exchanges and the results of any process of self-interested bargaining may not be efficient. In this case, the farmer and the rancher will not only have to reach an agreement, but they will have to agree upon how much damage is being done to the crops and whose cattle are causing the damage. They will have to agree on how and when compensation payments are to be made and will have to find a way to, for example, prevent the farmer from exaggerating the extent of the damage to his crops in order to extract additional compensation. All these represent potentially considerable transaction costs.

terms of the accuracy of its predictions. One such prediction is that the status quo cabinet in place at the start of a cabinet formation process will either remain in place at the end of that process or be replaced by a cabinet contained within its winset. Using data on cabinet formations between 1945 and 1989, they show that this prediction was true of 162 of 220 possible instances; a far better success rate, they argue, than could have been achieved by luck (for further empirical evidence on the portfolio-allocation model see Back, 2003).

So when judged in terms of this criterion, how does coalition theory perform? In a review of the portfolio-allocation model, one critic of the rational choice method, Paul Warwick (1999), has argued that it is possible to make far more accurate predictions about coalition formation and durability by statistically analysing the results of previous instances of cabinet formation and extrapolating from these results. In the case of, for example, cabinet durability, he argues that statistical analysis shows that just two factors account for most of the variance in cabinet survival. The first of these is whether or not the coalition commands a legislative majority, and the second is how ideologically compact it is. Knowing just these two pieces of information about any existing coalition, it is, Warwick argues, possible to make far more accurate predictions about the likely durability of that coalition than those derived from the portfolio-allocation model.

Now rational choice theorists might respond to this challenge by arguing that the predictive capacity of rational choice theory will continue to improve and eventually match or even surpass that of inductivists like Warwick. But can we really expect coalition theorists to develop formal models taking account of, for example, the transaction costs involved in policy discussions and to then derive from these models predictions about the likely outcome of particular negotiations? Our view is that we cannot. The number of factors likely to affect the course of negotiations is such that theorists will only be able to construct models whose predictions hold, all other things being equal (but see King et al., 1990) (see Chapter 9).

Yet it is, we think, a mistake to judge rational choice coalition theory simply and exclusively in terms of the accuracy of its predictions. As we argued in the opening section of this chapter, we might instead see it as being the role of rational choice theorists to explain why and when the empirical findings discovered by other political scientists hold. Rather than seeing inductive and deductive approaches to the study of politics as necessarily being in competition with each other, as is normally the case, we might instead see them as being complementary. Perhaps surprisingly given their positivist starting-point in *Making and Breaking Governments*, this is actually the position Laver and Shepsle themselves have come to adopt in recent years. Although disputing many of the technical details of Warwick's argument about the shortcomings of the portfolio-allocation model, they do, nevertheless, accept the basic premise of his argument: that it is possible to make more accurate predictions about the formation and durability of coalition governments using statistical induction. Yet they also argue that this form of analysis cannot be used to provide a coherent *explanation* of the coalition process. All this form of analysis can do, they maintain, is 'hint at some factors', like ideological diversity, which 'might be at work' but which 'do not hang together' and so cannot be used to provide an explanation of how or why particular events occurred (Laver and Shepsle, 1999: 396). The provision of such an explanation, one which will allow us to understand what is going on in the world around us, requires the construction of 'coherent and parsimonious analytical models' which can show us how different factors act and interact with each other (ibid.).

The explanatory, as opposed to predictive, value of the portfolio allocation model can be seen in its recent application to real-world coalition negotiations. Marc Debus (2011) argues that following the 2010 UK general election, the Conservative Party was a strong one in Shepsle and Laver's sense, with the salient and distinct policy dimensions being economic left–right and for/against decentralization. Debus argues that this position allowed Tories to secure almost all important cabinet positions. Just as the median voter theorem provides insight into why parties may seek the centre ground in one-dimensional, two-party systems, the portfolio allocation model provides insight into why parties might seek the centre ground when there is more than one dimension and more than two parties. In 2010 the Tories shifted to the left economically and became more favourable towards decentralization. Though they remained the most right-wing major party economically, their ideological distance from the centre was less than it had been previously. Where they had previously been the strongest opponents of further decentralization, the Tories shifted significantly in 2010 and replaced Labour as the median party on this dimension, with the Lib Dems being far more decentralist than the other two parties. If Debus's interpretation of events is correct, the portfolio allocation model does not simply provide predictive power; it also tells us something about *why* the Conservatives got the lion's share of ministerial posts.

Chapter 5

Kenneth Arrow and Social Choice Theory

Overview: In the two previous chapters we examined party behaviour in two-party and multi-party democracies. This chapter discusses the properties of democracy at a more general and normative level. Two key texts are examined. The first, Kenneth Arrow's (1951) *Social Choice and Individual Values*, has been interpreted as showing that it is impossible to provide a normative rationale for making social decisions when individual members of a society have different interests or opinions. The second, William Riker's (1982a) *Liberalism Against Populism*, uses Arrow's theorem and the work in social choice theory it inspired to defend a 'liberal' rather than 'populist' theory of democracy. Arrow and Riker's work has cast a 'very long, dark shadow over democratic politics' (Cain, 2001: 111). In the final section of this chapter we argue that this work does, however, need to be placed in context. Social choice theory may show that democracy is problematic and imperfect; it does not, however, show that democracy is impossible or necessarily undesirable.

Setting the stage: democracy and the public will

Democracy, according to Albert Weale (1999: 1) has 'ceased to be a matter of contention and become a matter of convention'. The number of countries in which citizens can remove their leaders through regular elections has increased remarkably since the late nineteenth century, and even thoroughly undemocratic regimes such as the Democratic People's Republic of Korea feel the need to pay homage to democracy in their official designations. Bryan Caplan (2007: 186) argues that democracy has become a sacred value beyond rational enquiry: 'Everyone from journalists and politicians to empirical political scientists and academic philosophers is willing to publicly profess his democratic fundamentalism without embarrassment.' Yet political theorists have often expressed a determined cynicism about or outright hostility to democracy (Mackie, 2003: 2; Dahl, 1989). Plato argues that democracy leads to social anarchy. Marxists and public choice theorists alike argue that representative democracy is a sham and that real power is monopolized by special interest groups (see Chapter 7). Critics have also routinely argued that voters lack the knowledge or determination to make rational and well-informed choices (see Chapter 8).

These critiques of democracy are often damning, but they all accept to varying degrees the idea that democracy can – for better or for worse – tell us something about what people want even if what they want is ill informed or is then ignored. The sub-branch of rational choice theory known as social choice theory, on the other hand, has offered a more foundational critique of democracy. Voting, whether it involves voting directly for some policy in, for example, a referendum, or voting indirectly for a candidate in a legislature, is a defining part of the democratic process. Voting reveals the 'public will' or 'collective interest'. The critique of democracy offered by the two social-choice theorists examined here, Kenneth Arrow and William Riker, is a critique of voting. Arrow and Riker argue that there is no way – even in principle – of fairly and accurately counting votes in order to reach a collective decision:

> Outcomes of voting cannot, in general, be regarded as accurate amalgamations of voters' values. Sometimes they may be accurate, sometimes not; but since we seldom know which situation exists, we cannot, in general, expect accuracy. Hence we cannot expect fairness either. (Riker, 1982a: 236)

It is worth emphasizing that this is *not* an argument about any particular method of voting. The target social choice theorists have in their sights is not plurality voting, proportional representation or some other specific way of counting votes. It is, rather, and more generally, the very idea of being able to aggregate the preferences of individual voters in such a way as to generate a fair and accurate decision or 'social choice'. Stated in this way, the concerns of social choice theorists appear both mysterious and fantastical. Mysterious because it is unclear what, precisely, such a sweeping claim might involve. Fantastical because the notion that voting might be an inherently flawed way of reaching social decisions seems, in this democratic age, a counter-intuitive one. Yet, as we will see, the basic argument involved here, although routinely presented in a technical way, is actually quite simple.

The precursors of social choice theory

Social choice theory did not emerge as a recognized subject area until the publication of Arrow's *Social Choice and Individual Values* in 1951. Yet as Iain McLean and Arnold Urken (1995) carefully demonstrate, many of the puzzles and inconsistencies associated with voting that Arrow carefully dissects were actually discovered and discarded in the eighteenth century. Of particular significance here is the work of two French mathematicians and members of the Paris Academy of Sciences, Jean-Charles Borda (1733–1799) and the Marquis de Condorcet (1743–1794). Borda, whose obituary records that he 'worked much and published little', delivered a paper to the Paris Academy in 1770 showing that the winner of a plurality or 'first-past-the-post' election might be opposed by a majority of voters. Consider, for example, the preferences of the seven (1–7) voters in Table 5.1 who must select between three options (x–z). The first, second and third preferences of the voters are shown. In a plurality election y will receive the votes of the third and fourth voters, z the votes of the fifth and seventh voters and the winner, x, the votes of the first, second and sixth voters. Yet a majority composed of the third, fourth, fifth and seventh voters clearly prefer both y *and* z to x.

The obvious problem with the plurality voting system is that it fails to take account of the full range of voters' preferences and, in this case, of the fact that x is the last choice of four voters. The solution, Borda argued, was to devise a method of voting taking account of this information. The result, the eponymous 'Borda count', works

Table 5.1   *Majority voting generates a majority-opposed decision*

Voters	Preferences			Borda count points score		
	1st	*2nd*	*3rd*	*x*	*y*	*z*
1	x	y	z	2	1	0
2	x	z	y	2	0	1
3	y	z	x	0	2	1
4	y	z	x	0	2	1
5	z	y	x	0	1	2
6	x	y	z	2	1	0
7	z	y	x	0	1	2
			Total	6	8	7

as follows. For any given number of options (n), assign $n - 1$ points to the option the voter ranks first on their ballot paper, $n - 2$ to the option they rank second and so on; the winner being the option receiving the most points. The right-hand part of Table 5.1 shows how this works by translating the preferences of the seven voters into point tallies. It shows that y is the Borda winner and that x receives the lowest score.

In an essay published in 1784, the Marquis de Condorcet, who was the Permanent Secretary of the Paris Academy until he fell to the Jacobin terror, showed that the Borda count is vulnerable to exactly the same problem as plurality voting. It will sometimes select as the social choice an option a majority of the electorate oppose. Table 5.2 shows the preferences of five (1–5) voters over five (a–e) options. As the right-hand part of the table shows, e wins the Borda count with 16 points. Yet a series of pair-wise comparisons shows that a majority composed of the first, third and fourth voters prefer d to e. The claim that e ought to be the social choice because it is the Borda winner therefore appears questionable.

It is a defect of both the plurality and Borda methods that they sometimes fail to select the majority-preferred option. It was therefore Condorcet's suggestion that the social choice ought to be determined by making a series of pair-wise comparisons between *all* the options

Table 5.2   *Borda count winner is majority-opposed*

Voters	Preferences					Borda count points score				
	1st	2nd	3rd	4th	5th	d	e	a	b	c
1	d	e	a	b	c	4	3	2	1	0
2	e	a	c	b	d	0	4	3	1	2
3	c	d	e	a	b	3	2	1	0	4
4	d	e	b	c	a	4	3	0	2	1
5	e	b	a	d	c	1	4	2	3	0
					Total	12	16	8	7	7

Note: The left columns of this table again show each voter's preference-ranking, whilst the right-hand columns translate this into point scores. With five options ($n = 5$) the first choice of each voter is assigned four points, the second choice three points and so on.

and selecting that one (the 'Condorcet winner') which is majority-preferred to all the others. This has become known as the 'Condorcet method'. In Table 5.2 we have already seen that a majority prefers d to e. By looking more carefully at this table, it can be seen that a clear majority also prefers d to either a, b or c.

There is, however, a problem here which Condorcet himself recognized and that has preoccupied social choice theorists ever since. In certain situations, the preferences of voters can be such that whilst one option is always majority-preferred to another, no one option is majority-preferred to *all* the others. This is known as 'Condorcet's paradox' or the 'paradox of voting'. Table 5.3 shows the preferences of three voters (1–3) over three options (a–c). Pair-wise comparisons reveal that a is majority-preferred to b (by virtue of the support of the first and third voters), that b is majority-preferred to c (by virtue of the support of the first and second voters) but that c is majority-preferred to a (by virtue of the second and third voters). There is therefore a 'cycle' such that a > b and b > c but c > a. In other words, collective preferences as revealed by the Condorcet method are intransitive. Even though each individual has a coherent (i.e. transitive) ranking of the options, the collective ranking just doesn't make any sense.

Table 5.3   *Condorcet's paradox*

Voters	Preferences		
	1st	*2nd*	*3rd*
1	a	b	c
2	b	c	a
3	c	a	b

In the 1870s the existence of voting cycles was independently rediscovered by an Oxford mathematician, Charles Dodgson, better known as Lewis Carroll, the author of *Alice's Adventures in Wonderland*. Modern social choice theory, it could be argued, began with a 1948 paper by Scottish economist Duncan Black (1908–1991) which not only provides an early formulation of the median voter theorem (see Chapter 3), but also demonstrates the possibility of cycles and defines some conditions under which they occur. As we will see in this chapter, the median voter theorem and voting cycles have a close logical relationship. Black (1948, 1958) applied the logic of economics to group decision making. To do this, Black (1948: 26) assumes:

that in a committee *m* motions are put forward, that each member carries out an evaluation of each motion in regard to every other, that in the voting each motion is put against every other, and that the committee adopts as its decision ('resolution') that motion, if any, which is able to get a simple majority over every other.

Like Condorcet and Dodgson, Black recognizes the possibility of cycles but moves beyond earlier work by specifying the conditions under which Condorcet's paradox can emerge. The key factor here is the 'shape' of individual preference orderings. Black shows that if individuals have 'single-peaked' preferences, voting cycles cannot occur. A preference profile is single-peaked if the preferences of all individuals can be aligned on a shared left–right scale, with each individual having an ideal point on the scale and judging other alternatives based on their ordinal distance from this point. If some voter's ideal point is a and point b is spatially between points a and c, single-peaked preferences require that the voter prefer b to c, or at least be indifferent between these options. Figure 5.1 shows the same set of preferences as found in Table 5.3, with the discrete alternatives a–c are arranged alphabetically along a single shared dimension (the horizontal axis). The vertical axis shows how individuals rank the choices, with a higher position signifying preference over a lower position. Figure 5.1(a) shows a ranking of b > c > a; Figure 5.1(b) a ranking of a > b > c. Although these rankings look quite different, both are single-peaked in the sense that as we move away from the first choice in either direction, options become increasingly less attractive. Figure 5.1(c), on the other hand, shows a multi-peaked ranking of c > a > b. Here we do not see a smooth decrease in desirability as we move away from the first preference; a is preferred to b even though b is closer on the scale to the individual's first choice of c.

If all voters have single-peaked preferences, cycles cannot occur and the Condorcet method always picks the first preference of the median voter. Consider the preference profile listed in Table 5.4 and shown graphically in Figure 5.2. We can see that all preferences are single-peaked. The Condorcet winner here is option c (beating option a with the support of voters 2 and 3; b with 2 and 3; d with 1 and 2; and e unanimously).

Black (1948: 26–30) proves that whenever preferences are single-peaked, there will always be a Condorcet winner, and that this will always be the median of voters' ideal points. At the peak of each preference curve is each voter's bliss point, and the median of these points

Figure 5.1 *Preferences and voting cycles*

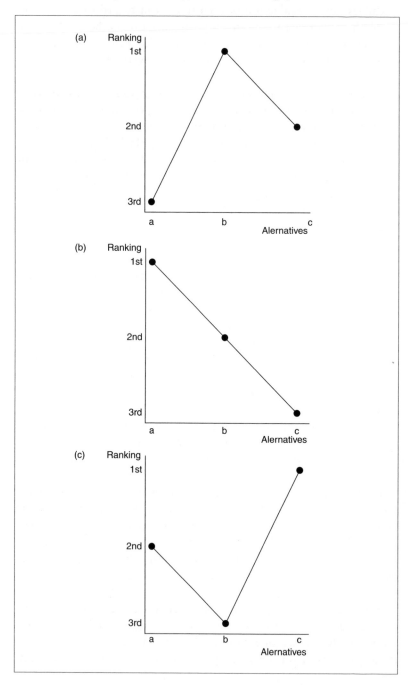

Table 5.4   *Single-peaked preferences and the Condorcet winner*

Voters	Preferences				
	1st	*2nd*	*3rd*	*4th*	*5th*
1	b	a	c	d	e
2	c	b	d	e	a
3	d	c	e	b	a

Figure 5.2   *Single-peaked preferences and the Condorcet winner*

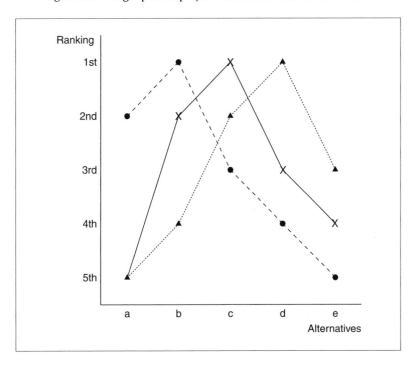

(in Figure 5.2 this is voter 2's first choice of c) there will by definition be the same number of other voters' ideal points on either side. Let's refer to the median ideal point (Black calls it the 'median optimum') in any preference profile as c, since this allows us to reuse Figure 5.2 as a graphical aid for a general but informal proof. For c to be the median optimum, it must be the case that there are exactly as many other voters with a bliss point to the left as to the right. Focusing just on first preferences and imagining that two parties compete for voters in a plurality system, we have the median voter result of Chapter 3, since c is preferred to any point to its right (i.e. d or e in Figure 5.2) by half of the non-median voters and to any point to its left (i.e. a or b in Figure 5.2) by the other half. These two groups cancel each other out and the median voter is decisive. With the Condorcet method, things are more complicated, but only slightly. Since we are assuming single-peaked preferences, we know that all voters with an ideal point to the right of c will vote for c over any alternative to the left of c. Otherwise, their preferences would not be single-peaked. The inverse applies to those voters with ideal points to the left of c, and this means that for any pairwise comparison involving c, the non-median voters will be split evenly and the median will again be left to decide.

After proving this version of the median voter theorem, Black (1948: 34) goes on to prove that 'when the shapes of the preference curves are subject to no restriction, the transitive property does not necessarily hold good'. Multi-peaked preferences allow cycles to emerge and the Condorcet method produces incoherent results. Not all types of multi-peaked preferences produce a cycle, but we know from Black's argument that cycling can *only* occur when the assumption of single-peakedness does not hold. As we will see later in this chapter, this is an important point when thinking about the normative implications of Condorcet's paradox and Arrow's theorem.

Arrow: social choice and individual values

Kenneth Arrow (born 1921) was educated in New York and has spent most of his working life at Stanford University. Awarded the Nobel Prize in 1972, Arrow made a number of fundamental contributions to economics, most notably in general equilibrium theory and welfare economics but also in information economics, choice under uncertainty, economic growth, and, of course, social choice theory (see Starr, 2008). Arrow wrote *Social Choice and Individual Values* as his doctoral thesis following a brief spell working at the Rand Corporation in the late 1940s. Economists and mathematicians at Rand were, at this time, pioneering the use of game theory to analyse international relations. When applied in this way, game theorists assume that it is possible to talk about the payoffs or utility accruing to countries under various outcomes. Given the commitment made to methodological individualism within rational choice in general and game theory in particular, the utility being invoked here can only refer to the combined utility of the individual citizens of those countries. But how can individual preferences be aggregated in such a way that we might talk about the utility of the citizens of a country? Arrow's intuitive answer was that a 'social welfare function' could be used to aggregate individual preferences in a fair and accurate way. A social welfare function, a concept developed by economists Abram Bergson (1938) and Paul Samuelson (1947), is a mathematical function which ranks all possible resource allocations by social desirability according to some individual-level determinants of welfare. Arrow began looking for the social welfare function which could be used to determine the collective will of a country but soon ran into problems and eventually concluded that there was no fool-proof way of doing so:

> For *any* method of deriving social choices by aggregating individual preference patterns which satisfies certain natural conditions, it is possible to find individual preference patterns which give rise to a social choice pattern which is not a linear [or transitive] ordering. (Arrow, 1950: 7; original emphasis)

Arrow (1951: 51) constructs his argument by identifying a number of 'unanimously acceptable' canons of democratic fairness, listed below, which any reasonable method of aggregating preferences must, he argues, satisfy. He goes on to show that no possible method of aggregating preferences can simultaneously satisfy all these principles for three or more alternatives. This finding, which has subsequently become known as the 'impossibility' theorem, has been interpreted as showing that 'majority rule is fatally flawed' (Wolff, 1970: 59) and that 'strict democracy is impossible' (Runciman, 1963: 133).

1 *Unrestricted domain.* Voters must be able to rank alternatives however they like (as long as their ordering is complete and transitive). Assume that there are three options (a–c) between which voters must choose. The condition of unrestricted domain simply requires that individuals should be free to rank these options in any order they want – an ordering of c > a > b is just as valid as a > b > c. This allows for multi-peaked preferences and thus generates intransitivity for some preference profiles.

2 *Transitivity.* Transitivity requires that the social choice be consistent in its ranking of alternatives. Consistency requires that if there are

three options (a–c) and a > b and b > c that a > c. Similarly, if a is ranked equally to both b and c, b and c must also be ranked equally.

3 *Completeness or decisiveness*. This condition simply requires that the social welfare function provides a complete ranking of alternatives. Given any two options, one must be preferred to the other or they must be ranked equally. That is, we must be able to give each option a definite place in the social ranking, although ties are allowed.

4 *Independence of irrelevant alternatives*. This condition requires that the ranking of two options is determined solely on the basis of individuals' ordinal ranking of those options. When deciding whether to rank a ahead of b, for example, the social welfare function cannot refer to individuals' ranking of c relative to either a or b. We will discuss the reason for and implications of this condition in more detail later. At this point we simply note that Arrow (1951: 93) includes it because he thinks the alternative is to allow the social welfare function to make interpersonal comparisons of utility, which he insists are impossible (Box 5.1).

5 *Weak Pareto principle*. If all individuals prefer a to b, the weak Pareto principle requires that the social welfare function chooses a over b. This provides a minimal guarantee that the social welfare function is responsive to individual preferences. It should be emphasized just how weak this condition is: if we have 100 voters, with 99 strictly preferring a to b and 1 being indifferent between them, the weak Pareto principle has nothing to say. Only when we have perfect unanimity of *strict* preference does the weak Pareto principle apply (see Box 2.2).

6 *Non-dictatorship*. This condition requires that there is no individual whose preferences are automatically the social choice independent of the preferences of all other individuals.

Arrow shows that no voting rule can simultaneously satisfy all six of these conditions. This does two things. First, it generalizes Condorcet's paradox to voting rules in general. Second, it shows that any attempt to escape the paradox will logically entail a violation of one or more of the conditions listed above. What Arrow shows is that *if* individuals' preferences are such that there is a cycle of the sort shown in Table 5.3 (a possibility allowed for by the first condition of unrestricted domain), then there is no possible voting rule which satisfies the other five conditions.

Proof of Arrow's theorem usually proceeds by demonstrating that there is one and only one social welfare function which satisfies the first five conditions listed above – dictatorship. Though the chain of reasoning required to arrive at this conclusion is long and convoluted, it does not require any complex mathematics. Before proceeding, however, we should pause to consider just what the axiomatic approach is trying to show, since it differs radically from the purpose of descriptive formal models which are in some sense designed to represent the real world. In critiquing Downs's formulation of the median voter model we asked whether his assumptions were reasonable approximations of the real world. This is because Downs was trying to build a predictive model of real political processes. Arrow's purpose, on the other hand, is not to describe or predict any empirical phenomenon, but rather to demonstrate the logical inconsistency of certain axioms. Proving the theorem is entirely a logical or mathematical exercise, and the steps taken in such a proof are not intended to represent in any sense the way real-world decision-making processes work. In some cases (like the median voter theorem), the simplest proof is in agreement with our intuition about how the process would work. In other cases, the simplest proofs have no easy intuition behind them. Arrow's theorem is an example of the latter case.

We here follow Sen's (Maskin and Sen, 2014) proof, which involves proving two intermediate theorems ('lemmas' in the language of mathematics). Assuming in both cases that the first five of Arrow's conditions are met, Sen proves that (1) any group of individuals which is decisive over the social ranking of *any* pair of options is decisive over *every* pair, and (2) that every decisive group with more than one member can always be split into two groups, one of which is decisive and one of which is not. From here, we can begin with some decisive group (perhaps containing everyone in society) and whittle it down until only one individual – the dictator – remains.

Define group D as a set of individuals which is decisive over the choice between two options. A group is decisive over a single pair of outcomes x and y if the social choice rule always ranks x over y when all members of D prefer x to y, regardless of how anyone outside D ranks these two alternatives. We know that all social welfare functions with a chance of satisfying all of Arrow's conditions must have some such group, since the weak Pareto principle requires that the group consisting of all members of society is decisive in the above sense – if they all agree, they get their way.

The first step in Sen's proof is to show that any group which is decisive over *any* pair of alternatives is decisive over *all* pairs of alternatives, and thus decisive over the entire social preference ranking. Take four

Box 5.1   Interpersonal comparisons of utility

Assume that there is just one person, Ben, and two goods, x and y. How can we determine whether Ben derives more utility from x than from y? If Ben is given a choice between x and y and chooses x, we can infer that he has 'revealed' a preference for x and so expects to derive more utility from its consumption. But can we know how much more utility? At this point, we could simply invite Ben to reflect upon the strength of his preference for x over y. Alternatively, we could rig the choice between x and y in such a way that it revealed something about his preferences. Assume, for example, that we give Ben the choice between getting y with absolute certainty or a 50 per cent chance of getting x and a 50 per cent chance of getting nothing. If Ben chooses x we can infer that he expects to derive at least twice as much utility from x. In this way, we can, in principle at least, derive a cardinal rather than ordinal preference-ranking for Ben.

Assume now that there are two people, Alice and Ben, and only one good, x. How can we tell whether Ben or Alice will derive more utility from consuming x? In *An Essay on the Nature and Significance of Economic Science*, Lionel Robbins argues that there is no rigorous, scientific way of making these kinds of interpersonal comparisons of utility. 'There is no means of testing the magnitude of [Alice's] satisfactions compared' with [Ben's] and so 'no way of comparing the satisfactions of different people' (Robbins, 1935: 124). There are two problems involved in making interpersonal comparisons. (1) We cannot see inside other people's minds and read their thoughts in a way that would allow us to directly compare utility streams. We can, Robbins (1932: 139) observes, test people's bloodstream and we can now measure endorphins and

→

distinct alternatives, a, b, x, y. Due to the weak Pareto requirement, there must be some group D which is decisive over the ranking of x and y. Unrestricted domain allows us to introduce any coherent set of preferences we want, so assume that all members of D have the preference ranking a > x > y > b. Assume also that for all those *not* in D, a > x and y > b, with no specification made of their ranking of the pairs (a, b) and (x, y). Since D is by assumption decisive over (x, y) and all members of D rank x > y, we know that the social choice rule ranks x > y. Since everybody agrees that a > x and y > b, the weak Pareto and transitivity conditions tell us that socially a > b. The independence condition tells us that this can only be because of the way individuals rank a and b (i.e. any information about rankings of x and y must be ignored). Since the only preferences we have specified over the pair (a, b) are members

→

record the firing of neurons within the brain. But these do not provide us with the direct measure of utility necessary to show that Alice derives more satisfaction from consuming x than Ben. (2) We cannot rig the choice between Alice and Ben in such a way that their behaviour reveals information about their utility. We might find that Alice is prepared to spend £10 on x whilst Ben is only prepared to spend £5, or that Alice is prepared to queue for two hours to get x and Ben only one. But we cannot infer from this that Alice derives twice as much utility from x because we cannot know that Alice and Ben place an equal value upon particular amounts of money or particular lengths of time spent queuing (for more details see Elster and Roemer, 1991).

Much to his apparent surprise, this argument about the impossibility of making interpersonal comparisons soon became economic orthodoxy (Robbins, 1971: 147–9). But Robbins' argument remains controversial. Some economists and many ordinary people would argue that it is a matter of 'plain common sense' (Cole, 1936: 149) that we can and do use language as a guide to making interpersonal comparisons of utility. Amartya Sen (1970a) has argued for 'partial comparability' of utility. Although we cannot precisely quantify the emperor Nero's glee at playing the fiddle while Rome burned or the suffering of other Romans, we can, and as a practical matter we must, make judgements about certain clear-cut cases and say that Nero's utility is quantitatively outweighed by the suffering of others. The approach of aggregating preferences in a 'fuzzy' way provides an incomplete ranking which does not allow us to compare any two alternatives but maintains that some alternatives can be considered unambiguously superior to others (Barrett et al., 1986; Gibilisco et al., 2014).

of group D, it must not matter what those outside D want. If the social welfare function is to produce a transitive and complete ranking of alternatives in this case it must find that a > b. Group D is therefore decisive over the pair (a, b) whenever it is decisive over (x, y). This logic can equally applied to any other pair, and we can thus conclude that any group decisive over a particular pair is decisive over the complete social ranking of alternatives for any social welfare function satisfying the first five of Arrow's conditions.

The second step in the proof is to show that any decisive group D consisting of more than one individual can be broken down into two groups, one of which is also decisive. Assume that we split D into two subgroups D_1 and D_2, with everyone in D_1 preferring x > y and x > z but with no assumption made about their preferences over the pair (y, z). For everyone in D_2, x > y and z > y. Since D as a whole is decisive and all members agree, we know that socially speaking x > y. Because of the completeness condition, it must be the case that either z ≥ x or x > z according to the social choice rule. If z ≥ x, transitivity requires that z > y. This makes D_2 decisive over (y, z), since we have not specified the preferences of anyone outside this group over this pair of alternatives. If, on the other hand, the social choice rule ranks x over z, then D_1 is decisive, since we have not specified any preferences over (x, z) other than those of members D_1. Thus, any decisive group can be partitioned in a way such that some subset of the group is decisive. Since this is true of all decisive groups with more than one member (and assuming the number of individuals is finite), we can keep partitioning until we find a decisive group with one member. This individual would be able to determine the social ranking of preferences regardless of others' rankings. They would be a dictator. Since this violates condition six and avoiding this result requires that we violate at least one of the other five conditions, Arrow's theorem is thus proved.

Again, it must be emphasized what this proof establishes and how it does so. The claim is not that real people would choose some electoral rule which satisfies important democratic norms but to their surprise gives some arbitrary individual absolute power. Rather, the proof shows that any social choice rule other than dictatorship violates at least one of Arrow's other conditions. Arrow's axiomatic method, which has since Arrow's contribution been the methodological core of modern social choice theory, can be described in broad terms quite simply (Sen, 1999: 353–4; Thomson, 2001). Imagine we start with the set of all possible social choice rules and want to know which we should choose. To do so, we impose some specific requirements we think the rule ought to meet. Adding some weak requirements will preclude some rules, but many possibilities will remain. Imposing more constraints will continue to narrow the field, and a 'characterization theorem' emerges when we conclude that only one rule or one family of rules satisfies the conditions. We briefly encountered such a theorem in Chapter 2 in the form of May's (1952) argument for simple majority rule in choices between two options on the grounds that it is the only social choice rule which is simultaneously decisive, responsive, impartial between individuals and neutral between options. Moving beyond a characterization theorem, we may impose further constraints and find that there is no possible rule which satisfies them. We then have an impossibility theorem such as Arrow's. Thus, the procedure for proving that only *one* voting rule (or family thereof) is consistent with certain normative requirements must, in a mathematical sense, always be a step along the way to proving that *no* voting rule is acceptable on slightly more restrictive grounds. As Sen (1999: 354) puts it in his Nobel speech, 'a full axiomatic determination of a particular method of making social choice must inescapably lie next door to an impossibility – indeed just short of it'. Conversely, slightly weakening the conditions of an impossibility result can produce a characterization theorem. As we will see later in this chapter (with respect to Donald Saari's argument for the Borda count) it is possible to argue that Arrow's conditions are slightly too restrictive and that with appropriate revision his theorem shows one voting rule to be uniquely preferable to all other possibilities.

Arrow shows that there is *no logically possible* way out of Condorcet's paradox which does not violate one or more of the six conditions listed. Arrow argues informally that the conditions are appropriate, but, being axioms, they are the unproved premises of his deductive argument rather than the conclusion. To consider the relevance of Arrow's theorem, we need to move beyond strictly axiomatic reasoning by considering the empirical likelihood of cycles, and whether the requirements he imposes on a reasonable social choice rule are acceptable. In the remainder of this chapter we consider how other social choice theorists – including economists, political scientists, mathematicians and philosophers – have tackled these topics. We begin with Riker's influential argument that Arrow's theorem shows populist democracy to be a sham before moving on to some defences of democracy against the claim of impossibility.

Riker: liberalism against populism

Although Arrow's work on social choice theory was lauded by economists, it was, initially at least, largely ignored by most political scientists and philosophers. This is no doubt partly because Arrow's presentation in *Social Choice and Individual Values* makes relatively few concessions to non-mathematicians. It is also because Arrow, who devoted himself almost exclusively to the study of general equilibrium theory in the years following the publication of his thesis, made little effort to relate his argument to existing debates about the nature and limitations of democracy (but see Arrow, 1967). One of the few political scientists who immediately recognized the importance of Arrow's work was, however, William Riker (1961, 1965) who, in *Liberalism Against*

Populism (1982a), eventually succeeded in establishing the significance of Arrow's work for a wider social science audience.

The first few chapters of *Liberalism against Populism* carefully document the perversities of a series of voting methods including plurality voting, proportional representation and the Borda count. The next few chapters then use Arrow's theorem to generalize these findings and show that *any* method of voting is flawed. But it would be a mistake to regard Riker as *simply* popularizing Arrow's work. For in two important respects, Riker's argument actually differs from Arrow's. In the first place, Riker is at pains to emphasize the practical significance of social choice theory. Arrow's contribution, as we have seen, is a theorem rather than a theory. It shows that there is no social choice rule which *guarantees* a coherent decision without violating one of the above conditions. Whether the Condorcet method, for example, *actually* produces intransitivity in any given case depends on the preference profile of the electorate. Arrow does not attempt to demonstrate that any actual set of voters have or have had these preferences. Using a combination of formal theory and detailed historical case-studies in which he reconstructs the preference-rankings of assorted politicians and voters, Riker claims that the cycles which give rise to Condorcet's paradox are actually quite common and that they disfigure democratic politics (Riker, 1982a: 197–202; Riker and Weingast, 1988).

As we saw in Chapter 3 and again in this chapter with respect to single-peaked preferences, the existence of more than one issue dimension opens the door to intransitivity. Black shows that majority intransitivity is impossible with single-peaked preferences and possible but not guaranteed with multi-peaked preferences. There has been important work in the axiomatic tradition defining the conditions under which multi-peaked preferences and transitivity can coexist (e.g. Sen and Pattanaik, 1969), but Riker's point on the ubiquity of cycles is best illustrated by returning to the two-dimensional spatial model of Chapter 3. Charles Plott (1967) showed that a two-dimensional version of the median voter theorem does exist, but that the conditions for its existence are extremely restrictive. Consider the case of three voters with simple Euclidian preferences (see Box 3.2) over two-dimensional policy space. If the three voters have preferences which form a straight line, policy space is effectively one-dimensional and the median voter result holds. This is because, as in the standard one-dimensional case, the voters on each side of the median have directly opposing interests which cancel each other out, leaving the median voter to decide.

For more than three voters, this pattern of balancing due to directly opposing interests can produce stability even if not all preferences are on a straight line. In Figure 5.3(a), we have five voters spread across the two issue dimensions. Notice that voter c's ideal point is on the line between the ideal points of voters a and b as well as that between d and e. This means that any movement away from point c supported by a will be opposed by b, and vice versa. This is because, since we have assumed symmetric and circular indifference curves, at no point on a straight line between two individuals' ideal points will their indifference curves intersect. As can be seen in Figure 5.3(a), there is tangency between a's and b's indifference curves at point c, and thus any gain to one must come at the expense of the other. Voters a and b will never join an alliance which moves away from c. Since d and e find themselves in a similar conflict with respect to moves away from c, their preferences also balance each other out and no three-voter majority prefers any point to c. Another way of making this point is to say that the majority winset of c is empty (graphically, no three voter's indifference curves passing through c ever overlap). As in the median voter case, all others cancel each other out and the central voter is left to decide.

This requires quite a specific distribution of preferences, however. Note that the distance between voters a and b or d and e makes no difference at all; the requirement is that a straight line between the two points passes through c. If we keep adding voters, c will remain an equilibrium if and only if the new arrivals can be paired off one against the other such that their interests directly oppose. Even a slight movement of any voter in a direction which is not directly toward or away from their 'opposing' voter will destroy the equilibrium. In Figure 5.3(b), e has shifted and the line connecting e and d no longer passes through c. As a consequence, d and e are no longer directly opposed when it comes to movements away from c, and a majority of a-d-e would prefer any point in the shaded winset. Since there is now no voter at the intersection of all the lines connecting pairs of opposing voters, McKelvey's chaos theorem applies and we can conclude there is no majority rule equilibrium in this case (see Mueller, 2003: 87–93 for a proof that symmetry of this type is necessary for equilibrium in two dimensions). It should be obvious that with a large number of voters, the likelihood of preferences being perfectly arranged around a single point is extremely slim. Riker (1980: 442) thus concludes that 'the conditions for equilibria are so restrictive as to render equilibria virtually nonexistent'.

It is important to note that Riker's use of Plott and McKelvey is concerned with intransitivity in the underlying preferences of individuals

Figure 5.3   *The Condorcet winner in two dimensions*

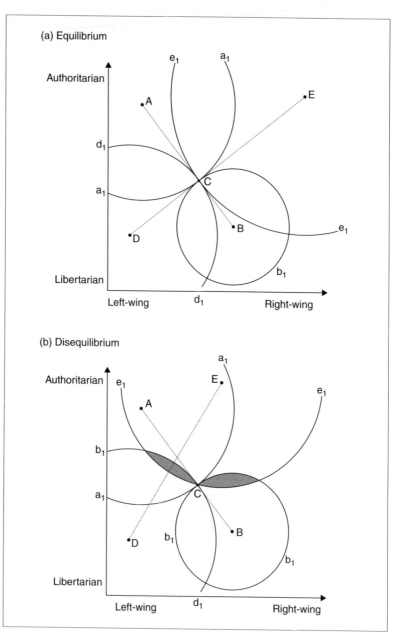

(a) Equilibrium

(b) Disequilibrium

when political space is unconstrained. The restrictive conditions required for spatial equilibrium in two dimensions tells us that it is likely that any platform can be beaten by some other *logically* possible alternative, but predictions of chaos cannot be straightforwardly applied to collective choices involving a fixed set of alternatives or ideologically-constrained parties (see Chapter 3). As we saw in Chapter 4 with respect to the portfolio allocation model, structural constraints on collective choice can produce stability when the underlying preferences would otherwise produce chaos. Riker (1982a: 188–92) insists, however, that such structural constraints are not themselves democratic and must in some sense be arbitrary.

The virtual nonexistence of equilibria means that elections often generate intransitive results. This, in turn, means that elections 'fail to make sense' because they result in the selection of candidates or policies to which there are majority-preferred alternatives (Riker, 1982a: 115). How do we know this? Arrow's theorem tells us that when there is a voting cycle one or more of the previously listed conditions have been broken in the process of aggregating preferences. It would not appear to be the case that the conditions of unrestricted domain, the weak Pareto principle or non-dictatorship are being routinely broken. The problem, Riker concludes, must therefore be that elections are generating intransitive results. The argument at this point may still seem a little fanciful. We do not, after all, regularly encounter newspaper reports that in some election the socialists were majority-preferred to the centre party, the centre party to the conservatives and the conservatives to the socialists. But, as Riker emphasizes, this is because the incoherence of democratic choice is usually hidden from view. Elections produce winners, and, since we do not have access to all voters' complete preference ordering, we do not see what the outcome would have been under an alternative social choice rule or if some irrelevant alternative were added to the ballot. We cannot conclude that intransitives do not exist because we do not look for them. Furthermore, and because we do not know which election results would, if we checked, generate intransitive results, we cannot have confidence in the results of *any* election.

Riker's argument differs from Arrow's in a second way. Arrow simply looks at the problem of preference aggregation posed by voting cycles. Riker, however, wants to show how self-interested political actors can exploit those cycles through by manipulating the agenda, adding new issue dimensions, and voting insincerely. Riker (1986) uses the term '*heresthetic*' to refer generally to this 'art of political manipu-lation'. Whereas rhetoric is the art of changing preferences for political advantage, heresthetic, deriving from the Greek word for choosing or electing, involves changing the structure of the choice situation for political advantage while leaving preferences unchanged.

Agenda control

In most democratic bodies, whether they are committees, legisla-tures or executive cabinets, one person is usually given control of the agenda. Political scientists have previously recognized that this person may be able to secure their preferred outcome by excluding certain options from formal consideration (Lukes, 1974; Bachrach and Baratz, 1970). Riker (1982a: 169–92), following the argument of McKelvey (1976, 1979) we encountered in Chapter 3, shows that the agenda setter may also be able to secure their preferred outcome by determining the *sequence* in which options are considered. Assume that there are four options (w–z) and three voters (1–3) with the following preferences:

Voter 1: $w > x > y > z$
Voter 2: $x > y > z > w$
Voter 3: $y > z > w > x$

There is a cycle here such that $z > w$, $w > x$, and $x > y$ but $y > z$. But assume that voter 3 is the chairman of the committee and thus controls the agenda. They can arrange for an initial contest between x and w (which w will win), then one between w and y (which y will win) and, finally, one between y and z (which y will win). In doing so, they can secure the eventual triumph of their preferred option.

Agenda control is also important when all options are considered simultaneously, as in plurality voting and the Borda count. Here, it is the options on the ballot which can influence the outcome, and for most issues there is no 'natural' set of alternatives which everyone agrees should be considered. In referenda, for example, those with the power to specify the options may be able to manipulate the result. In elections with the free entry of parties there is no central agenda set-ter, but the result depends on which parties choose to enter. Since no voting rule satisfying Arrow's five other conditions produces results independently of irrelevant alternatives, there is no way around this problem.

Strategic voting

Drawing on the work of Allan Gibbard (1973) and Mark Satterthwaite (1975), Riker (1982a: 137–62) demonstrates that any method of voting is vulnerable to strategic manipulation by voters who, by misrepresenting their preferences, can try to secure their preferred outcome. To see what this might entail, look again at the preference-rankings of the three voters above. If voter 1 can spot what it is that voter 3 is trying to achieve in sequencing the votes in a particular way, they can thwart their ambitions by voting strategically for x during the initial contest between x and w, so ensuring the victory of x. During the subsequent contests between x and y, and x and z, x will again triumph. In this way, voter 1 can secure their second rather than, as would otherwise be the case, third choice.

Adding issue dimensions

At times, the preferences voters have are such that there will be a stable equilibrium manifesting itself in a clear and enduring majority for one particular party. Such equilibria are, however, extremely fragile (Riker, 1982a: 136–9, 1984, 1986, 1996). By either reframing or reigniting a previously dormant policy issue, politicians can undermine existing equilibrium by introducing new issue dimensions. In Chapter 3 we saw how parties must sometimes compete in a multi-dimensional setting and how this can engender instability. At that time, the existence and number of dimensions was treated as being exogenous to the process of competition itself. Riker shows why parties sometimes compete *by* trying to create new issue dimensions. In the case of, for example, the American Civil War, Riker argues that the Republicans, led by Lincoln, were able to overcome their political isolation by introducing a new and previously dormant issue, slavery, that split the existing and winning coalition between the north-western states that were against the admission of new slave states to the union and the south, which argued that this was a matter for the states themselves.

Democracy is supposed to embody a certain notion of political equality; every person has one vote and that vote is supposed to count equally. Riker (1982a: 200–1) argues that heresthetic shows that this equality is a chimera:

> The absence of political equilibria means that outcomes depend not simply on participants' values and constitutional structures, but also

on matters such as whether some people have the will or the wit to vote strategically, whether some leader has the skill, energy, and resources to manipulate the agenda, or whether some backbencher – in a committee or out – has the imagination and determination to generate a cyclical majority by introducing new alternatives and new issues. These are matters of perception and personality and understanding and character.

Such is the ferocity of Riker's denunciation it might seem that he must be opposed to democracy itself. This is not, however, the case. Riker distinguishes between what he calls a 'populist' and a 'liberal' theory of democracy. The populist theory, which he associates (rather unfairly) with Rousseau as a political theorist and Britain as a country, interprets democracy as requiring the translation of the public will into public policy. The liberal theory, which he associates with Madison, is understood as requiring, firstly, that voters be given the opportunity to remove from office an incumbent government which has offended their sensibilities, and, secondly, the existence of constitutional checks and balances such as a bill of rights, the separation of powers, federalism, a multicameral legislature and fixed terms of office, limiting the power of the executive.

Social choice theory shows that the populist theory of democracy is flawed 'not because it is morally wrong, but because it is empty' (Riker, 1982a: 236). There is no reliable way in which voters' preferences can be aggregated and because any election is vulnerable to heresthetical manipulation, we simply cannot equate democratic rule with the translation of the public will into public policy. The liberal theory of democracy is not however compromised in the same way, because instead of demanding that a government embody the public will it requires only that it be possible for voters to remove a government from office (Riker, 1982a: 243). Although Riker insists that there is no neutral and meaningful method of aggregating preferences when they are multi-peaked, he argues that democratic voting does place limits on elected officials. Voters are quite likely to have coherent and homogenous preferences over whether politicians should exploit them for their personal gain, and so voting can perform a disciplinary role. In Riker's (1982a: 9) liberal interpretation, 'the function of voting is to control officials, *and no more*': an argument that carries obvious implications for the kind of work on constitutional political economy surveyed in Chapter 2.

The possibility of social choice

Arrow and Riker's work strikes at the very heart of democracy, and we have argued in the previous sections that their work does deserve to be taken seriously. At the very least, Arrow's impossibility theorem shows that the idea of a collective will is more complicated and contingent than democratic theorists might have thought. Riker and his followers make the stronger claim that the very idea of collective choice is meaningless. In this section we consider two major responses to Arrow's theorem and Riker's interpretation of it. First, we look more closely at Arrow's independence condition, suggesting that it is more restrictive than it initially seems. We then consider the unrestricted domain requirement and look at arguments which suggest real-world preferences may be effectively restricted in ways which make democratic cycles unlikely.

Independence of irrelevant alternatives

Although each of Arrow's conditions has been subjected to criticism, the most controversial among social choice theorists has been independence. On the surface this seems like an uncontroversial assumption – how could anyone deny that the choice between two options should be based only on individual preferences between those options? The way in which this intuitively appealing requirement is formalized, however, is stronger than this. As Mackie (2003: 137) observes, the independence condition 'would be better named the pair-wise comparison condition, as it requires that choices among several alternatives be carried out only with information about choices between pairs'. This is important because the reliance upon pair-wise comparisons precludes the use of preferential methods of counting votes like the single transferable vote or the Borda count.

   Donald Saari (2008) argues that this requirement is excessive. A reasonable social choice rule should not be prevented from consulting individuals' complete preference rankings when making social choices, since only by looking at the complete ordering of alternatives can the rationality of underlying individual preferences be appreciated. Saari agrees with Arrow that in ranking two alternatives, a social choice rule should consider only individual's preferences over those outcomes but insists that preference *intensity* should matter in addition to simple ordinal rank. Voting rules, of course, do not provide direct information about preference intensity. If ballots asked voters how much they wanted their preferred outcomes, there would be strong incentives to strategically exaggerate. Saari (2008: 58–64) argues, however, that the position of an alternative in a global ranking provides important information about preference intensity.

Gerry Mackie (2003: 133) provides a useful illustration of when it might make good sense to take even infeasible alternatives into account. Suppose a reception is to be held and the caterers will only provide one drink, either beer or coffee. To save time, the organizer copies a form from the previous year's event which asks people to rank their preferences over beer, coffee, water, tea, milk and fruit juice. Assume that only two families reply and that they indicate the following preferences:

> Family 1 (5 people)   beer > coffee > water > tea > milk > fruit juice
> Family 2 (4 people)   coffee > beer > water > tea > milk > fruit juice

Given the caterer's requirements, there are only two feasible (relevant) alternatives and beer is majority-preferred to coffee. Assume now that at the last moment the second family pulls out and a third family with the following preferences decides to attend in its place:

> Family 3 (4 people)   coffee > water > tea > milk > fruit juice > beer

What should the organizer now do? In terms of the simple pair-wise comparison, beer is still majority-preferred to coffee (family 1 is larger than family 2) and so nothing has therefore changed. If the other infeasible alternatives are to be considered as simply irrelevant, the organizer will have to choose beer. But surely it is relevant that the third family rank beer last? Now we need to be careful here. The difficulties involved in making interpersonal comparisons of utility are such that we cannot necessarily assume that the members of the third family derive less utility from the consumption of beer than the first family simply because they rank it lower (see Box 5.1). It may simply be that the members of the third family derive exceptional amounts of utility from all the other drinks. But given the limited amount of information available, there is nevertheless a plausible case for making coffee the social choice. Consider what would happen if we were to conduct a Borda count here. There are six options ($n = 6$), so five points should be awarded to the first-ranked option, four points to the second and so on. Beer is the first-ranked option of five people (5 × 5 = 25) and the last-ranked option of 4 (4 × 0 = 0) and so scores 25 points. Coffee is the first-ranked option of four people (4 × 5 = 20) and the second-ranked option of five (5 × 4 = 20) and so scores 40 points.

Saari argues that Arrow's independence condition should be replaced with an intensity adjusted version which requires that alternatives be ranked purely on their ordinal ranking and the intensity of their preference for one over the other, with intensity being defined by the number of alternatives between the two options in the total ranking. This allows a variety of social choice rules to satisfy the modified version of Arrow's condition, but among positional voting rules (i.e. those which consider only the ranking of alternatives), the Borda count emerges as a uniquely desirable choice. Thus, by slightly relaxing Arrow's impossibility theorem Saari arrives at a characterization theorem which tells us, should we accept the underlying conditions, that the Borda count is not only *a* fair voting rule, but *the only* fair voting rule.

Arrow and Riker, of course, reject such a move on the grounds that position in a global ranking is not a reliable indication of preference intensity. In addition to the problem of interpersonal comparisons of utility and strategic voting, a particularly troublesome problem is that the results of a Borda count depend crucially on the alternatives which make the ballot. In some cases there may be a natural set of alternatives to be voted upon and the problem will not arise. But many real-world policy issues have an almost unlimited number of potential responses. Consider the case of climate change policy. One option would be to do nothing, others would be implementing a carbon tax of $20/ton, a carbon tax of $21/ton, and green energy subsidies of various sorts. Clearly a Borda count on this issue would only work if the uncountable options are whittled down to a manageable number, but this would give those in charge of the whittling a great deal of power.

Unrestricted domain

Another popular target has been Arrow's first condition of unrestricted domain, which requires that voting rules are able to deal with multi-peaked preferences. Critics argue that an assumption of single-peakedness is quite plausible in a number of contexts (Gaertner, 2001; Mackie, 2003: 5). Imagine that there are three parties: a left-wing party (lw), a right-wing party (rw) and a centre party (ce). If voters have as their first choice the party 'closest' to them in political space and as their last choice the party furthest away from them, they will either rank the parties:

(i)   rw > ce > lw,
(ii) lw > ce > rw,
(iii) ce > lw > rw, or
(iv) ce > rw > lw.

Nobody will rank the parties:

(v)　rw > lw > ce, or
(vi)　lw > rw > ce,

for if spatial proximity is what counts how could a person who most preferred the right-wing party prefer the left-wing party to the centre party? This is significant because when voters agree in this way about the criteria by which to rank options, cycles and Condorcet's paradox cannot arise. We need to be careful, however, because some seemingly one-dimensional choices might give rise to multi-peaked preferences. Consider the case of military spending. Although many individuals may have single-peaked preferences on this issue, it is not difficult to think of ways in which a reasonable person might have a multi-peaked preference. Suppose that Jim most prefers a strong military (spend $10b) but thinks that having a weak military (spend $1m) is pointless and wasteful and would prefer no military at all (spend $0). Jim's preference ranking would therefore be $10 billion > $0 > $1 million. In general, if some individuals think thresholds are important, even simple numerical choices with a natural scale might allow for individually coherent multi-peakedness capable of generating social intransitivity.

Another interesting possibility is raised by Egan (2014), who argues that voters will on certain 'do something' policy issues demand that virtually *any* action be taken rather than remaining with the status quo. For many policy issues such as crime and education, there is widespread agreement about the *goals* of the policy and dissatisfaction with the status quo but much disagreement and uncertainty on the best means of achieving the goal. Those on the left, right and centre all want education improved and crime rates reduced, but many voters will be uncertain whether shifting to the left or the right is the better approach. For 'do something' policies, Egan uses survey data to show that many people have multi-peaked preferences in the sense that they prefer something be done regardless of whether that something means moving to the right or left of the status quo.

Of course it is implausible to assume that *every* voter will employ the same criteria in judging candidates or policies. What happens if *most* voters have single-peaked preferences on a shared scale? Intuitively we might expect to see democratic cycles emerge less frequently under such conditions, and this is indeed what analytic models and simulations have found (Gehrlein, 2004, 2005; List et al., 2013: 83; Niemi, 1969): the probability of a Condorcet winner increases as preferences become 'closer' to single-peaked in the sense that a high proportion of voters make their decisions on the basis of a single underlying dimension.

The idea of approximate single-peakedness has led some to argue that democratic deliberation has an important role to play in avoiding democratic cycles. Deliberative democrats argue that legitimate decision-making requires not simply the aggregation of preferences but a period of careful reflection upon and debate about those preferences prior to voting. During this period of deliberation, participants, it is argued, should not simply assert their own claims and viewpoints; they ought instead to frame their arguments in terms of common interests whilst responding to the force of the better argument (Dryzek, 2010; Elster, 1998; Gutmann and Thompson, 2009).

On one reading, deliberation is meant to lead to substantive agreement on policy issues. Many deliberative democrats see this view as hopelessly naïve and instead argue that deliberation works through a type of 'meta-agreement' on the relevant *dimension* of choice rather than agreement on concrete policy options (Dryzek and List, 2003; Miller, 1992). The claim most often made here is that deliberation may increase 'structuration': that is the degree to which individual preferences are aligned along the same shared set of underlying dimensions. Deliberation may increase preference structuration in two main ways (Farrar et al., 2003). Firstly, as people talk and learn from each other, they may come to adopt criteria for judging alternatives that they recognize it is conventional to use. Secondly, through careful deliberation they may influence each other's thinking and acquire more of a shared understanding of what an issue involves.

This is important because increased structuration reduces the chances that voters' preferences will generate a cycle. In particular, deliberation may often produce approximate single-peakedness on particular policy dimensions. List et al. (2013) investigate this possibility empirically by using 'deliberative polls', which involve opinion polls taken before and after individuals deliberate on some issue. Their study finds that deliberation does indeed make preferences on specific issues more single-peaked. The obvious problem is that many collective choices as we currently make them involve more than one policy issue. The obvious solution for the deliberative democrat is to disaggregate these choices wherever possible. Even if preferences over comprehensive policy bundles are unlikely to be approximately single-peaked, it is plausible that through deliberation most people will come to judge each issue along a single dimension. If this is the case, direct democratic mechanisms such as referenda could be used to meaningfully aggregate preferences on specific issues (Miller, 1992). Deliberation would not produce consensus, but it would produce coherent aggregate rankings which would allow for a coherent and reasonably fair compromise between competing values.

In any case, it may be that political preferences more broadly are sufficiently unidimensional that cycling will be unlikely or restricted to a small central region of policy space. As we saw in Chapter 3, politics in contemporary democracies is never entirely one-dimensional but the salience of secondary and tertiary dimensions varies across time and place. It is, of course, difficult to know when close enough is good enough when it comes to single-peakedness in real-world elections, and there has so far been little work attempting to answer this important question. This reflects a more general absence of good empirical evidence on the real-world prevalence of majority cycles.

As we have already noted, Riker (1982a, 1986) illustrates and defends his claim that voting cycles are extremely common by way of a series of historical case-studies. These include the American Civil War, the introduction of a school construction bill in the US House of Representatives in 1956, the adoption of the Seventeenth Amendment to the US Constitution (on the direct election of senators), the Roman trial of the servants believed to have killed Afranius Dexter in about 100 AD and C.P. Snow's fictional account of a Cambridge University college election in *The Masters*. Yet as Mackie (2003: 197–309) demonstrates, these accounts depend upon contestable interpretations of politicians' preference-rankings and ignore alternative and usually more obvious explanations of the same event. Furthermore, and even if we accept that these accounts do actually illustrate cases of majority cycles, it is unclear how representative they are. Although there has been more empirical work documenting the presence of cycles, it remains unconvincing. In reviewing the evidence of Condorcet's paradox, Adrian Van Deemen (2014) concludes that the 47 empirical studies he considers jointly provide little insight into the likelihood of majority cycles. Of the 265 elections (ranging from large elections to small committee decisions) considered in these studies, 25 were categorized by their authors as having no Condorcet winner. What are we to make of these findings by Riker and others? The very obscurity of at least some of Riker's stories suggests not only that he is extremely erudite but perhaps also that he had to search long and hard for some of his examples. This is at least partially explained by the general inaccessibility of complete individual preference rankings, but it may also be because democratic cycles are uncommon in real-world elections.

Assessment

In Chapter 1, we suggested that rational choice theory has polarized political science and that its proponents and opponents have been reluctant to engage with each other. This has been particularly true of social choice theory. Despite a growing body of theoretical work clearly relevant to democratic theory and practice, the insights of social choice theorists have not entered the canon of democratic theory. Indeed, more than half a century after the publication of *Social Choice and Individual Values*, many textbooks on democracy simply fail to mention Arrow's theorem (e.g. Eagles, 2008; Held, 2006; Johnston, 2011). In this chapter we have tried to show why this is unfortunate. Social choice theory has important implications for democratic political theory; political scientists may have good reasons to doubt the claim that social choice theory shows democracy to be 'impossible', but this is a claim that they ought to address and use to sharpen their own definitions and discussions of democracy. Democratic theorists have been improving in this regard (e.g. Dryzek and Niemeyer, 2006; Estlund, 2009; Gaus, 2010; Landemore, 2013; Mackie, 2003; Shapiro, 2009), but social choice theory remains a peripheral idea.

What, then, does social choice theory have to tell democratic theorists and political scientists? The first important lesson, in our view, is that no voting system is perfect or appropriate for all situations. Although Arrow sees each of his conditions as necessary for a good voting rule and Riker argues that violation of any of these conditions renders populist democracy meaningless, those interested in evaluating or designing electoral systems may be better advised to treat them as important considerations which need to be evaluated according to the situation at hand. If for example, a committee is interested in choosing among a number of discrete 'natural' alternatives, the independence of irrelevant alternatives as used by Arrow might be too strong, and we might instead accept Saari's argument for the Borda count as satisfying all relevant requirements in this case. The Borda count is not an infallible method of aggregating preferences. As Condorcet first recognized, it sometimes fails to select the majority-preferred alternative. But a great deal of comparative research by social choice theorists into the relative merits of different methods of voting has shown that the Borda count most frequently delivers fair and defensible election results (Dummett, 1998; Saari, 2000). In particular, and given the sort of preference-profile which sustains the Condorcet's paradox, the Borda count has the great advantage of reporting a tied result rather than an intransitive cycle. This is important because there is, in principle, no difficulty in dealing with tied results by agreeing, at a prior constitutional stage, to flip a coin or giving a casting vote to the speaker or longest-serving member. In those cases where there is no natural and fixed set of alternatives, the situation may be very different. A national referendum on climate change policy would be highly vulnerable to agenda manipulation if conducted using a Borda count and we might want to focus on the trade-offs between other democratic values. Arrow's theorem can reasonably be interpreted as showing that there is no unique and impartial collective will waiting to be revealed through voting, but that does not mean that there are not more or less fair means of balancing competing interests through voting.

The second important lesson is that evaluation of voting rules cannot be entirely divorced from evaluation of their non-electoral institutional supports. If, as Riker argues, agenda setters are able to manipulate elections to get their own way, the question of whether to worry too much about this possibility depends crucially on what other non-electoral mechanisms we have to ensure that the agenda is set fairly. If we have trust in these other institutions, agenda manipulation may not be much of a problem. Similarly, if we have a direct democracy which considers one issue at a time, the arguments of deliberative democrats suggest that fair compromise through simple majority of plurality voting rules will be enhanced by institutions encouraging rational deliberation. This is one of Riker's central points: equilibrium cannot always come from *within* democratic choice; it must in some sense be *imposed* by institutions which set rules relating to agenda setting or the admissibility of particular preference rankings. One interpretation of this point is that such impositions are anti-democratic, but an equally valid one is that democracy as voting can only survive when embedded in a well-designed constitutional structure and suitable political culture. Riker's Madisonian vision of liberal democracy is one conception of how non-electoral institutions should support electoral ones, but there is nothing unique in Riker's view in this respect. Indeed, it seems to us that this broader view of democracy as something more than simply an electoral phenomenon has been characteristic of political science throughout its history. Though political theorists occasionally talk of an institution-free collective will, the conventional wisdom in political science has always been that coherent collective choice is only possible when some institutional or cultural prerequisites are in place.

Chapter 6

Mancur Olson and the Logic of Collective Action

Overview: Individuals must sometimes act collectively in order to achieve their goals. The collective action problem, often known as the free-riding problem, arises when it is better for all the members of a group that they act collectively even though it is in nobody's individual interest to contribute to the provision of the collective good. Within rational choice theory, credit for the identification of the collective action problem is usually given to Mancur Olson whose doctoral thesis, *The Logic of Collective Action*, was first published in 1965. In what has become an emblematic statement of the collective action problem, Olson (1965: 2) suggests that 'unless the number of individuals is quite small, or there is coercion or some other special device to make individuals act in their common interest, rational, self-interested, individuals will not act to achieve their common or group interests'. In this chapter we introduce Olson's general framing of the collective action problem and consider more recent contributions, particularly those of Elinor Ostrom, which have built on Olson's framework while challenging many of his conclusions.

Setting the stage: individuals, groups and rationality

If individuals are rational and groups are made of individuals, we might intuitively conclude that groups are rational. Consider the empirical and normative study of interest groups, which during the 1950s and 1960s was dominated by pluralists like David Truman (1951) and Robert Dahl (1956). Although pluralism is an easier position to caricature than characterize, pluralists believe that power should be dispersed throughout society, that public participation in political processes should be encouraged, and that government policy should command the consent of the public (Baggott, 1995: 13). Pluralists argue that interest groups are important policy actors *and* that they are instrumental in achieving these goals. Interest groups allow people to express their preferences over policy issues on a sustained basis and to become personally involved in the political process. They also act as a check upon and a balance to any concentrations of power within society.

The idea that groups uniformly represented the interests of their members has been attacked by neo-pluralists (Galbraith, 1972; Lindblom, 1977) and Marxists (Block, 1977) who, in different ways, argued that business interests had privileged access to the policy-making process. The most enduring, and in our view powerful, critique of pluralism came from rational choice theory in the form of Mancur Olson's *The Logic of Collective Action*. Pluralists assumed that people would always and everywhere mobilize in support of their interests, and that the pattern of interest group activity on any particular policy issue could therefore be taken as indicative of the state of public opinion. Olson showed that we cannot conclude groups are rational in this sense simply because their members are rational – this inference involves a fallacy of composition (i.e. assuming that objects and their constituent parts share all properties). People with shared interests must overcome a collective action problem if they are to organize in defence of that interest. Because some groups are more likely to overcome that problem than others, it cannot be assumed that larger and more powerful interest groups necessarily represent people who feel more intensely about some issue.

Olson's *The Logic of Collective Action*

Collective action is necessary whenever a group of people can or must work together in order to achieve some goal. Olson (1965: 1), who was a professor at the University of Maryland from 1968 until his death in 1998, opens *The Logic of Collective Action* by observing that 'it is often taken for granted ... that individuals with common interests usually attempt to further those common interests'. Yet, as he shows, this is not always the case. In the case of collective goods, the benefits of which are non-excludable (see Box 6.1), collective action is compromised, sometimes fatally, by the existence of a collective action problem. Faced with the choice of whether or not to contribute to the provision of a collective good, each individual may well reason that their contribution will make little, if any, difference to the overall

Box 6.1   Excludability, rivalry of consumption and types of economic goods

Economists often classify goods in terms of (1) their 'excludability', and (2) their 'rivalness' (Mankiw, 2014: 216–17). A good is excludable if its owner can prevent its consumption benefiting anyone else. To use a standard example, the beam of light emitted by a lighthouse is non-excludable because any passing ship can potentially benefit from it. A good is rivalrous when its consumption by one person reduces the amount available to others. A television signal is non-rivalrous because the quality of the signal one person receives is unaffected by the number of other people receiving it. This two-way classification generates four possible types of goods, as shown below.

	Rivalrous	*Non-rivalrous*
Non-excludable	Common pool resources (e.g. over-harvested fisheries, the environment, congested non-toll roads)	Public goods (e.g. national defence, unencrypted television signals, uncongested non-toll roads)
Excludable	Private goods (e.g. cars, chocolate bars, congested toll roads)	Club goods or toll goods (e.g. golf courses, encrypted television signals, uncongested toll roads)

'Private goods' are the stuff of standard economics and raise no collective action issues. Of the other types of good, economists focus most often on 'public goods', which are both non-excludable and non-rivalrous. Perhaps the best example of a public good is national defence. A military force capable of deterring or preventing an attack on your next-door neighbour will also deter or prevent an attack against you – you cannot be excluded from enjoying the benefits of national defence. Further, the fact that you benefit from this defence does not reduce the benefit to your neighbour or anyone else – the good is non-rivalrous in consumption. It is generally believed that public goods, if they cost anything to produce, will not be provided in the absence of government intervention, since the lack of excludability prevents anyone producing the good from charging consumers for its use.

'Common pool resources' like fishing grounds are non-excludable to the extent that it is very difficult to stop boats exploiting them but are rivalrous in the obvious sense that the fish caught in one boat cannot then be caught in another. It is a common feature of such goods that they are, up to some point, naturally self-sustaining. Fishermen are able

→

> →
>
> to catch a certain number of fish each year without reducing the over-all size of the population. Yet beyond a certain level of consumption, common goods become degraded and eventually destroyed (Box 6.3). Again, economists generally assume that government action is required here – either nationalizing or privatizing in order to control access to the resource (i.e. making it excludable).
>
> 'Club' or 'toll' goods are excludable but non-rivalrous in consumption. Examples include encrypted television signals and, at sufficiently low levels of utilization, golf courses, toll roads and movie theatres. Club goods can often be provided voluntarily by the market, although economists may worry that firms will charge too much for club goods to generate efficient results. Since there is no rivalry in consumption, the marginal cost of providing the good to one more person is zero. Efficiency requires that in such circumstances the good be provided to everyone valuing it at all. But if the provider of the good cannot alter prices to the demand of each individual, they will set prices such that some of those valuing the good positively will not be willing to pay. This leaves potential mutually beneficial trades unrealized (i.e. the outcome is Pareto inferior to some alternative).
>
> The line between club goods and private goods is not a clear one. Many goods will be non-rivalrous at low levels of utilization but suffer 'congestion' at higher levels. A movie theatre might be a club good on Monday morning but a private good on Saturday night. The same holds for the distinction between public goods and common pool resources. A small population of fisherman working a large lake might see the fish population as a public good, since their efforts are not large enough to
>
> →

amount of the good provided and that by free-riding they can benefit from the contributions made by others:

> Any group or organization, large or small, works for some collective benefit that by its very nature will benefit all of the members of that group in question. Though all of the members of a group therefore have a common interest in obtaining this collective benefit, they have no common interest in paying the cost of providing that collective good. Each would prefer that the others pay the entire cost, and ordinarily would get any benefit provided whether he had borne part of the cost or not. (Olson, 1965: 21)

The danger here is of course that if everyone attempts to free-ride that there will be no collective action.

As examples of the collective action problem, consider the following:

→

make a dent in the number of fish. If the population increases, however, the public good may be transformed into a common pool.

Just as rivalry comes in degrees, excludability is not an all-or-nothing thing. In most cases excludability is a matter of cost. In principle most goods can be rendered excludable. If they wanted to, the owners of a lighthouse could arrange for a series of ships carrying giant black-out screens to sail directly in front of any boat which had not paid to use the lighthouse beam. But this would obviously cost the owner more than they could hope to charge for their services. Technological change can have serious effects on excludability, however. The invention of barbed wire made grazing land for cattle an excludable good (Anderson and Hill, 1975), and effective digital rights management (DRM) for music and software allows creators to prevent pirates from free-riding on their efforts.

In *The Logic of Collective Action* Olson suggests that the collective action problem afflicts the provision of public goods. Yet he defines public goods solely in terms of their excludability. 'A public good is here defined as any good such that, if any person X_i in a group $X_1, \ldots, X_i, \ldots, X_n$ consumes it, it cannot feasibly be withheld from the others in that group. In other words, those who do not purchase or pay for any of the public or collective good cannot be excluded or kept from sharing in the consumption of the good' (Olson, 1965: 12). To the extent that public goods are usually defined in terms of their non-excludability and non-rivalrous, this suggests that the collective action problem affects the provision of both public goods and common pools. In this chapter we use the term 'collective good' to refer non-excludable goods, regardless of their rivalry of consumption.

- Five students sharing a flat would each prefer that they all pitch in on housework, but since each person's messiness contributes only slightly to the inconvenience of a filthy kitchen, each person may slack off in their cleaning duties in the hope that others will clean up after them.
- All citizens would be better off if all voters thought carefully about what policies would best promote their common interests. Since each voter has only a small probabilistic impact on electoral outcomes, however, each has an incentive to free-ride on the political knowledge of others by remaining 'rationally ignorant' (see Chapter 8).
- The concentration of carbon dioxide in the atmosphere has increased by 40 per cent since pre-industrial times, primarily due to fossil fuel emissions. This has increased global temperatures and is likely to continue to do so for the foreseeable future (IPCC, 2013). Though there is much uncertainty and debate on the level of harm this is

likely to cause and the appropriate policy solutions, there is widespread agreement that climate change is a very bad thing (Lomborg, 2007; Stern, 2007). Yet even if it is in every country's interest that overall emissions of carbon dioxide are reduced, it may not be in any one country's interest to reduce *their* emissions as doing so would retard national economic growth.

- 'Realists' argue that in an anarchical international system, states confront a 'security dilemma'. In order to protect their economic, political and territorial integrity, states will want to arm themselves. Yet the more one state arms itself, the more reason other states then have to either accelerate their own rearmament or contemplate a pre-emptive attack. Yet even if it is in the interests of every country that every country disarms, it may not be in the interests of any one country to be the first to do so (Booth and Wheeler, 2008; Bull, 1981; Mitzen, 2006).

- Marxists traditionally assume that a revolution will somehow simply happen when the objective economic conditions are right (see Elster, 1985: 437–46). Yet even *if* the working-class believe that they would be better off in a communist system, it does not necessarily follow that it would be in the interest of any one worker to become a revolutionary. Revolutions are both difficult and dangerous; why would any one person risk their neck on the barricades when they could stay at home and free-ride?

One way of thinking about collective action problems is with game theory and, more specifically, the prisoners' dilemma game (see Box 2.1). With more than two players we cannot represent a prisoners' dilemma in a two-dimensional matrix as we did earlier, but the same logic applies. Just as the two prisoners would be better off if they could credibly agree to stay quiet but were led by their individual interests to confess, each person in the above example prefers that everyone protest but are led by their individual interests to stay at home. An N-person prisoners' dilemma requires that we have N players each able to choose whether to cooperate or defect, with two important conditions on their payoffs: (1) each of the N players prefers the outcome in which all N players cooperate to the outcome in which they all defect; (2) regardless of what the other N-1 players do, each of the N players must individually prefer to defect rather than cooperate, that is, defection must be a dominant strategy. The two-person prisoners' dilemma introduced earlier is just a special case of this broader class of strategic situations.

To see the connection between the prisoner's dilemma and the collective action problem assume the members of a group all favour a revolution and that they all face the choice of whether or not to join a proposed street protest (cooperate) or stay at home (defect). If the protest is successful, every person will benefit from the removal of the government and will do so whether or not they attend. Because joining the protest takes time and effort and may be quite dangerous, each person prefers the outcome in which they defect but that a sufficient number of other people cooperate that the protest is successful. That is, each person will prefer to 'free-ride'. Because each person is committed, in principle at least, to the revolutionary cause, everyone's second-best outcome is that everyone cooperates. Everyone's third-best outcome is that everyone defects. Finally, and because they would not want to be the only person left standing at the barricades, everyone least prefers the outcome in which they cooperate and join the protest and everyone else defects.

The strategic situation is somewhat more complicated here than in the two-person case, since each player needs to consider the possible actions of a number of other people. In many collective action problems there will be some threshold of participation required for success. For example, it might be that 100 people are needed for a successful protest. If an individual knows that exactly 99 others are planning to cooperate and would prefer the situation in which they cooperate and the protest is successful to the one which they stay at home and it fails, they would be better off cooperating and pushing the protest over the threshold. If this possibility exists, the situation is not a prisoners' dilemma, since defection is not a dominant strategy. Unless there is no chance that an individual is individually decisive in bringing about the preferred outcome, the situation is not strictly speaking a prisoners' dilemma.

If defection *is* a dominant strategy, if the game really is one-off, and if none of the mechanisms we discuss later are available, the logic of the prisoners' dilemma will ensure that collective action does not occur. Olson does not claim that all collective action problems are of this nature, and his argument is best seen as an exploration of the factors which influence the gap between individual incentives and group interests. Others have modelled collective action problems game theoretically but using other game types (Box 6.2). Olson, however, builds a more general and abstract account by using the tools of neo-classical economics to consider the individual costs and benefits of collective action.

Box 6.2 Game-theoretic models of collective action

The prisoners' dilemma is not the only game-theoretic form the collective action problem can take (Taylor and Ward, 1982). Imagine a situation in which the survival of two farmers' crops depends upon the maintenance of a dam. We will start here by assuming that both farmers must work for one day if the dam is to be maintained. If each farmer has the choice of whether or not to cooperate, there are four possible outcomes. Both prefer the outcome in which they both cooperate and the dam is maintained. Both are indifferent between the outcomes in which they defect and the other person cooperates and the one in which they both defect. Finally, they least prefer the outcome in which they cooperate and the other defects. Mapping these outcomes on to a two-by-two matrix generates the 'assurance' game shown below. What will happen here? The first point to note is that there is no dominant strategy. If each farmer believes that the other farmer is going to cooperate, they are better off cooperating (3 > 2). If each farmer believes that the other is going to defect they are better off defecting (2 > 1). Yet given that each farmer prefers the outcome in which they both cooperate, it is unclear why either might believe the other would defect. If the farmers are rational, know each other to be rational and know the payoffs associated with each outcome, collective action should be easily achieved.

Assume now that the dam still needs repairing but that only one day's labour is required. This can be supplied by either one farmer working a whole day or from both farmers working for half a day. Once again, we have a collective action problem, albeit of a slightly different sort. Both now prefer the outcome in which the other farmer does all the work and they defect. In turn, both prefer this to the outcome in which they both cooperate and share the work. Both prefer this to the outcome in which they do all the work and the other farmer defects. Finally, the worst possible outcome for both farmers is that they both defect and the dam eventually collapses. Mapping this on to a two-by-two matrix generates the game of 'chicken'.

In this game there is, once again, no dominant strategy. Whether or not a farmer is better off cooperating depends on what they believe the other farmer will do. If they believe that the other farmer will cooperate they are better off defecting (4 > 3). If they believe that the other farmer will defect they are better off cooperating (2 > 1). So what will happen? One possibility here is that one farmer will try to pre-commit themselves to defecting by, for example, claiming to have hurt their hand. They will do this in the knowledge that if they can persuade the other farmer of the sincerity of their intention to defect (regardless of whether they can persuade them that they really have damaged their hand) that the other

→

→

Farmer 2

Cooperate   Defect

		Cooperate	Defect
Cooperate (mend dam)		I 3,3	II 1,2
Defect (stay at home)		III 2,1	IV 2,2

Farmer 1 (labels the rows, at left of first grid)

Farmer 2

Cooperate   Defect

		Cooperate	Defect
Cooperate (mend dam)		I 3,3	II 2,4
Defect (stay at home)		III 4,2	IV 1,1

Farmer 1 (labels the rows, at left of second grid)

farmer will then find it in their interests to do all the work themselves (2 > 1). Yet if both try to pre-commit in this way, there is of course a danger that each will thereby achieve their worst possible outcome (1, 1). But if one farmer realizes this and so calculates that the other will eventually back down and cooperate, they will be tempted to defect (4 > 3). Yet if one farmer realizes this, then, given the assumption of a common knowledge of rationality, the other one will do so as well. If they both realize that they both realize it, then both will have to recognize that neither might cooperate. In short, and in a single play of the game, anything can happen.

Consider the case of the five students sharing a flat. Keeping the flat clean or at least tolerably hygienic poses a potential collective action problem. The cleanliness of the communal areas can be considered a collective good for this group – if any cleanliness is produced it will inevitably be shared equally among all five flatmates. The collective good is non-excludable with respect to members of the group. Intuitively, this non-excludability combined with the individual costliness of cleaning raises the possibility that the flat could end up filthy even if everyone would in theory be willing to do their part. Olson's logic considers the characteristics of individuals and groups which influence the likelihood of collective action failure.

Olson's logic asks us to assume that we can assign cardinal values to the benefits to individuals of the collective good and the costs of individual effort to produce it. Let's simplify the lazy flatmates example a great deal and say that there is a stack of plates which need to be washed. Each plate left unwashed makes each flatmate feel a little bit worse about their life, and they would each be willing to pay exactly $1 for each plate washed. Washing up is time-consuming, however, and 'costs' each individual $2 worth of effort and boredom – that is, they would be willing to pay $2 but no more in order to avoid washing each plate. Given these preferences, it is clear that the individually rational approach is laziness – the decision to wash a plate produces $1 of benefit for $2 of cost. Since this is not a good deal, nobody will make any effort and the dishes will pile up. At the group level, however, this produces an outcome everybody would prefer to avoid. The problem is that each flatmate individually pays the full cost of cleaning but captures only one fifth of the benefit. A clean plate is worth $1 to each flatmate but $5 to the flatmates as a group. All flatmates would be better off if everybody did their share of cleaning, but the individual incentives are for laziness. Without some way of solving this collective action problem, the equilibrium outcome will be Pareto dominated by an alternative.

In the example above, none of the collective good of 'cleanliness' was produced. Other assumptions about the costs and benefits of collective action produce situations in which some of the collective good is produced, but less than the members would prefer. Suppose, as economists often do, that the marginal benefits of a collective good are decreasing. As the flat gets cleaner and cleaner the additional benefit of further cleaning gets smaller and smaller. Decreasing marginal benefits are common in many situations and quite plausible in the case of cleaning – five minutes spent removing the dead cat from under the couch is likely to make a greater contribution to happiness than the same five minutes cleaning skirting boards or dusting the top shelf.

Suppose our lazy flatmates have five potential chores each costing $2 in disutility but producing benefit to each flatmate of $10, $5, $3, $1 and $0.10 respectively. In the language of economics, we have constant marginal cost but decreasing marginal benefit. When we consider the benefit to the group as a whole, the optimal solution is for the flatmates to complete four of the five chores. Since we need to multiply the individual benefit by five to find the group benefit, all chores except the last pass the cost-benefit test – marginal group benefit exceeds the constant marginal cost of $2. For the first three chores, the *individual* marginal benefit also exceeds the marginal cost. Setting aside strategic considerations for now, any flatmate would be individually willing to perform these first three chores. It is in no individual's interest to perform the fourth chore, however. The marginal *group* benefit of this chore exceeds the marginal cost, but the marginal *individual* benefit does not. In this situation we might see a reasonably clean flat, but cleanliness would nevertheless be underprovided relative to the group optimum due to a collective action problem.

At the centre of Olson's logic is this distinction between group and individual benefit. Collective action problems arise wherever individuals must undertake costly action in order to benefit a group. By speaking generally of costs, benefits, members, and groups, Olson creates a framework of analysis with very wide applicability. Though this generality does limit the specific predictions of Olson's analysis, the simple framework allows us to say some interesting things about when collective action problems are likely to emerge and when they might be overcome.

Group size and the taxonomy of groups

For Olson, the most important factor influencing the likelihood of collective action occurring is the *size* of the group. In larger groups, the fraction of group benefits captured by each individual is smaller, and this makes it less likely that any of the collective good will be produced or that it will be produced at an optimal level. Each of the flatmates above captured one fifth of the total benefit of their own production; the average individual reducing their carbon emissions to fight global warming would capture less than one seven-billionth. Olson's logic points to a potential problem in both cases but predicts the latter will be much more serious.

When group members differ in their valuation of a collective good, it is not simply the number of members that matters. What determines the likelihood of collective action is the fraction of total benefit captured by individuals, and if one or more individual captures a large share of the benefit they will have strong incentives to produce the good. Suppose that one of our flatmates has a pathological hatred of squalor and derives $4 of utility from each clean plate while the other four continue to value each clean plate at $1. If the cost of cleaning is again $2, we would expect to see the collective action problem resolved by the clean flatmate. Although this individual constitutes only one fifth of the group, they capture one-half of the benefit of cleanliness. We might still see too little of the collective good produced, but the existence of at least one person who captures a significant share of the benefit will make any production more likely and bring the level of production closer to the group optimum.

Olson distinguishes between three broad types of group: *privileged* groups, *intermediate* groups and *latent* groups. A privileged group is one in which at least one individual values the good to such an extent that they are prepared to bear the entire costs of providing it and, in doing so, to tolerate the free-riding of others (Olson, 1965: 48–50). The flatmates described above are a privileged group if one of them values cleanliness enough to clean without assistance from the others. A group in which *every* member values the good highly enough to bear the costs of providing it is also a privileged group. Olson concludes that in privileged groups there is a presumption that the good will be provided. There is, however, a strategic problem when more than one member values a good highly enough to provide it themselves. As Olson (1965: 50) recognizes, even if each individual would be willing to provide a good if nobody else does so, *each* individual might try to free-ride in the expectation that one of the others will eventually provide all of the good. Olson does not integrate such strategic consideration into his analysis, but game theoretic extensions of his work have considered strategic interaction of this kind via the analysis of assurance and chicken games (see Box 6.2).

The theory of hegemonic stability developed by international relations theorists offers a substantive application of the idea of the privileged group. Liberals argue that a secure and prosperous international order depends upon the provision and maintenance of an open trading regime, a stable international currency and a sense of security. These are all collective goods (Keohane, 1984). For whilst every country will be better off in a world of free trade, every country will gain from erecting tariff barriers so long as it can continue to export to the rest of the world. Charles Kindleberger (1981) maintains that in an anarchic international system, this collective action problem is most likely to be resolved when there is a 'hegemonic' power. The idea here is that such a power will benefit from the existence of a liberal international order to such an extent that it will be willing to bear the costs of maintaining it. It will do this by allowing its currency to act as an international reserve currency and its army to act as an international police force, preventing territorial attacks and ensuring free trade. The periods of international peace and prosperity which characterized the nineteenth and late twentieth century were, it is then argued, secured through first British and then American hegemonic power. Britain's loss of its hegemonic status in the first part of the twentieth century, it is concluded, led to a period of protectionism and financial crisis and, eventually, world war.

Although the possibility a strategic interaction as demonstrated by the chicken game creates some problems for certain types of privileged groups, Olson's logic suggests collective goods will generally be provided without any need for formal organization or informal coordination. The distribution of costs and benefits across individuals is itself sufficient to produce the good.

An intermediate group is one which no individual has sufficient incentive to produce the good themselves but whose members (or at least some of them) are noticeably affected by the behaviour of each other individual member. A noticeable effect, here, is one which members *know* about and *care* about. That is, members must be able to see what others are doing and be strongly enough affected by it to have an incentive to alter their behaviour in order to influence the behaviour of others. Olson suggests that the production of collective goods in intermediate groups is possible but not guaranteed, insisting that *if* collective goods are produced in intermediate groups it must be through some sort of formal organization or informal coordination. Since his analysis tries to be as general as possible, he does not go into any detail on what form such coordination might take. We saw one type of this coordination in Chapter 2 – conditional cooperation in iterated prisoners' dilemma games (pp. 41–4). We will consider others later in this chapter.

Latent groups are those in which no member has an incentive to unilaterally produce the good and no member's behaviour has any noticeable effect on any other. This means that 'if one member does or does not help provide the collective good, no other one member will be significantly affected and therefore none has any reason to react' (Olson, 1965: 50). If this is the case, coordination in the sense of mutual adjustment cannot happen. Olson does not argue that collective goods cannot be provided in such groups, but that they can be provided only through the use of 'selective incentives' – individual rewards or punishments tied to the individual's contribution to the collective good.

Olson (1965: 65) summarizes his central theoretical conclusion by saying that 'large or latent groups will *not* organize for coordinated action merely because, as a group, they have a reason for doing so, though this could be true of smaller groups'. By applying the same simple cost and benefit logic to all groups, Olson shows that size is a crucial determinate of the collective rationality of groups. Members of small groups may well be able to voluntarily work out their differences and cooperate for their common good without using external incentive schemes; members of large groups will not.

Resolving collective action problems

A superficial reading of Olson's first two chapters would suggest that collective action is impossible in large groups. Olson argues that there is a collective action *problem*. He does not suggest that groups will *always* fail to overcome it. Indeed many of the most interesting and innovative parts of the *Logic of Collective Action* specify the ways and circumstances in which latent groups manage to act collectively through selective incentives. In the rest of this chapter we review these arguments and some more recent variations before returning to the question, largely ignored by Olson, of how coordination might happen in intermediate groups.

Selective incentives in latent groups

Olson insists that latent groups will be unable to provide collective goods without some system of incentives distinct from the collective good itself. Remember, a collective good is one which by definition is available equally to all members of the group, meaning that no individual can be denied access if they refuse to contribute. If such exclusion *is* possible, we are not dealing with a collective good in Olson's sense and his analysis does not apply. For an individual in a latent group to contribute, they must get some non-collective good in return. These 'selective incentives' can be either positive or negative. A positive selective incentive takes the form of a reward extended to those, and *only* those, who contribute to the provision of a collective good. In the case of, for example, the collective good of collective workplace bargaining, Olson suggests that workers join unions in order to secure private benefits such as free legal representation and dispute resolution.

Although Olson (1965: 60–63) is sceptical of their relevance, social incentives may produce selective benefits capable of mobilizing latent groups. In addition to the mundane economic goals of consumption and leisure, people are motivated by the desire for prestige and friend-ship. If contributions to a collective good increase the contributor's social standing in some way, social incentives are selective and could in theory mobilize a latent group. Although Olson does not explicitly rule this possibility out, he argues that social incentives are generally only effective in privileged and intermediate groups. Small groups are thus 'doubly blessed' by non-selective economic incentives and selective social incentives, while large latent groups have neither. The claim that social incentives are stronger in small groups is intuitively plausible, but Olson's claim that they have little or no impact in large groups is far from self-evident. Individuals do seem to be motivated by esteem in a variety of contexts (Brennan and Pettit, 2004). Consider contempo-rary attitudes towards voting. Many argue that political participation is a public good. Democracy only works when the public participates, but each voter has an incentive to free-ride on the participation of oth-ers (see Chapter 8). Why then do people vote? One plausible answer is that people vote because they want others to think well of them. Anecdotally, many see voting as a duty and look down on those who abstain. Wearing an 'I voted' sticker might provide social benefits only to those who vote, thus overcoming the collective action problem of democratic participation. Although empirically testing this possibility is quite difficult, there is some revealing evidence. For example, in a large-scale field experiment involving registered voters in Michigan, turnout was significantly higher among those told that their participa-tion would be made public (Gerber et al., 2008).

A negative selective incentive takes the form of a punishment or cost extended to those, and *only* those, who fail to contribute to the provi-sion of a collective good. Unions able to implement a 'closed shop' are using negative selective incentives in preventing those who fail to pay dues from working. Threats of violence for those crossing the picket line are another negative selective incentive. The most obvious negative selective incentive is, of course, state coercion. As individuals we do not have to decide whether to contribute to the cost of providing defence forces, roads or social security programmes. The state requires us to contribute to their cost and threatens those who refuse to pay their taxes with jail.

It is not only the state which can play the role of coercive Leviathan. Criminal gangs and warlords can sometimes perform the same function. Diego Gambetta (1993) argues that the Mafia prospered in Southern Italy in the nineteenth century because it was trusted to oversee and enforce market exchanges. To follow the logic of this argument, assume that a peasant farmer wants to sell one of his sheep to the local butcher. Although the exchange may be mutually beneficial, the butcher may not trust the farmer to sell them a healthy sheep. The butcher could of course pay a veterinarian to inspect the sheep but because this would add to the transaction costs of the exchange, so deterring them from dealing with the farmer (Box 4.4). If it is operating effectively, the state reduces transaction costs and so facilitates exchange by providing a legal framework within which actors can, for example, claim damages from each other (see North, 1990). Yet in Southern Italy, the state was, at this time, inherently weak and mistrusted. In these circumstances Gambetta argues that the Mafia was able to prosper by promising to exact revenge on anyone who acted dishonestly in return for a share of the profits of every exchange.

David Skarbek (2011, 2014) provides a fascinating twist on Gambetta's story. In Los Angeles there are roughly 400 drug-dealing Hispanic street gangs in competition with one another. Those dealing in illicit drugs have as much need for dispute resolution and contract enforcement as anyone else but, for obvious reasons, cannot rely on government-provided police and court services. Skarbek argues that the 'Mexican Mafia' prison gang has stepped in to provide governance for the street gangs, ensuring cooperation on the outside by acting as a Leviathan on the inside. The Mexican Mafia is an extremely powerful force within the California penal system. Because drug dealers expect to spend future time in prison and usually have incarcerated friends, the gang can extort money from street gangs on the outside – demanding 'taxes' in exchange for protection of incarcerated members. Since its income depends on the profitability of tax-paying street gangs, the Mexican Mafia has an incentive, like the Sicilian Mafia had with respect to non-criminal market exchanges, to enforce property rights and adjudicate disputes among rival gangs.

Latent groups 'mobilized' by selective incentives overcome collective problems by introducing non-collective goods into the mix, but this requires some individual or organization willing and able to provide selective incentives. As Olson (1965: 133) points out, this means either (1) the capacity for coercion, or (2) the resources to provide positive inducements. When either of these conditions is met, the individual or organization can attempt to alter individual incentives such that the collective good is produced as a by-product of the pursuit of rewards or avoidance of punishment: 'The common characteristic which distinguishes all of the large economic groups with significant lobbying organizations is that these groups are also organized for some *other* purpose' (Olson, 1965: 132).

Elinor Ostrom and common pool governance

Olson argues that collective action is *possible* in intermediate groups but, due to the abstract and general nature of his argument, spends little time considering the mechanisms intermediate groups might use to coordinate their behaviour. Those drawing on Olson's work have taken up this issue from a variety of perspectives. We saw one such perspective in Chapter 2 – Michael Taylor and Robert Axelrod's work showing that cooperation is possible in iterated prisoner's dilemma games. This work demonstrates that coordination on the cooperative equilibrium can in principle happen quite straightforwardly when players are concerned with the future and realize that their actions will influence the actions of others. It is important to keep these results in mind, but in this section we take a broader view of conditional cooperation in intermediate groups, drawing in particular on the work of political scientist Elinor Ostrom (1933–2012), who won the Nobel Prize in economics in 2009.

In a series of detailed case-studies of the management of common pool resources, Ostrom (1990, 2005, 2010a; Poteete et al., 2010) has shown how groups of individuals have, over time, developed complex formal rules of allocation as well as subtle informal norms which allow them to overcome collective action problems. Ostrom's primary foil is Garrett Hardin (1968) and his 'tragedy of the commons' (see Box 6.3), which can be considered a restatement of Olson's argument with respect to latent groups and common pool resources. Hardin's conclusion that common pool situations invariably end tragically has been used as an argument for both government intervention on the one hand, and privatization on the other. Ostrom (2010a: 648) rejects the

Box 6.3 The tragedy of the commons

Garrett Hardin's (1968) analysis of 'the tragedy of the commons' has proven to be immensely influential. His original argument – which, strangely, contains no references to Olson's work – concerns the possibility of human population growth in the face of limited resources. Hardin argued that the welfare state and other social supports designed to feed the hungry prevent natural selection from discouraging excessive breeding. Since the poor can have children and push the cost onto others, Hardin argues, the freedom to breed produces a collective action problem resulting in excessive population.

The idea of the tragedy of the commons has since become more associated with the use and misuse of environmental resources like common pasture land, fisheries and water basins which are rivalrous but non-excludable. Take the case of common land. This good is rivalrous in the sense that grass eaten by one farmer's sheep or cattle cannot then be eaten by another's. It is non-excludable in the sense that no farmer can stop another from grazing their animals on the land. The farmers have a shared interest in regulating the use of the land because if too many cattle are left to graze, the land will be damaged. The farmers must however confront a collective action problem. For even if each of them were aware of the total number of animals that the land could sustain, each farmer would find it in their interests to graze as many of their animals as possible. Furthermore, this will be so whether or not each farmer believes the others will exercise any restraint:

> Therein is the tragedy. Each man is locked into a system that compels him to increase his herd without limit in a world that is limited. Ruin is the destination to which all men rush, each pushing his own best interest in a society that believes in the freedom of the commons. (Hardin, 1968: 1244)

Hardin (1968: 1246) argues that if the tragedy of overpopulation and environmental destruction is to be avoided and the commons saved, 'people must be [made to] be responsive to a coercive force outside their individual psyches, a "leviathan" to use Hobbes' phrase'. Caught in a collective action problem, people must be forced to act in their own interests. By implication, the state ought to control access to the use of common pool resources. Hardin's conclusion in the case of population is that the 'intolerable' freedom of procreation must be eliminated. Contemporary environmentalists take the view that the freedom to pollute must be eliminated.

conventional assumption that 'the momentum for change must come from outside the situation rather than from the self-reflection and creativity of those within a situation to restructure their own patterns of interaction' and instead argues that groups of individuals are capable of resolving their own collective action problems without recourse to Leviathan or the market. Collective action is a challenge, but for Ostrom (1998: 16) '[w]e are neither trapped in inexorable tragedies nor free of moral responsibility for creating and sustaining incentives that facilitate our own achievement of mutually productive outcomes'. Individuals can escape collective action problems by converging on informal norms or crafting formal rules which facilitate cooperation.

To understand Ostrom's contribution, we need to consider just how interdisciplinary and methodologically pluralistic her work is. Though she was trained as a political scientist, she borrows methods from a variety of social and physical sciences. In order to understand how collective action problems can be resolved in any particular instance, she contends, we need to consider not only the social properties of the group but also the physical properties of the good and the environment in which it is embedded.

One way groups can overcome collective action problems is through the use of social norms. Instrumental rationality is concerned with outcomes. It tells people that if they want to achieve X, they ought to do Y. Action guided by a social norm is not outcome-orientated. Norms simply tell people to do (or not do) Y, or to do (or not do) Y if people do X (Brennan et al., 2013; Elster, 1989b). Ostrom (2005: 5) sees a social norm as a type of preference over one's own behaviour which is adopted as part of a community or culture. By working alongside economic motivations, norms can encourage cooperation when it would otherwise not be forthcoming.

Norms as understood by Ostrom can be seen as a type of selective social incentive in Olson's terms. Though Olson is sceptical of the relevance of such incentives, Ostrom's work demonstrates that shared standards of acceptable conduct are important determinants of cooperation. Whereas game theory predicts that unenforceable agreements are nothing but cheap talk, Ostrom emphasizes the importance of communication. When participants in lab experiments involving collective action problems are given a chance to communicate before playing – and particularly the chance to communicate face-to-face rather than via written messages on paper or computer screens – they are much more likely to cooperate, even when their individual interests would be better served by feigning cooperation while actually defecting

(Balliet, 2010). Indeed, a number of studies have demonstrated that the presence of *pictures* of eyes can encourage cooperation (for example, Burnham and Hare, 2007; Francey and Bergmüller, 2012).

It is easy to imagine that an appropriate set of social norms might encourage cooperation where narrow self-interest would otherwise produce a tragedy of the commons; it is more difficult to see why we should expect these norms to arise. As Elster (1989b: 140) comments, 'even if a norm does make everybody better off, this does not explain why it exists, unless we are also shown some feedback mechanism that specifies how the good consequences of the norm contribute to its maintenance'. The creation and maintenance of the norm gives rise to a second order collective action problem at least as serious as the one it is purported to solve. Why would individuals adopt such a norm? Ostrom's answer to this question is subtle and easy to misinterpret. First off, it needs to be emphasized that she in no way suggests that norms will always arise to solve collective action problems – in the real world many problems go unsolved. If a norm of reciprocity is to spread among the users of a common pool resource, it must in some sense be in their individual interest to adopt such a norm. Ostrom draws on the work of Taylor and Axelrod on conditional cooperation in repeated games, outlining the conditions under which we might expect such cooperation to emerge.

Ostrom argues that our evolutionary history has equipped us with a tendency to adopt norms. Our ancestors survived not only by solving individual problems but also by cooperating to solve collective action problems. If norms provide a mechanism for such cooperation to emerge, those without a tendency to adopt norms would not have survived long enough to pass on their genes. The human propensity to adopt norms can be likened to the human propensity to acquire rules of grammar. Humans are not born with specific grammatical rules, but they do seem to be hard-wired with a tendency to easily grasp whatever rules of grammar those around them use (Chomsky, 1965; Pinker, 1994). Similarly, Ostrom (2000: 143–4) argues, we have been conditioned by our evolutionary history to identify and adopt social norms, though the substance of the norms we adopt will depend on the culture in which we grow up and the groups in which we interact. If a small number of conditional cooperators can identify each other and adopt a norm of reciprocity in a small group, others may wish to adopt this norm in order to secure higher payoffs from group membership. As the size of the cooperating group grows, membership will become more attractive. As more and more individuals adopt a norm of reciprocity, the short-term temptation to cheat will be tempered by social incentives mandating cooperation.

When is this self-reinforcing cycle of norm adoption likely to happen? Ostrom suggests that individuals' ability to monitor and sanction each other is an important factor. If conditional cooperators cannot recognize one another there will be strong incentives to free-ride and we should expect to see a world consisting entirely of rational egoists. If monitoring and sanctioning is perfectly reliable and costless, we should expect to see a world consisting entirely of conditional cooperators. Between these two extremes we will see varying levels of cooperation and free-riding (Ostrom, 2000: 145).

Though Ostrom (2005) emphasizes the need for rules tailored to the social and biophysical context of the collective action problem and rejects the idea of 'one size fits all' solutions, her empirical research (see especially Ostrom, 1990) along with that of her collaborators and colleagues (Poteete et al., 2010) has revealed eight general 'design principles' which all successful and robust solutions to collective action problems share:

(1) *Clearly defined boundaries.* The distinction between the controlled resource and the surrounding environment is clearly defined, as is the distinction between those who do or do not have a right to use the resource.

(2) *Proportional equivalence between benefits and costs.* The contribution expected of an individual is in some way related to the benefits they derive from a collective good.

(3) *Collective-choice arrangements.* Most or all individuals affected by rules are able to participate in decisions over their modification.

(4) *Monitoring.* Some or all individuals are responsible for monitoring the compliance of others, and these individuals are accountable to other group members.

(5) *Graduated sanctions.* Isolated and minor infringements are punished lightly, with more serious and repeated violations earning harsher punishments.

(6) *Conflict-resolution mechanisms.* There must be some low-cost means of resolving conflicts among group members.

(7) *Minimal recognition of rights to organize.* Group members must be able to devise and enforce their own rules without excessive coercive interference from outside groups such as government.

(8) *Nested enterprises.* For large-scale resources, governance mechanisms must be organized in multiple layers of nested organization.

Ostrom suggests that groups able to satisfy these conditions in a way suitable to the environment, group and resource in question will be able to overcome collective action problems. When these conditions are met, users can find their own way out of the tragedy of the commons without the need for central government or markets. Ostrom shows not simply that privatization or nationalization will often be *unnecessary*, but also that they will sometimes be counterproductive. If a common pool resource is being effectively managed by a community, nationalization will make outcomes worse if, for example, the government does not solve the problem of effective monitoring. Similarly, creating complete private property rights might be inferior to more subtle rules which restrict access to some scarce aspect of an environment while leaving other aspects uncontrolled. Privatizing a lake, for example, might solve the problem of overfishing while also preventing non-rivalrous use of the lake for transport. A system which directly controlled access to the fish rather than the lake might be better in this instance.

Whereas traditional approaches to governance and collective action saw a sharp conceptual barrier between markets and states, Ostrom's work on common pool governance showed that individuals working together to overcome collective action problems can devise solutions which do not fall neatly into this dichotomous classification scheme. More generally, her work suggests that governance need not be provided by a unitary government, but rather through a variety of state and non-state actors. This line of research was initiated by Ostrom's husband Vincent in his work on metropolitan governance (Ostrom et al., 1961), which questioned the conventional view among public administration scholars that metropolitan governance was inefficient due to multiple and overlapping jurisdictions (for example, Gulick, 1957). Such fragmentation not only duplicated services, but also produced chaos as each jurisdiction imposed externalities on others. A single centralized metropolitan government, it was argued, would promote efficiency by internalizing such interjurisdictional externalities and exploiting economies of scale. Though Olson had not yet written *The Logic of Collective Action*, this is clearly a collective action problem between jurisdictions.

Ostrom et al. (1961) argued that this ignored the scale of public goods. Consider the difference between four goods – a clean flat, a neighbourhood police patrol, national defence and global warming mitigation. In each of these cases there is some geographic area in which the good is non-rival and non-excludable, but the relevant 'public' is very different in each case. For a clean flat, the relevant public is the inhabitants of the flat; for global warming mitigation, the inhabitants of the planet. In each case there might be some need for governance in order to provide the public good, but there is no reason to think that all should be provided on the same scale.

On this view, the relevant question is not the optimal scale of metropolitan government in general but rather the optimal scale of governance for each public good. Just as there is no single scale of governance best able to deliver clean flats and a clean atmosphere, the differences between rubbish removal, local pollution control, fire prevention, policing and the myriad other goods provided by metropolitan governments are too large to allow efficient provision for all through a single jurisdiction. Rather than consolidated jurisdictions in which decisions flow from one central point, Ostrom et al. (1961: 831) argue for a *polycentric* political system, in which there are 'many centers of decision-making which are formally independent of each other' (see also Bish and Ostrom, 1973; Boettke et al., 2011; Oates, 1972). A highly decentralized system would give rise to a number of externalities and inefficiencies, but the possibility of 'contracting up' and interjurisdictional agreement suggests that decentralization will be preferable if collective action problems among local governments can be solved (Feiock and Scholz, 2009).

This patchwork of overlapping jurisdictions further blurs the line between public and private. In an earlier paper, Charles Tiebout (1956) modelled local governments as firms in a market. As individuals may choose where to live partly on the basis of public services like schools, parks and the quality of local regulations, they could be considered consumers who vote with their feet for the local government they most prefer. When we consider homeowners' associations, condominiums and other voluntary governance arrangements, the distinction becomes even less clear. A homeowners' association seeks to solve collective action problems in a particular geographic area, much like local and national governments. The difference is scale – a difference of degree rather than kind (Boudreaux and Holcombe, 1989; Nelson, 2005).

Shortly before her death, Elinor Ostrom (2010b, 2012; Ostrom and Cox, 2010) wrote a series of papers applying the concept of polycentric governance to the issue of global climate change. This work is highly instructive, since it provides an important application of polycentric governance and clarifies what is distinctive about the polycentric governance approach. The conventional logic of collective action would suggest that since the action on climate change is a global public good, that is, the relevant public contains everyone on the planet (Sandler,

2004), the only way of successfully resolving the problem is governance at the global level (Held and Fane-Hervey, 2011; Nordhaus, 1994). Ostrom's polycentric approach, on the other hand, sees global action as potentially desirable but insists that it should not be the sole focus.

There are, for Ostrom, two problems with an exclusive focus on the global level. First, there is no guarantee that global action will be successful, and it seems almost certain that it will take some time: 'Given the failure to reach agreement at the international level ... continuing to wait without investing in efforts at multiple scales may defeat the possibilities of significant abatements and mitigations in enough time to prevent tragic disasters' (Ostrom, 2012: 354). Second, global action is only likely to be successful if backed up by action at more local levels. This is most obvious with climate change adaptation. The collective action problem of reducing greenhouse gas emissions is global in scale, but the benefits of responding to changing climate – by, for example, diversifying food production or enabling migration away from vulnerable areas – are more local (Agrawal, 2010).

Efforts to reduce greenhouse gas emissions have been undertaken with limited but real success at the local, national and regional level. The collective action problem has not been completely overcome, but nor has there been a complete lack of action by individuals, local communities and national governments. Through norms and social preferences, it seems that the dire prediction of zero contribution to climate change mitigation has proven false (Brennan, 2009; Brekke and Johansson-Stenman, 2008; Gsottbauer and van den Bergh, 2011). Though a more comprehensive solution would no doubt be desirable, the polycentric approach draws our attention away from *the* solution to *the* problem of climate change and focuses instead on how actors at various levels can come together to solve collective problems.

Assessment

Although the basic idea that groups must confront and surmount a collective action problem now seems quite obvious, this is only because Olson has made it seem so. Olson is still sometimes interpreted as arguing that collective action is impossible or somehow irrational. Yet this is not the case. Indeed one of the most positive legacies of Olson's work is a number of detailed case-studies of specific instances of collective action showing how selective incentives and conditional cooperation operate can make a real difference. Such studies, a number of which have already been referred to in this chapter, include explanations of the household division of labour (Carling, 1992), the American Civil Rights movement (Chong, 1991), East Asian peasant uprisings (Popkin, 1979), the evolution of the firm (Miller, 1992), the military draft (Levi, 1997), ethnic conflict (Hardin, 1995), the management of common pool resources (Ostrom, 1990), the success of strict churches (Iannaccone, 1994), the origins of the Mafia (Gambetta, 1993), cooperation among pirates (Leeson, 2009), the existence of hate groups (Mulholland, 2010) and the power of prison gangs (Skarbek, 2014).

Olson's framework cannot, however, explain everything. Olson distinguishes in very broad and general terms between types of groups and how their characteristics affect the likelihood of successful collective action. His general analysis revealed one important factor – group size – but obscured many others. More recent work by Elinor Ostrom and her colleagues has led to a much richer understanding which complements some aspects of Olson's analysis and sheds serious doubt on others. Olson was no doubt correct that the size of the group and the excludability of the good are important aspects, but he was incorrect in claiming that social incentives are unimportant and that voluntary cooperation is out of the question in large groups. *The Logic of Collective Action* tells us something about the ways and circumstances in which groups can overcome the collective action problem posed by free-riding, yet Olson's book does not (and does not claim to) provide a comprehensive theory of collective action. It cannot tell us about how individuals acquire interests which lead them to identify with a particular group; how the members of a group agree on particular policy platforms; how and when particular forms of collective action induce changes in government policy; or how and why groups sometimes collapse. There is no reason why rational choice theorists cannot address these topics. But it would be a mistake to think that *only* rational choice theorists can do so.

In addition to her vigorous use of multiple methods of analysis, Ostrom's subtle understanding of the strength and limits of narrow rational choice is instructive here. Although she consistently recognizes human beings as purposeful and active choosers, she insists that thin conceptions of rationality as calculative selfishness is only one limiting case on the spectrum of motivation we see in the real world. When individuals are isolated from one another and competitive pressures are strong, humans do behave roughly, though not completely, as game theorists predict (Ostrom, 2010a: 655). As soon as we relax these requirements by, for example, allowing conversation, humans often take actions which are irrational when considered in isolation but which allow for 'better than rational' outcomes in the long run. Olson's groundbreaking analysis provided an important first step in this line of research, but recent work has moved beyond its rigid analytical structure to provide new insights into whether, when and how individuals are able to overcome collective action problems in the wild.

Chapter 7

Gordon Tullock, Rent-Seeking and Government Failure

> **Overview:** Business firms and interest groups are influential actors in the policy process. In 'The Welfare Costs of Tariffs, Monopolies and Theft', Gordon Tullock (1967) argued that the way in which they exercise this influence is economically crippling. Rent-seeking takes place when firms or interest groups try to extract special privileges from government. Rent-seeking is damaging because it entails the expenditure of resources which might otherwise have been used to benefit consumers. In this chapter we outline Tullock's original argument and subsequent work by Tullock and others asking why the rent-seeking 'industry' of lobbying firms, public relations companies and lawyers so small. We then consider other rational choice models of interest group behaviour and extend the rent-seeking approach to influence within private organizations and public bureaucracies.

Setting the stage: government without angels

As we saw in Chapter 2, government can usefully be seen as a response to the problems caused by individual selfishness. Without laws backed by the coercive power of the state, many would find plunder an attractive career option, and this would ultimately make everybody worse off. But if government is empowered to prevent private predation in the form of theft and murder, we need to beware the possibility of predation by government. James Madison elegantly summarizes the problem in the 51st *Federalist* paper:

> If men were angels, no government would be necessary. If angels were to govern men, neither external nor internal controls on government would be necessary. In framing a government which is to be administered by men over men, the great difficulty lies in this: you must first enable the government to control the governed; and in the next place oblige it to control itself.

It may be, as Hobbes argued, that a certain amount of public pre-dation is simply the price we pay for civilization, but if government can be controlled or if life in the state of nature is tolerable, it is worth thinking carefully about the extent to which the self-interest of those in government can lead to exploitation and inefficiency. A good deal of rational choice scholarship, and particularly that of the so-called Virginia School associated with the work of Buchanan, Tullock, Robert Tollison and Leland Yeager at Virginia Tech and later at George Mason University, takes such a 'government failure' approach to polit-ical analysis, considering the individual incentives of political actors and pointing to the ways in which such incentives conspire to produce undesirable outcomes.

The most well-known government failure argument, and the one around which we frame this chapter is 'rent-seeking' by special inter-ests. Tullock (1967) argued that when government has the ability to provide special privileges, interest groups have incentives to use resources attempting to secure such privileges. Quite apart from any unfairness which arises from political corruption, lobbying produces a great deal of economic waste. As we will see shortly, Tullock argues that government-sanctioned monopolies and other forms of special priv-ilege are much more inefficient than economists recognize. Similarly, Tullock and others have analysed the incentives of bureaucrats, poli-ticians, voters and interest groups and documented a number of ways in which individually rational action fails to produce socially optimal outcomes. In this chapter we review some of this work, beginning with Tullock's work on rent-seeking, and discuss the normative implications which have been drawn from the idea of government failure.

Prior to 'the public choice revolution' (Lemieux, 2005) of the 1960s, welfare economics and public finance operated under the assumption that government is a benevolent dictatorship. When formulating policy advice, economists did not pause to look at the incentives of political actors and ask whether the optimal policy solution is politically feasible or likely to be competently implemented. Identifying a market failure and a logically possible government solution was as far as economists went: effectively assuming that men are not angels but that angels are to govern men. There is thus an obvious asymmetry in the assumptions made by economists regarding economic and political behaviour. Tullock, Brady and Seldon (2002: 5) rejects this asymmetry, arguing that 'people are people':

> People in the supermarket mainly buy the food and other goods that are, granted the price, found to benefit themselves and their families.

However, when individuals become politicians, a transformation is assumed to occur so that a broader perspective guides them to make morally correct decisions rather than follow the course of behaviour that pleases the interest groups that supported them or the policies that may lead to reelection.

It is against this backdrop that Tullock's arguments regarding the implications of selfishness in politics were formed. In rejecting the prevailing 'benevolent despot' model of government held by welfare economists, Tullock and other public choice theorists took issue with not only the assumption of benevolence, but also the assumption of despotism. Policy outcomes, even in autocracies (see Mesquita and Smith, 2011) but especially in democracies, are never determined by a single individual, but by a variety of individuals each guided by their own diverse goals. As Tullock (2006: 34) puts it in his non-technical introduction to public choice theory *The Vote Motive*, first published in 1976:

> Government is seen as an apparatus, like the market, by which people attempt to achieve their goals. Instead of assuming that government aims at some particular goal – say, the most health per pound of expenditure – and then calculating how it should be achieved, students of economics of politics assume that all the individuals in government aim at raising their own utility, that is, serve their own interests within certain institutional limits, and then inquire what policies they can be expected to pursue.

Clearly, Tullock's positive view of politics has serious implications for his normative evaluation. We will discuss these implications later, but for now we will introduce his positive arguments.

Rent-seeking: the welfare costs of tariffs, monopolies and theft

Economists have long recognized that monopolists are able to charge excessive prices which undermine efficiency. Consider Figure 7.1 in which the quantity of some good being produced is shown on the horizontal axis and price and cost on the vertical axis. Assume that a perfectly competitive industry produces output Q at a price P equal to marginal cost. Notice that at this price some consumers are paying less

Figure 7.1   *The efficiency costs of monopoly*

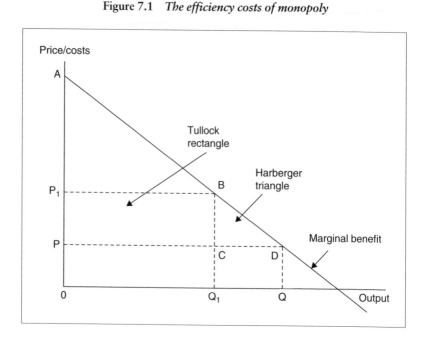

for the good than they would be willing to pay. The resulting consumer surplus is shown by the triangle A–P–D. Assume now that the industry is, for whatever reason, transformed into a monopoly. Because the monopolist needs to be less concerned with losing customers as a result of increasing prices, it can increase profit by raising price to P_1, though at this price it can only sell output Q_1. Less of the product will now be sold and that which is sold will be sold at a higher price. This has two consequences. The first is a loss of consumer surplus measured by the triangle B–C–D. The second is a transfer of income to the monopolist in the form of excess profits (or producer surplus) measured by the rectangle P_1–B–C–P.

Economists traditionally conceived of the efficiency costs of monopoly in terms of the triangle, which, in honour of the first economist to measure its size, Arnold Harberger (1954), is known as the Harberger triangle. The redistribution of surplus from consumers to producers might be morally problematic, but the economist has nothing to say against pure transfers on efficiency grounds. Although economists had generally held that monopoly was a significant economic problem, the costs of monopoly were actually found to amount to no more than a fraction of 1 per cent of gross domestic product (Johnson, 1958; Schwarzman, 1960). Did this mean that monopoly was economically unimportant? Tullock argued that it did not and that those economists who had been attempting to calculate the costs of monopoly had been looking in the wrong place.

At the time he wrote 'The Welfare Costs of Tariffs, Monopolies, and Theft', Gordon Tullock (1922–2014), who completed his doctoral studies in law at the University of Chicago, was a lecturer at the University of Virginia. His article – which was rejected by a number of more prestigious journals before eventually appearing in the *Western Economic Journal* (Tullock, 1993: 11–13) – starts with the observation that governments tend not to create monopolies of their own accord but 'have to be lobbied or pressured into doing so'. This raises the following question. How much will firms invest in order to acquire a monopoly privilege? Tullock suggests that they will be willing to invest as much in the acquisition of a monopoly as they believe that monopoly is worth. In other words, they will be willing to invest resources to the value of the area P_1–B–C–P. The critical step in Tullock's argument then comes with the claim that resources invested in this way are wasted:

> These expenditures, which may simply offset each other to some extent, are purely wasteful from the standpoint of society as a whole; they are spent not in increasing wealth, but in attempting to transfer or resist transfers of wealth. (Tullock, 1967: 227)

The efficiency costs of monopoly are therefore not simply the Harberger triangle (B–C–D), but also what is now known as the 'Tullock rectangle' (P_1–B–C–P) (see Figure 7.1). It is important to note that not all competition is rent-seeking. Tullock (1989: 55) defines rent-seeking as the costly pursuit of proposals which have a negative social impact. Rent, on this view, is profit which produces losses to other people which exceed the gain to the profit maker, and rent-seeking is a pursuit of such profit. When firms compete for a fixed pool of customers by advertising or engage in research in order to secure a patent, there may well be wasteful zero-sum effort, and Tullock (1989: 50–51) is even willing to support heavy taxation on advertising in order to reduce such waste. But, he insists, the 'rent-seeking' label should be applied only to cases in which the outcome sought is itself undesirable regardless of the effort wasted in pursuing it. Lobbying for monopoly is harmful, because the monopoly itself produces inefficiency (i.e. the Harberger triangle), and for Tullock this makes a zero-sum effort to secure the monopoly (i.e. the Tullock rectangle) unambiguously and irredeemably wasteful.

Tullock (1967) initially suggested that the total amount spent in pursuit of a rent would be equal to the value of that rent: that rents would be entirely 'dissipated' in the process of rent-seeking. Tullock's hypothesis about the dissipation of rents was formally restated by Richard Posner (1975). He constructed an example in which ten firms must compete to capture a monopoly rent worth a million dollars. He demonstrated that if (1) actors are risk-neutral, (2) the value of the rent-seeking prize is known and fixed, and (3) the chances of any one firm acquiring the rent are a positive and monotonic function of the amount invested, then each firm will invest $100,000 in rent-seeking.

The assumption that rents would be fully dissipated during the process of rent-seeking was challenged by Tullock (1980) himself who argued that whether or not this happens will depend upon how competitive the rent-seeking industry is. He constructed a very different example using the analogy of a lottery. There is a $100 prize; there are two firms competing to acquire that prize; firms can buy as many tickets as they want at a cost of $1 each; once every firm has bought as many tickets as it wants, one ticket is then randomly drawn and the prize given to its owner. How many tickets should each firm buy? Intuitively the answer is 50. But Tullock argues that this is not the case; if there is a common knowledge of rationality, each firm ought to buy 25 tickets. To see why, consider the following explanation. When each firm has bought 25 tickets each firm will have a 50 per cent chance of winning the $100 prize. At this point, the expected value of each firm's tickets will therefore be $50. Consider the position of firm A as it contemplates buying an additional 25 tickets. A total of 75 tickets will then have been bought, of which it will own 50, giving it a two-thirds chance of winning the prize. The expected value of firm A's tickets is therefore $66. But this $16 increase in the value of their tickets will have cost the firm $25.

Tullock went on to show that whether rents are under-dissipated, dissipated or even over-dissipated will depend upon the number of people in the rent-seeking game and the relationship between the number of tickets each firm buys and its chances of winning the prize. When there are a small number of players and the chances of any one ticket being drawn only depend upon the total number of tickets sold, rents will be under-dissipated. When there are a large number of players or the chances of any one ticket being drawn depend partly upon the total number of tickets that firm has already bought, rents may be over-dissipated. Hillman and Katz (1984) build on Tullock's lottery model of rent-seeking to show that rents will be under-dissipated when rent seekers are risk averse.

More recent models have recognized that rents are not assigned randomly as in a lottery, but to whoever spends the most resources seeking it (Congleton, 1980; Hillman and Riley, 1989; Hillman and Samet, 1987). Rent-seeking has therefore been modelled as an auction, albeit an unusual one in that the losers are nevertheless required to pay what they bid and receive nothing in return. The intuition behind this 'all-pay auction' model is that rent-seeking expenditure happens before the winner is decided and cannot be recovered after the fact: it is a sunk cost. Auctions of this type can induce rational actors to behave in peculiar ways, as Martin Shubik (1971: 109) demonstrated with the 'extremely simple, highly amusing, and instructive parlor game' of the dollar auction (see Box 7.1). These models show that predicting the outcome of rent-seeking contests is a complicated affair involving strategic interaction among bidders in which the degree of dissipation depends on the institutional structure in which competition takes place.

Though formal models of rent-seeking differ on the extent to which rents are dissipated, they generally agree that the Harberger triangle enormously underestimates the social costs of monopoly. Estimates of the costs of rent-seeking run to 50 per cent of American gross domestic product (Laband and Sophocleus, 1988), 20–40 per cent of Indian gross domestic product (Mohammad and Whalley, 1984) and 12 per cent of American domestic consumption expenditure (Lopez and Pagoulatos, 1994) (see Del Rosal, 2011 for a review of the empirical literature). There is however a significant problem here. Given the number of special privileges government dispenses, we would therefore expect the amount spent by firms and interest groups on lobbying, public relations and campaign contributions to be equally large, or at least of the same order of magnitude. Yet this is very obviously not the case:

> During the time I was living in Washington D.C., I was impressed with the size and general prosperity of the rent-seeking industry in that city. As I grew to know more about it, however, I began to wonder why it was not much bigger. Not far from my apartment, for example, was the headquarters building of the dairy lobby. It was a moderate-sized office building, nowhere near as big as one would

Box 7.1   The dollar auction

How much would a rational person pay for a dollar? In normal circumstances we might suppose the answer to be a dollar. Martin Shubik (1971), however, showed that this is not always the case. When a dollar is auctioned off under the understanding that the two highest bidders will each forfeit their bid but only the first highest bidder will receive the prize, it will sometimes be rational to buy one dollar for two, five or even a million dollars. As long as two people enter a bidding war, they will be stuck in an 'arms race' (see generally Baumol, 2004; Khalil, 1997) in which a series of individually reasonable decisions produce a disastrous outcome. The game is thus 'usually highly profitable to its promoter' (Shubik 1971: 109).

Suppose that Alice bids 5 cents and Bob, sensing the opportunity for a cheap dollar, bids 10 cents. Alice will presumably up her bid to 15 cents, and the bidding war will continue. After a few more rounds of bidding, Bob is in the lead at 50 cents, with Alice having previously bid 45 cents. If Alice bids 55 cents in the hopes of gaining rather than losing 45 cents from the auction, the auctioneer is able to breathe a sigh of relief in the knowledge that they will certainly make a profit, since the sum of the two highest bids now exceeds a dollar and can only grow larger. In fact, there is nothing special about the 1 dollar mark. If Alice has bid 95 cents and Bob a dollar, common sense would suggest that Alice should not offer any more than a dollar for a dollar. But since prior bids are sunk costs this is not the case: by bidding $1.05 Alice has the chance to lose 5 cents rather than 95. At some point somebody will presumably decide to cut their losses, but there's no guarantee of when this will be. Shubik (1971: 111) describes his experience with the game at cocktail parties with apparent glee:

> Bidding proceeds fairly briskly until the point when the sum of the two top bids is greater than a dollar, after which a look of realization comes onto the faces of many participants. There is a pause, and

$\rightarrow$

think justified by the roughly $500m a year the dairy farmers were taking out of the taxpayers' pockets ... given these figures, the rent-seeking industry is surprisingly small. (Tullock, 1989: 3)

Other examples of large rents apparently being offered cheaply are not difficult to find. The lobbying expenditure of defence contractors in the United States is in the tens of millions, but the money up for grabs in the hundreds of *billions* (Ansolabehere et al., 2003: 110). Now as

> → hesitation in the group when the bid goes through the one dollar barrier. From then on, there is a duel with bursts of speed until tension builds, bidding then slows and finally peters out.
>
> What does this tell us about rent-seeking? Suppose the government has committed to spending $1 billion on clean energy subsidies but has yet to decide whether the money should go towards solar or wind power. If the solar and wind industries are both represented by effective lobby groups, each should be willing to invest up to $1 billion in trying to convince politicians that their industry is best. Assuming that such investments happen incrementally, however, the strategic situation here is similar to the dollar auction. If both industries have spent $1 billion, their efforts will cancel each other out and the incentive to invest more in order to secure the subsidy will be as strong as ever. This explains how we could see over-dissipation of rents.
>
> An important lesson of the dollar auction for rent-seeking theory is the institutional environment matters a great deal. The potentially disastrous outcome for bidder in this auction is driven by the fact that bids are made sequentially, leading to a type of escalation which makes the whole exercise thoroughly unprofitable, even though each bid seems reasonable. If bidders had instead been asked to provide a single sealed bid, nobody would be willing to pay more than a dollar and escalation would not be a problem. Another issue raised by the dollar auction is whether we should think of participation in rent-seeking contests as voluntary or compulsory. This may seem like a strange question, since nobody forces interest groups to lobby for preferential treatment. When one group lobbies for a policy which would harm another, however, the issue becomes more complex. Suppose that the local manufacturing industry lobbies government for increases in import tariffs in order to increase the monopoly power of its members. This would be costly for importers, who have effectively been placed as a bidder in an all-pay auction. If they refuse to lobby against tariffs, they will be harmed by the manufacturers' successful rent-seeking.

Tullock goes on to suggest, some of the resources invested by firms and interest groups will be spent on expensive meals, foreign travel and other more shady services that are not a part of the visible rent-seeking industry. Yet, if rent-seeking consumes anything close to 50 per cent of American gross domestic product, it nevertheless seems odd that there are not far more lobbying firms in Washington DC. Does this mean that rent-seeking is less of an economic problem than initially envisaged? Tullock (1989) argues not. The costs of rent-seeking are, he now suggests, to a significant degree explained by the need to transfer wealth to interests groups in covert and inefficient ways.

Rent seeking, ignorance and ideology

Politicians create and dispense rents in the expectation of acquiring campaign contributions, political endorsements and perhaps future employment. Though there remains a great deal of disagreement on the size and generality of the effect, it seems to be the case that campaign spending does improve electoral prospects (Mueller, 2003: 481–6; Stratmann, 2005). So politicians can benefit by selling policy promises. But politicians presumably have to set these benefits against the electoral costs moving away from public opinion and possibly being found selling policy favours (Culpepper, 2011; Smith, 1999; Trumbull, 2012). Now cynics may object that the risks of exposure and punishment for creating and selling rents are actually quite small, but politicians and the media presumably have some incentive to highlight the misdemeanours of their opponents (Wittman, 1995). Tullock (1989: ch. 2) argues that one way in which politicians can minimize their political exposure is by constructing a public interest 'cover' for their actions that appeals to voters. By making it appear that there are actually good reasons for granting some privilege, politicians can immunize themselves from criticism. Tullock suggests that the construction of a public interest cover usually precludes direct cash payments to firms and interest groups and often requires the adoption of inefficient production methods which reduce the value of the rents being sought and so reduces the amount groups are willing to invest to acquire them.

It may be that politicians use such covers in a purely instrumental way without believing their own rhetoric, or it may be, as Bruce Yandle (1983) suggests, that ideologues and rent-seekers will form implicit coalitions which provide politicians with both ideological and financial support. Yandle gives the example of bootleggers and Baptists implicitly joining forces to support alcohol prohibition. Baptists favoured prohibition for moral reasons; bootleggers for simple profit. Any politician promising to support prohibition has a public interest cover and could also expect (presumably anonymous) campaign contributions from organized criminal groups. Even if no politician compromises their morals in order to sell policy favours, the greater availability of campaign funds and other resources for those agreeing with special interest groups will give them a better chance of being elected and successfully pushing through their preferred policies. Lobbying can take the form of electoral and legislative subsidy rather than bribery (Hall and Deardorff, 2006).

Is prohibition the most efficient way of providing bootleggers with monopoly rents? No. Having to produce and distribute liquor covertly increases production costs a great deal, and many potential customers will refuse to buy illegal alcohol. It would be much more efficient to give the mafia a legal monopoly over the sale of alcohol in return for a cut of the profits, but politicians would presumably recognize the electoral costs of advocating such a policy. Prohibition increases the cost of production and exchange, and thus a portion of the Tullock rectangle is wasted on inefficient production and contract enforcement. This makes the value of the rent to the bootleggers less than would be the case if more efficient methods of transfer were available.

A contemporary example is the European Union's Common Agricultural Policy. Although subject to several rounds of reform which have weakened its impact somewhat, this policy has, until recently, cost European taxpayers around 30 billion pounds a year whilst adding about nine pounds a week to the average family's weekly food bills. The excesses of this policy were such that at one point the average income of a European Union dairy cow exceeded that of half the world's human population. Now imagine that politicians had simply proposed giving farmers 30 billion pounds a year in direct cash payments. There would have been political uproar. So instead payments are hidden through subsidies, quotas, price supports and set-aside measures justified as being necessary to stabilize income, protect the interests of hill farmers and preserve the environment. The problem with these measures is not, however, simply their cost but their inefficiency. Subsidies paid through the Common Agricultural Policy create perverse incentives to over produce and this leads to the accumulation of rotting surpluses which were once 'dumped' on markets in developing countries. The Common Agricultural Policy may cost 30 billion pounds a year but it is not worth this amount in additional profits to farmers. Hence farmers have no reason to invest 30 billion pounds a year in the pursuit and defence of this policy. This does *not* mean that rent-seeking is economically insignificant; it means that the costs of rent-seeking reveal themselves in the commitment to this hugely inefficient policy.

A formal version of this argument is provided in Figure 7.2 (Tullock, 1990), which shows the usual demand and supply curves for an industry with the supply curve (CC) in this case showing variable cost. At the initial equilibrium output, Q will be produced at price P. Suppose that the industry seeks and obtains a government-mandated price rise to P_1. As a

Figure 7.2   *The costs of rent-seeking*

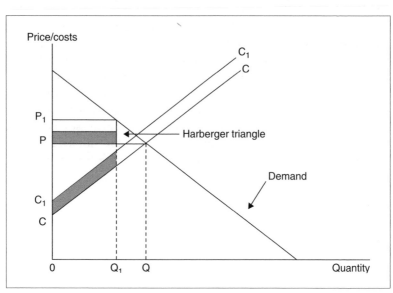

Source: Adapted from Tullock (1990), p. 197.

result, the quantity produced falls to Q_1. The Harberger triangle measures the direct costs of granting this special privilege in terms of lost consumer surplus. Once again, the Tullock rectangle to its left (which, for reasons that will become apparent, is divided into two parts) measures the additional profits the industry stands to make and so, in theory, the amount it will be willing to invest in pursuit of the rent.

Assume now that the public interest cover used to justify this price rise requires the adoption of a less-efficient method of production. Because prices are now fixed, this increase in costs cannot be passed on to the consumer and will have to be met by the industry; reducing overall profitability and the value of the rent. More precisely, assume that costs increase from CC to C_1C_1. At the new equilibrium, total additional costs will be equal to the shaded area between the two cost lines. Looking now at the Tullock rectangle, this increase is equivalent to a reduction in profits of the amount shown in the lower and shaded part of the rectangle (the size of this part of the rectangle is equal to the size of the shaded area between CC and C_1C_1). The total costs of rent-seeking are therefore: (1) the Harberger triangle; (2) the amount invested in pursuit of the rent (that is the upper part of the rectangle); and (3) the additional costs which come from using the less-efficient method of production. The most the industry will be willing to invest in the pursuit of the rent is however the smaller, upper, and not shaded, part of the rectangle. The rent is fully dissipated, but mostly by inefficient production rather than lobbying expenditure.

If voters want these inefficient policies, however, it is not clear that we ought to be criticizing them. Tullock (1989: 29) recognizes that 'democracy is supposed to give the voter his choice, not what some economists think that they should choose'. Given that rational choice theorists see preference as revealed through choice, can we accept that voters voluntarily take actions which are on balance costly to themselves? Intuitively, it seems that if we are claiming voters are choosing incorrectly, there must be some objective standard of rationality which rational choice theorists can divine independently of choice (Hindmoor, 1999). Tullock does not come down firmly one way or the other on this issue – seeing the costs of rent-seeking as 'a metaphysical problem' for which he has no solution. He does, however, argue that the relationship between choice and preference is much less obvious when it comes to collective decisions such as voting.

For Tullock's ideological cover explanation to work in the long run, voters must be systematically deceived by politicians and rent-seekers (Tullock, 1989: 5). There is some tension with rational choice theory here (Wittman, 1995), but we will see in the following chapter that rational choice theory has a plausible (but controversial) explanation for ignorant, and even irrational, voters. This is essentially an application of Olson's logic of collective action we encountered in the previous chapter: no individual voter has much incentive to monitor the conduct of politicians, but concentrated interest groups do have such incentives. Voters remain 'rationally ignorant', and rent-seekers are able to eke out a living in the gaps of public opinion.

Given that rent-seeking requires voter ignorance, we should expect rent-seeking to be more common on policy issues with low salience to voters. This suggests that the broad contours of policy will be guided by voter preferences, but the intricacies of various policies will tend to favour special interests (Olson, 1982: 27–8). There is a reasonably widespread and salient demand among voters for action on climate change, but the specifics of such proposals are far less salient, however, and this gives special interests the opportunity to lobby for preferential treatment. By lobbying for tradable permits with grandfathered emission rights rather than a carbon tax, for example, existing emitters can not only avoid the costs of climate change mitigation but also increase the costs of competitors hoping to enter their industry. Likewise, technology companies can lobby for subsidies on research into clean energy (see Helm, 2010 for a discussion of the situation in the UK). If voters are equally happy with any number of plausible policy options but special interests have strong preferences over policy details, politicians will likely do best by tailoring broad goals to public opinion and narrow implementation to interest groups.

Whereas Tullock focuses on the short-term efficiency costs of rent-seeking, Mancur Olson's (1982) later work focused on the long-run dynamics of interest group activities. Olson extended the *Logic of Collective Action* to think about what happens as societies subject to rent-seeking grow old. Though organizing for collective action is difficult, inefficient policies, once implemented, are generally quite resilient. Due to the fact that no individual has much incentive to lobby against inefficient policies with dispersed costs, they will tend to remain in place in the absence of major institutional change. Policies may persist even when the organized interests which once lobbied for their implementation no longer exist. Over time, stable democracies will accumulate ever more inefficient policies which are individually trivial to each citizen but which collectively produce a great deal of inefficiency.

Corruption, slack and bureaucracy

Rent-seeking is possible because voters are unable to control the legislators charged with representing them. This is a general problem in the private and public sectors known as the 'principal–agent problem' (see Box 7.2). Voters would like politicians to pursue their preferences and will punish those who do not by withdrawing support. Due to information asymmetries, monitoring costs and collective action problems, however, politicians have some slack to pursue other preferences in their private decisions. Candidates may pursue their own ideological preferences, private wealth through corruption or reelection prospects by offering policy favours for campaign contributions. Principal–agent problems are not restricted to the relationship between voters and their representatives, however. Tullock and other public choice economists such as William Niskanen (1933–2011) have also analysed bureaucracy from a rational choice perspective, focusing on the scope bureaucrats have to pursue their own interests at the expense of their official duty to implement government policy.

Box 7.2   Principals and agents

A principal–agent (P–A) relationship arises when one person, the principal, contracts with another person, the agent, to undertake tasks on their behalf. P–A relationships are a pervasive feature of life. Employers hire employees; homeowners sign contracts with estate agents to market their house; and patients pay doctors to diagnose and treat their illnesses. Within the political arena, voters select representatives to represent their interests; in parliamentary systems representatives then select governments; and governments must then rely upon bureaucrats to implement their policies. For two reasons, economists generally expect P–A relationships to generate P–A problems. First, principals usually have incomplete information; they cannot know, or can only find out at a great cost, whether agents are acting in the way that they would want them to act. Second, agents will not necessarily act in their principal's interests unless induced to do so; agents have conflicting interests whether in 'shirking' or in pursuing their own policy preferences.

P–A problems can be managed in a number of ways. (1) Principals can devise contracts that link an agent's payment to their performance. But if this performance depends upon the agent's effort *and* some random variable then risk-averse agents may well require higher overall payments to compensate for the resulting uncertainty. (2) Agents can sometimes be deterred from shirking by principal's threats to terminate their relationship if performance falls below some level. (3) P–A problems will be most acute in short-term relationships. By offering agents the prospects of entering into long-term relationships, agents can be given an incentive to acquire a reputation for being trustworthy. (4) Through the design of careful selection procedures principals may succeed in hiring agents who share and so naturally pursue their interests. It is, however, unlikely that principals will be able to (or want to) eliminate P–A problems. This is because it may well cost the principal more to eliminate the P–A problem than they gain from doing so. In such cases the existence of some agency costs may well be economically efficient.

Tullock published *The Politics of Bureaucracy* in 1965. He argues that the crucial feature of bureaucracies is not simply that they are hierarchies, but 'pyramidal' hierarchies with fewer people at the top than in the lower ranks (Tullock, 1966: 33). The relationship between junior and senior bureaucrats is one of principal and agent. Bureaucracies work efficiently to the extent that bureaucrats in junior positions pass on the 'right' information to their superiors. Once this information has been collated, those at the top of the pyramid are then meant to reach a decision which is communicated back down the pyramid before being implemented by those at the bottom. One problem with this account is that it ignores the potentially conflicting interests those in subordinate positions have. Junior bureaucrats have an interest in impressing their superiors, and those superiors have an interest in impressing their superiors, and so on. Most bureaucrats will therefore filter any information they receive and only pass on that part of it which they believe shows them in a good light or which their superiors want to hear. Rather than information being passed up the pyramid, this means that 'factual information tends to flow from the top down instead' (Tullock, 1965: 70). Each bureaucrat will have more interest in finding out what their superiors think about particular issues than they will in finding out about what is happening in the outside world. Problems of this sort mean that bureaucracies are generally extremely inefficient. They usually 'accomplish something, but [they] will not perform the task for which they are designed' (Tullock, 1965: 97).

Tullock's book, which was originally drafted in 1957 before he knew much economics (Niskanen, 2012), was pioneering in its use of the *Homo economicus* assumption but offered no systematic theory of bureaucratic behaviour. Niskanen (1971) provides a more formal account in which budget-maximizing bureaucrats are able to expand the scope of operations beyond what legislators and citizens would prefer.

The budget-maximizing bureaucrat

Niskanen's argument in *Bureaucracy and Representative Government* is that public sector bureaucrats attempt to maximize the size of their budget and to a significant extent succeed. Niskanen (1971: 38) assumes that bureaucrats value a range of goods including 'salary, perquisites of the office, public reputation, power, patronage, output of the bureau'. Since these goods are in most cases positively related to the total size of the bureaucrat's budget, Niskanen assumes that they will seek to make these budgets as large as possible. Since legislators and voters prefer a smaller budget, other things equal, this is a classic principal–agent problem.

Niskanen's argument about budget-maximizing ought to be seen in the context of an existing debate within economics. In the 1950s and 1960s a number of economists began to argue that the rise of the giant corporation had rendered the assumption of profit-maximization redundant. Salaried managers with no stake in the ownership of a firm had, it was argued, no real incentive to maximize their employer's profits. But what did managers maximize if not profits? The alternatives canvassed at this time included the number of staff, autonomy from shareholders and perks such as overseas conferences and plush offices. But as William Baumol (1959) first observed, many of these variables are positively related to the size of the corporation. For this reason, managers will, he argued, be growth-maximizers. In response, critics argued that whatever it is that managers may *want* to do, the discipline of market competition and the need to retain the confidence of shareholders actually gives managers no alternative but to maximize profits. But, as Niskanen grasped, whether or not this is true, the same discipline does not exist within the public sector where there is no requirement to return a profit and no guarantee that those who succeed in cutting costs will actually be rewarded:

> The rationality of budget maximization by bureaucrats may best be illustrated by considering the consequences of contrary behaviour. Consider the probable consequences for a subordinate manager who proves without question that the same output could be produced at, say, one-half of the present expenditures. In a profit-seeking firm this manager would probably receive a bonus, a promotion, and an opportunity to find another such economy ... in a bureau, at best, this manager might receive a citation and a savings bond, and the suspicion of his new colleagues. Those bureaucrats who doubt this proposition and who have good private employment alternatives should test it ... once. (Niskanen, 1971: 38)

At some point in the budgetary cycle, senior bureaucrats submit budget requests to their political patrons in government. Bureaucrats will want to acquire as large a budget as possible. Politicians will have some interest in resisting their demands. Niskanen (1971: 64) argues that the resulting negotiations conclude with public bureaucracies supplying 'an output up to twice that of a competitive industry faced by the same demand and cost conditions'. So what advantage do bureaucrats have over politicians which allows them to inflate budgets in this way? Niskanen offers two answers to this question. The first is that bureaucrats have more information about the costs of supplying particular levels of output. The second is that they can make 'take-it-or-leave-it' offers to their political patrons. We will consider each of these in turn.

Private sector firms sell particular units of output – be it pints of milk or ocean liners – at a given price. Public sector bureaucracies instead offer to provide a total output – a certain number of hospital beds, army divisions or school meals – in return for an agreed budget. In bargaining about the level of budget and output, Niskanen credits politicians with the possession of four powers or capacities. The first is that of selecting the overall level of output to be produced. This means that bureaucrats cannot budget-maximize by simply selecting a level of output requiring an enormous budget. The second is ensuring that bureaucrats fulfil any promises they make about the level of output they will deliver in return for an agreed budget. This means that bureaucrats cannot budget-maximize by promising to provide 100 hospital beds in return for a budget of one million pounds even if they know that they cannot achieve this. The third is ensuring that the total benefits individuals derive from consuming whatever output it is that the bureaucracy provides are equal to or greater than the total costs of providing it. This means that bureaucrats cannot budget-maximize by setting a budget which is so high that the costs of the resulting output exceed its benefits. The fourth is that of ensuring that the marginal benefits of any output are not negative.

The existence of these capacities implies that politicians have access to detailed information about bureaucratic output and costs. Politicians need to know a great deal in order to know when the total costs of providing a particular level of output will exceed the total benefits individuals derive from consuming it. Yet Niskanen critically assumes that *only* bureaucrats know what the minimum costs of producing particular levels of output are. When a senior bureaucrat tells a politician that it will take a certain level of budget to provide a certain level of output, the politician will not know whether it would be possible to provide that level of output at a lower cost. Because bureaucrats know that politicians do not know what the minimum costs of producing various levels of output are, they can budget-maximize.

Niskanen's second argument is that bureaucrats can inflate their budgets by making 'take-it-or-leave-it' offers. In Figure 7.3 the quantity of some good which is being produced is shown on the horizontal axis and price and cost on the vertical axis. Notice that the marginal benefit consumers derive from the consumption of a good (from which can be derived the demand curve) declines as output increases and that marginal costs (from which can be derived the supply curve) increase as production costs rise. Economists generally argue that profit-maximizing firms will produce additional units of output up to that point at which the marginal benefits of doing so are equal to marginal costs. In Figure 7.3 such a firm will therefore produce output Q at price P. At this equilibrium total consumer 'surplus' – which measures the difference between what some consumers have paid for the good

Figure 7.3 *The profit-maximizing firm*

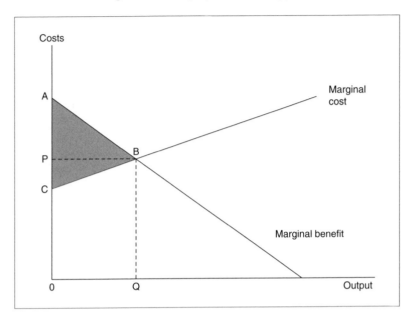

and the amount they would have been willing to pay – is shown by the shaded area A–B–C.

How much will a budget-maximizing bureaucracy produce? We will follow Niskanen in *initially* assuming that politicians accurately represent individuals' demand for particular goods and services and that the marginal benefit schedule for a bureaucratically produced good is therefore the same as it is for a privately produced one. Assume now that bureaucrats can make take-it-or-leave-it offers; in other words that they can offer to produce a certain level of output in return for a certain budget and credibly threaten not to produce *anything* if this request is rejected. In Figure 7.4 assume that bureaucrats demand a total budget of 0–C–D–Q_1 in return for a promise to produce output Q_1. This budget corresponds to the *total* costs of producing output Q_1, that is a total output of the area 0–C–D–Q_1. This budget and output combination is clearly sub-optimal because the marginal costs of producing output Q–Q_1 are greater than the marginal benefits. In this particular case the resulting 'waste' B–D–E is exactly equal to the surplus A–B–C. This is in fact the equilibrium output because if bureaucrats

Figure 7.4   *The budget-maximizing bureaucrat*

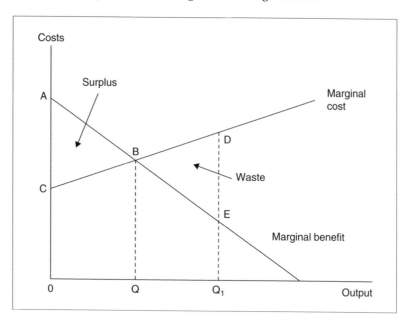

were to ask for a larger budget, total waste would be greater than the total surplus. Faced with a take-it-or-leave-it offer, the vote-maximizing politician would have good reason to reject such an offer because at this point they would prefer zero output with zero benefits and costs to an output whose costs were greater than its benefits. If, on the other hand, the bureaucrat were to ask for a budget of less than this amount, consumer surplus would be greater than total waste and the politician would accept the budget offer. Yet bureaucrats will not make such a budget offer precisely because they could ask for and receive more.

What are we to make of Niskanen's arguments? The idea that bureaucrats possess more information than their political patrons is a venerable one which can be found in, for example, Max Weber's sociological analysis of bureaucracy (see Beetham, 1987). The claim that bureaucrats can make 'take-it-or-leave-it' offers appears, on the other hand, entirely fanciful. Niskanen defends it by suggesting that these two arguments have the same consequences; it makes no difference whether it is assumed that bureaucrats can make take-it-or-leave-it offers or whether only bureaucrats know what the minimum costs of producing certain levels of output are. By implication, the assumption that they can make take-it-or-leave-it offers can be regarded as little more than a presentational device and defended on the instrumentalist grounds that theories ought to be judged in terms of the accuracy of their predictions rather than the realism of their assumptions (Niskanen, 1971: 191). This suggestion seems implausible because there is one very obvious difference between these two arguments. In the information-based argument politicians choose the level of output to be produced. In what might be called the blackmail argument, wherein bureaucrats can make 'take-it-or-leave-it' offers, this responsibility is however given to bureaucrats. Yet in *both* cases, the limits placed upon bureaucrat's capacity to budget-maximize derive from the assumption that politicians know enough to prevent the total costs of bureaucratic output exceeding its total benefits. In the case of the information-based argument this assumption stops bureaucrats extracting too large a budget in return for any specified output. In the case of the blackmail argument, this assumption provides the cut-off point beyond which politicians will reject any budget demands.

Other models of bureaucratic behaviour

In one of the first published critiques of *Bureaucracy and Representative Government*, Jean-Luc Migue and Gerard Belanger (1974) argued that bureaucrats maximize not the size of their budget *per se*, but the size of their discretionary budget which they define as the difference between the total budget and the minimum costs of producing the output expected by the bureau's sponsor. Although this discretionary budget cannot be appropriated as personal profit by the bureaucrat, it can, Migue and Belanger argue, be used to secure greater power, patronage, prestige and so on. In a formal reassessment of his work, Niskanen (1991) has now accepted their argument and suggested that he was always uncomfortable with the behavioural assumption that bureaucrats are budget-maximizers. This concession might, however, be regarded as entailing a revision to, rather than a repudiation of, the original budget-maximizing argument.

The claim that bureaucrats want to maximize their discretionary income is, after all, still consistent with the underlying claim that bureaucrats are self-interested actors who attempt to maximize their salary, perquisites of the office, public reputation, power and patronage. In a sense, all Niskanen is now arguing is that bureaucrats are more likely to achieve these goals by maximizing their *discretionary* budget. Furthermore, this concession does not significantly affect Niskanen's overall conclusion that bureaucracies are inefficient. It does, however, alter the details of that argument. If bureaucrats maximize their total budget then, as we have seen, output will be too large relative to the level of demand and cost.

The most interesting and plausible alternative to the assumption that bureaucrats maximize their discretionary income is that they are 'bureau-shapers'. Patrick Dunleavy (1985, 1991) argues that senior bureaucrats care more about the kind of work they do than their terms and conditions. Bureaucrats prefer innovative work with longer time horizons and high discretion over routine work with short time horizons and low discretion; small-sized work units with cooperative working relationships over large-sized units with coercive work relationships; and work which entails proximity to political power centres and confers high-status social contacts to work in regional locations conferring low-status contacts (Dunleavy, 1991: 202). Senior bureaucrats will sometimes be able to achieve these goals by applying for new jobs or redefining their existing ones. At other times they will, however, act collectively to offload or contract out unattractive parts of their work. Far from attempting to maximize their budget and output, 'bureau-shaping' bureaucrats will sometimes welcome budget cuts.

More recently, bureaucrats have been modelled as active participants in the policy process who, through their influence over implementation, are able to shape the direction of policy. In this literature bureaucrats are modelled as having preferences over policy space just like voters in Downs's model and candidates in some of the work which followed (see Gailmard and Patty, 2012 for a review). Principal–agent problems remain relevant here, since bureaucrats are meant to be the agents of elected politicians, who are themselves agents of voters. If a bureaucrat has preferences which diverge from the politicians and citizens they are meant to serve, opportunism by policy shifting may be as much of a concern as opportunism through corruption or laziness.

Political agency, constraint and selection

Rent-seeking and bureaucratic slack are principal–agent problems, and rational choice theorists have generally seen such problems in terms of moral hazard and their solution in terms of sanctions or incentive design. Politicians and bureaucrats have the ability to engage in *ex post* opportunism, and the way to prevent them from doing so is to adjust the environment in such a way as to make it in their self-interest to serve the interests of the agent. Generally speaking, this can be done by punishing bad behaviour or increasing the value of good behaviour. For Tullock, Niskanen and many other public choice theorists, the best incentive scheme in this respect is privatization and liberalization. If politicians abuse their power, it should be taken away from them and placed in the hands of individuals interacting in the marketplace. Although almost all public choice theorists accept that there is *some* role for the state, it is not uncommon to argue that market competition provides more effective restraints on power than electoral competition or constitutions and that we should therefore reduce the size and scope of government.

This sanctions-based model of political control is grounded in the assumption that political actors are homogeneous agents. Indeed, the use of such 'representative agent' models is so common in rational choice theory that it is easy to see the assumption of homogeneity as a defining characteristic, at least when it comes to Virginia School public choice who have been particularly reluctant to base explanations on differences in preferences or capabilities or suggest that government can be improved by selecting better politicians (Buchanan, 2008). If all possible agents are essentially the same – competent and self-interested – the means of preventing or mitigating the effects of rent-seeking or bureaucratic slack will need to be focused on constraining political opportunism.

Although there might be good pragmatic reasons for thinking particularly carefully about what might happen when knaves control government, it is clear that not everyone is motivated by precisely the same factors. Even if nobody is guided entirely by civic duty, it is difficult to deny that people vary in terms of civic motivation and competence. It may be unwise to assume that men will be governed by angels, but it is entirely reasonable to think about the ways in which institutions might discourage the relatively angelic from seeking and gaining office. In an 1813 letter to John Adams, Thomas Jefferson argued that there is a 'natural aristocracy' of men with superior virtue and talents, suggesting that 'that form of government is the best, which provides the most effectually for a pure selection of these natural *aristoi* into the offices of government'. Jefferson thought democracy was a good system for selecting the virtuous and talented, but others such as Hayek (1944: 10) have argued that the worst inevitably get to the top in politics. Recent work by rational choice theorists has pursued the idea that selection as well as sanctioning can be used as a tool for improving government performance (Besley, 2006; Brennan and Hamlin, 2000; see generally Fearon, 1999).

Generally speaking, selection models of electoral accountability assume that candidates vary in some desirable trait such as virtue, talent or ideological proximity to voters. We might talk here of 'good' and 'bad' candidates where good candidates can be thought of as honest and competent and bad candidates as dishonest and incompetent. This is obviously a gross simplification. Honest and dishonest and competent and incompetent are not binary categories. Furthermore, they may not come packaged together. Candidates may be honest but incompetent or dishonest but competent. For the purposes of our analysis however these simple distinctions will suffice. Voters want to elect good candidates, but bad candidates will run for office, and there is often no fool-proof way of telling them apart. In sanction-based models of electoral discipline, it would not matter whether politicians were good or bad, since the sanctions in place are meant to force good behaviour regardless of the underlying preferences. Yet sanctioning is beset by principal–agent problems. In selection-based models, sorting the good from the bad becomes key. Rather than encouraging the bad to behave like the good (i.e. produce a 'pooling equilibrium'), selection works when good and bad candidates behave differently and those differences make the good more likely to seek and win office (a 'separating equilibrium'). In general, selection can happen when institutions are designed to attract good candidates or when electoral competition allows voters to sort the wheat from the chaff.

There are a number of factors which might influence the extent to which good and bad types seek office. If we focus on the issue of honesty, the general challenge is that if a dishonest type enters government they will be able to sell policy to special interests rather than pursue the public interest. If sanctioning dishonest behaviour is not a viable option, there may be ways of selecting for honest candidates by designing institutions in such a way that the dishonest find politics an unattractive vocation. The strength and likelihood of sanctions is obviously important here – dishonest politicians are less likely to seek office when they expect dishonesty to be swiftly and severely punished – and the selection models we outline here are really models combining sanctions and selection.

In order to think about how to model this selection problem, we need to define the preference of honest and dishonest potential candidates. Honest politicians, we can assume, care about the public interest and the wages they receive for holding office. Dishonest politicians do not care about the public interest but instead about wages and available rents. A useful general concept developed by Besley (2005: 53) is the attractiveness ratio: A = (rents + wages) / (public service motivation + wages). High values of this attractiveness ratio will tend to attract dishonest politicians, while low values will tend to attract honest ones. If there were no rents available, for example, the attractiveness ratio would be low and the public service motivation of honest candidates would make them more likely to run for office.

Suppose that we hold public service motivation and rents constant. How should politicians' salaries be set in order to attract honest candidates? For Besley (2005: 54), the answer depends on the relative strength of rents and public service motivation in attracting honest or dishonest politicians. If available rents are high relative to public service motivation (i.e. the attractiveness ratio is greater than one), low wages will discourage the honest from entering politics and leave electoral competition to the corrupt. If this is the case, increasing political salaries would increase the average honesty of candidates, since higher wages reduce the weighting of other factors in the attractiveness ratio. The same logic tells us that if public service motivation is more important than rents, low wages would discourage the dishonest from entering. In this case higher salaries would lead to an increase in dishonest politicians seeking office. If we want to think about whether we should increase or decrease salaries in order to select for honest politicians, then, we need to think about the non-wage reasons people enter politics. Other institutional factors such as electoral finance rules and term limits influence selection by altering the rents and wages available over a political career, but we do not review this literature here (see instead Braendle, 2013).

Unless selection mechanisms of the type discussed above work perfectly to ensure only the best seek office, there will remain good reason for voters to attempt to distinguish between good and bad candidates during an election campaign. If voters can costlessly distinguish good candidates from bad, they will presumably elect the good and there will be no problem. If, on the other hand, good and bad candidates are indistinguishable, selection will be impossible. Between these two extremes is the analytically interesting case in which voters can get information about candidate quality, but only fallible and/or costly information. If this is the case, voters may use various imperfect cues in order to assess candidate quality and high quality candidates may attempt to honestly signal their type to voters while low quality types attempt to disguise their type. We will discuss voters' use of informational shortcuts in the next chapter, so here we will focus on the issue of candidate signalling.

For a signal of quality to be credible, it must be possible for high quality candidates to send a signal in a way which cannot be faked by low quality candidates. When it comes to competence, the general purpose tools of education and professional experience may be used by politicians to signal competence. Earning advanced degrees or occupying high status jobs is much easier for highly competent individuals, making these factors credible signals of competence. When it comes to honesty, things are more complicated. It is easy to claim to be morally good, but absent reliable public tests of morality as exist for competence, such statements will amount to nothing more than cheap talk. There are, however, some signals of moral character or ideology which are more costly for those not intrinsically motivated to help others or pursue some political goal. Lifelong voluntary campaigning for a political cause is often a useful qualification, as is public-spirited work for NGOs or public interest law firms for below market wages.

Although sanctions and selection may sometimes push in opposite directions (e.g. Ashworth, 2012: 188–90; Besley and Smart, 2007; Smart and Sturm, 2013), they generally seem to work together. An institutional environment which both selects for virtue and competence as well as taking precautions against opportunism seems like a clearly superior approach to the extent that such an environment is possible (Besley, 2006; Braendle, 2013; Brennan and Hamlin, 2000). The relative effectiveness of sanctions and selection will no doubt continue to be a major source of debate in rational choice theory and political science more generally, however.

Assessment

Critics of the rational choice method often suggest that it is in some sense 'inherently' right-wing (King, 1987: 92: also see Dunleavy and O'Leary, 1987; Self, 1993; Stretton and Orchard, 1994). The two most politically charged areas of rational choice theory are rent-seeking and budget-maximizing. In both cases, public choice theory has been used to justify cutbacks in public expenditure and privatization. It is worth noting, however, that the *laissez-faire* implications of these theories can be found not so much with the core assumptions of self-interested behaviour or political individualism, but in the auxiliary comparative analysis of the public and private sectors. Public choice theorists rightly criticized welfare economists for unfairly comparing the fiction of a perfectly efficient and benevolent government with the reality of market failure. Although neither Tullock nor Niskanen explicitly assume that markets work perfectly, it is important to note that even if we accept that rent-seekers and expansionist bureaucrats are responsible for large and genuine welfare losses we cannot conclude that privatization or deregulation are the correct responses without conducting a thorough comparative analysis. If regulation and public provision were implemented in order to solve some market failure, we need to weigh the costs of market failure against those of government failure. Traditional welfare economists very clearly failed to do this in treating government as a benevolent dictatorship, but it might well be argued that theorists like Tullock and Niskanen have overcorrected by focusing on government failure and neglecting the obvious fact that markets also fail.

In claiming that public sector bureaucracies 'will supply an output up to twice that' of a private sector industry, for example, Niskanen explicitly assumes that the private market is perfectly competitive. This assumption is important insofar as it provides a yardstick for evaluation, but those producing and consuming public choice theory must be careful not to confuse this standard of evaluation for a feasible alternative. Public choice theory cannot, as one of its practitioners has claimed, show that government 'usually make things worse' (Simmons, 2011: 49). Many individual theorists may be well placed to compare market failure and government failure, but it needs to be emphasized that a demonstration of rent-seeking or bureaucratic inefficiency can never be any more than half a normative argument.

Consider the issue of how we recognize rent-seeking costs when we see them. Although rent and profit are simply different words for the same economic concept (Buchanan, 1980), Tullock and his compatriots want to draw a categorical distinction between rent-seeking which has a 'negative social impact' (Tullock, 1989: 55) and profit-seeking which does not. At an analytic level this is an important and meaningful distinction, but how, in practice, can profit-seeking be distinguished from rent-seeking? Consider the two following examples. First, that of a firm investing resources in the attempt to discover a cure for cancer (Tullock, 1993: 22–3). If the investment is successful the firm will acquire a monopoly patent and large profits. Is this investment therefore rent-seeking? No, because the discovery of a cure for cancer is obviously socially desirable. Second, that of a struggling American steel firm which invests resources in the attempt to secure a ban on the imports of a rival Korean firm on the 'grounds [that they] are environmentally dangerous' (Tullock, 1989: 55). Is this rent-seeking? Yes, because whilst the ban will help the American steel firm it will harm a far larger number of American consumers. What about the environmental damage caused by the Korean imports? Well there is no problem here because Tullock helpfully adds that the argument about 'purported' environmental damage is, 'entirely spurious'.

In these two cases the distinction between rent-seeking and profit-seeking is, by assumption, entirely straightforward, but most of the policy questions politicians are called upon to resolve do not come so neatly packaged (Hindmoor, 1999). Consider the following policy choices. Should education be subsidized? Should imports from countries using child labour be banned? Should unlicensed medical practitioners be prohibited? Should churches be exempt from taxes? If the answer to any one of these questions is yes, the competitive market will be compromised and a particular group – teachers, domestic manufacturers, doctors and the clergy – will be given access to a rent. Should we therefore define any expenditure of resources by any of these groups in pursuit of any of these privileges as rent-seeking? Given Tullock's definition, the answer to this question will depend upon whether the policy in question creates or destroys social surplus.

As Tullock recognizes, there are serious conceptual and empirical problems here. In practice it will often be impossible to know whether a given policy is socially destructive (Tullock, 1989: 5) and in any case it is unclear whether economic efficiency should trump the wishes of voters (Tullock, 1989: 3). Many people believe, sincerely believe, that the future of the countryside ought not to be determined through the interplay of market forces. No doubt many of the people who believe this are farmers but it is simply not the case that the only people who support farm subsidies are farmers. The point is this. Those who believe that farming ought to be subsidized will regard subsidies as creating value in so far as they free us from reliance upon vulnerable foreign imports, help preserve a valuable rural way of life and ensure that city dwellers have a beautiful countryside to visit at weekends. They will therefore not regard any investment by farmers in pursuit of additional subsidies as rent-seeking. Without a comprehensive economic analysis to ground the claim, attributions of rent-seeking are a matter of political taste. To accuse someone of rent-seeking is to say that you do not approve of what it is their investment is intended to secure. Tullock believes that the free market should be protected from government intervention and so considers resources invested in the pursuit of rents to be rent-seeking. Tullock, seeing a Harberger triangle, also sees a Tullock rectangle. Others who believe that some proposed intervention is in the public interest will however see neither.

Chapter 8

Anthony Downs (again) and *The Economics of Information and Voter Choice*

> **Overview:** Rational choice theorists generally see individuals as well informed and rational. Decades of survey research by political scientists has found, however, that voters are in most cases extremely uninformed about basic political matters. If voters do not know what policies best serve their interests or whether a candidate can be trusted, can they be said to be making a reasoned and rational choice? If not, must we conclude that rational choice theory is not applicable to the behaviour of voters? In this chapter we suggest not. Drawing again on the work of Anthony Downs we show that on one interpretation rational choice theory can not only accommodate voter ignorance but *requires* it. Because a single vote is very unlikely to have any electoral impact whatsoever, individuals have little or no incentive to think about how they vote. This chapter lays out the logic of this 'rational ignorance' argument along with some of its extensions and critiques. We show that although these arguments are sometimes overplayed by critics of democracy, they do present a very real concern which deserves to be taken seriously.

Setting the stage: motivation, information and rational choice

As we saw in Chapter 3, Anthony Downs based his spatial model of electoral competition on the assumption that voters are rational in a fairly narrow and instrumental sense – voters know what they want and know which candidates will give it to them. In Downs's view, electoral competition is much like market competition, with political parties selling policy platforms to voters. Politicians are assumed to be office-seeking and citizens are assumed to judge candidates rationally and comprehensively when casting votes. Although nobody in their right mind would claim that voter choices are actually and completely rational in this way, many rational choice theorists have found the simple assumption of calculative and omniscient rationality extremely useful in predicting political outcomes and explaining patterns of political behaviour. Indeed, it is difficult to reject Downs's assumptions without also rejecting the entire methodology of modern economics, which generally assumes rational profit-maximizing firms and welfare-maximizing consumers. The value of simple assumptions is widely accepted in the analysis of economic markets, and since voters and consumers are simply the same people in different contexts, there is no obvious reason to treat voters and consumers differently: 'The initial burden of proof must surely rest with anyone who proposes to introduce differing behavioral assumptions in different institutional settings' (Brennan and Buchanan, 2000: 56).

Yet many political scientists and philosophers do routinely make different and intuitively more plausible assumptions about economic and political behaviour. Does this place their analyses in conflict with rational choice theory? In this chapter we will suggest not, by pointing to Downs's own discussion of the peculiarities of collective choice and more recent theoretical and empirical work which builds on these insights. We will argue that rational choice theorists can legitimately produce very different *behavioural* models in different institutional settings while making the same *motivational* assumptions (Brennan and Hamlin, 2000: 9).

Electoral competition may be analogous to market competition in the sense that we can liken voters to consumers and politicians to entrepreneurs, but this does not mean that these two markets are analytically equivalent. One important difference here relates to the underlying logic of individual choice. In an economic market, consumers – subject to constraints upon their budget – can choose what to buy and, by and large, get what they pay for. This is not the case with collective political choice where, in a democracy at least, no individual gets what they want simply by voting for what they want. Voters decide which box to tick, but, except in extremely rare circumstances, their choice does not directly affect who ends up in government. If voters are interested only in electoral outcomes (and restricting our attention to majority or plurality voting systems), a vote only matters when it makes or breaks a tie. Electorally, it makes no difference whether a party wins or loses by one vote or one million, what matters is whether they cross the threshold for victory. In real-world elections, the probability of casting a decisive vote will generally be extremely small. Mulligan and Hunter (2003) looked at the historical record and found that 1 in 89,000 votes in US congressional elections between 1898 and 1992 were pivotal, while 1 in 15,000 votes in US state legislative elections between 1968 and 1989 made a difference to the outcome. Gelman et al. (2009) estimate the probability of pivotality in the 2008 US presidential election. The average voter had a 1 in 60 million chance of making a difference, while those in small and important states had a chance as high as 1 in 10 million.

Although electoral *outcomes* are often extremely important to individuals, individual electoral *choices* are normally profoundly unimportant in an instrumental sense. Consider the situation of a wealthy and passionate partisan in a battleground state during the 2012 presidential election, and assume she would be willing to pay $1 million to have her preferred party win. How much is her vote worth? Since the million-dollar benefit of a desirable outcome needs to be discounted by the 1 in 10 million chance of bringing it about, the vote is worth ten cents in expected value terms. Since most people would be unwilling to spend a million dollars to swing an election, we must conclude that individual votes are not worth much in instrumental terms.

This raises two important questions. First, why do so many people bother to vote? Voting is a costly activity. 'It takes time to register, to discover what parties are running, to deliberate, to go to the polls, and to mark the ballot' (Downs, 1957a: 266). The existence of these costs is significant because whilst it may matter a great deal to people whether or not their preferred party is elected, rational actors will realize that the chances of their vote making any difference to the eventual outcome are incredibly low: lower indeed than their chances of being knocked down by a car whilst crossing the road to get to the polling station (Meehl, 1977). Now, as Downs (1957a: 266) and, more recently, Bernard Grofman (1993) have observed, the existence of such costs gives rational choice theorists the opportunity to explain why turnout increases when the costs of voting are lower either because the weather is sunny, the polls are open longer or postal voting is possible. But there is an obvious problem here. In any reasonably sized electorate the chances of any one person's vote making a difference to the result are so small that the costs of voting are almost certainly going to exceed the possible discounted benefits of doing so no matter how good the weather is. This means that for most people it is simply irrational to vote. But of course millions of people do vote. This is the 'paradox of not voting' or, as it is sometimes called, the 'paradox that ate rational choice' (Fiorina, 1990: 334).

So why do people vote? Possible answers include the following. (1) People vote because they value democracy and recognize that democracy will collapse if nobody votes (Downs, 1957a: 267–8). But this is hardly an answer because, as Downs (1957a: 270) himself recognizes, voters will 'actually get this reward [of living in a democracy] even if [they] do not vote as long as a sufficient number of other citizens do'. (2) Voters are risk averse and are driven to the polls by the fear of not voting and then seeing their preferred candidate lose by one vote (Ferejohn and Fiorina, 1974). Yet if people are so risk averse why would they ever leave their house (Beck, 1975)? (3) People vote because they think that other people will calculate that it is not rational to vote and that their vote will therefore be decisive (see Mueller, 2003: 306–7). But would rational people really think it likely that nobody would vote when millions of people have consistently done so in previous elections? (4) People vote because the costs of voting are extremely low, and below some threshold people do not bother to calculate whether the costs of low-cost activities are greater than their benefits (Barry, 1978: 23). To put the same point in a slightly different way, people vote because they 'satisfice' and the costs of voting are so small that people do not bother to adjust their behaviour to maximize their returns (Bendor et al., 2003). (5) People vote because they want to demonstrate to others that they can be trusted to behave in a non-selfish manner (Overbye, 1995). (6) Voters are driven to the polls out of a sense of duty; out of a sense that they ought to vote (Riker and Ordeshook, 1968). But if people are prepared to eschew self-interested calculations here, why assume that in other areas of their economic and political life they act in a purely instrumental and self-interested manner? (7) People vote 'expressively' to demonstrate (to themselves and others) their support for a particular candidate (Brennan and Lomasky, 1993). We will return to the paradox of not voting later in this chapter and consider what the answer to the question of *why* people vote might tell us about *how* they vote.

The second question raised by the apparent insignificance of voting is whether (and if so, why) voters have any incentive to gather enough information or think carefully enough to make a reasoned democratic choice. Recognizing that voters, like consumers, need to gather information in order to make wise choices, Downs argued that the collective nature of democratic choice made it rational for voters to remain ignorant. As information economists later came to emphasize, information is costly and this means that instrumentally rational actors will need to balance the costs of acquiring new information against its expected benefits (Stigler, 1961). Gathering a great deal of costly information in order to make trivial decisions optimally would not be instrumentally rational, and it is entirely reasonable to make many choices you expect to be suboptimal in order to economize on decision-making costs.

Given that the chance of deciding an election is normally very small, the expected cost of picking the wrong candidate will also be small. Suppose instead of the rich partisan in the 2012 presidential election described above we have a ruthlessly calculating investor who knows that the candidate with the best economic policy would increase her wealth by $1,000,000 relative to the alternative and was otherwise indifferent between the parties. Unfortunately, she does not know which candidate has the best economic policy and without gathering better information would have no basis for voting either way. Suppose that she could hire a consultant for $100 to discover for certain the question of which party would increase her wealth. If we ignore the fact that her vote is unlikely to be decisive, this seems like an excellent investment in information: voting randomly would give her a 50 per cent chance of picking the right candidate while hiring the consultant would increase that probability to 100 per cent and for $100 she would gain $500,000 of expected wealth. We know from the study of Gelman et al. (2009), however, that voters in pivotal states during the 2008 presidential election had roughly a 1 in 10 million chance of deciding the outcome. This makes the expected value of the consultant's report $500,000/10,000,000, or five cents. This is significantly less than $100 and the voter would be better off not buying the consultant's report.

No actual voter faces such a well-defined decision, of course, but the logic of this example can easily be generalized. The desirability of alternative political parties is often far from obvious, and it would take a great deal of time and effort to make a well-informed electoral choice. This leads Downs (1957b: 147) to 'the startling conclusion that it is irrational for most citizens to acquire information for purposes of voting'. There is a great deal of survey research and other empirical evidence backing up the claim that voters are generally ignorant (Campbell et al., 1960; Converse, 1964; Delli Carpini and Keeter, 1996). In the 2010 US mid-term election, only 33 per cent of respondents knew that the economy had grown over the previous year, with 61 per cent incorrectly thinking it had contracted, despite the fact that a majority of voters saw the economy as the most important issue in this election. Meanwhile only 34 per cent of respondents knew that the TARP bailout bill was enacted under Bush rather than Obama, with 47 per cent incorrectly believing the opposite (Somin, 2013: 22).

During the 2000 presidential election, only 44 per cent of respondents to the American National Election Survey knew that Al Gore was more supportive of environmental regulation than George W. Bush (Somin, 2013: 31). Ferejohn's (1990: 3) statement that '[n]othing strikes the student of public opinion and democracy more forcefully than the paucity of information most people possess about politics' is representative of the view of many political scientists.

The issue of how voters make choices is important not only in an empirical and predictive sense, but also normatively to the evaluation of democracy. The competence and motivation of citizens has always been a central problem in democratic theory. Plato rejected democracy on the grounds that the masses lacked the knowledge and judgement required for wise political decisions. Governing should be left to those with the requisite skills, meaning that society should be ruled by philosopher kings. More recently, those generally favourable to democracy have seen democratic ignorance as an important challenge which needs to be overcome. James Madison, for example, wrote in an 1822 letter to William T. Barry that a 'popular government without popular information, or the means of acquiring it, is but a Prologue to a Farce or a Tragedy; or perhaps both'.

Some have seen the citizens of contemporary democracies as generally incompetent and argued on this basis that democracy should be seen not as a mechanism through which rational and well-informed voters make collective choices, but as a mechanism though which ignorant voters exercise imperfect control over political elites (Dahl, 1956; Riker, 1982a; Schumpeter, 1942). Others have insisted that political knowledge must be increased through civic education (Barber, 1993; Galston, 2001). Deliberative democrats in particular have been critical of current levels of political knowledge and engagement, arguing that democracy will only work well if citizens can become more knowledgeable, reasonable and engaged. On this view, deliberation performs an educative role by forcing citizens to confront conflicting views and state reasons for their own position. In doing so, errors and fallacies will be exposed and citizens will become more competent (Dryzek, 2010; Gutmann and Thompson, 2009).

Rational ignorance

Gathering and processing information takes time, and Downs (1957b: 145) argues that this means that 'no decision-maker can afford to know everything that might possibly bear on his decision before he makes it'. When deciding whether or not to gather information, voters, like any rational actors, should compare the marginal costs and marginal benefits of information. The marginal cost of a piece of information is the time and energy used in getting it, which could otherwise have been used doing something else. The marginal benefit of a piece of information is the additional utility the individual can expect due to making better decisions. Standard economic logic tells us that it would be irrational to learn new things when the marginal cost of such learning exceeds the marginal benefit. Downs (1957b: 145–7) argues that for voting decisions the marginal benefit of information is normally extremely low. Since an incorrect voting choice will almost certainly have no effect on the outcome, the information which could help voters avoid such mistakes is virtually worthless and rational actors will therefore normally refuse to gather any costly information whatsoever.

Downs (1957b: 146–7) recognizes that not all information is costly in an economic sense, however. Political junkies and policy nerds may gather a great deal of information simply because they enjoy learning for its own sake, and anyone not living under a rock is exposed to a great deal of 'free' information through discussion, news and advertising. Downs's argument is not that voters are completely ignorant, but that they are less informed than they ought to be from a social perspective.

The problem of rational ignorance is perhaps best understood as a collective action problem (see Chapter 6). Insofar as a well-informed electorate leads to desirable policy outcomes, political knowledge is a public good which will be underprovided by individually rational action. A well-informed vote has only a miniscule chance of mattering, but if it does matter it will affect everybody in society and this makes the expected social benefit of political knowledge much greater than the expected private benefit. It may be that everyone would be better off if everyone could credibly agree to gather a reasonable amount of political information and vote wisely, but individual incentives prompt voters to free-ride on the political knowledge of others (Downs, 1957b: 147–9; Hardin, 2009: ch. 3; Olson, 1990: ch. 4). As Downs (1957b: 147) explains,

> the benefits which a majority of citizens would derive from living in a society with a well-informed electorate are indivisible in nature. When most members of the electorate know what policies best serve their interests, the government is forced to follow those

policies in order to avoid defeat (assuming that there is a consensus among the informed). This explains why the proponents of democracy think citizens should be well informed. But the benefits of these policies accrue to each member of the majority they serve, regardless of whether he has helped bring them about. In other words, the individual receives these benefits whether or not he is well informed, so long as most people are well informed and his interests are similar to those of the majority. On the other hand, when no one else is well informed, he cannot produce these benefits by becoming well informed himself, since a collective effort is necessary to achieve them.

The conclusion Downs (1957b: 148) draws from this argument is that 'democratic political systems are bound to operate at less than maximum efficiency'. Depending on the level of free information people are exposed to, democracy may nevertheless work tolerably well, but the point Downs wishes to make is that informational incentives are always such that the level of political knowledge held by citizens is always less than optimal. This argument is a *comparative* one. No choices, individual or collective, are made with perfect knowledge, but some decisions are more informed than others. The claim is that collective decisions are subject to a collective action problem which makes them less well informed than otherwise similar individual decisions.

Some have interpreted Downs's rational ignorance argument as implying that democracy is seriously and fundamentally flawed and that we should replace collective with individual choice wherever possible (e.g. Pennington, 2010; Pincione and Tesón, 2006; Somin, 2013; Tullock, 1989). To borrow Riker's distinction (see Chapter 5), 'populist' notions of democracy are obviously rendered questionable if the votes cast do not represent the underlying preferences or interests of citizens. Not even minimalist 'liberal' conceptions of democracy escape the problem, for if citizens are to hold politicians to account for misdeeds they must have some idea what it is that politicians are doing. Rational ignorance loosens the constraints of democratic competition and thereby allows politicians and special interests to exploit the ignorant majority (see Chapter 7). Just as imperfect and asymmetric information in the marketplace can produce market failures, many free-market economists use rational ignorance to argue that democracy's failings are so serious that it should be abandoned wherever possible. Although these theorists generally accept that democracy is the only reasonable system for making collective choices and reject in no uncertain terms the argument of Plato, Lenin and Hitler that voter ignorance justifies dictatorship (e.g. Caplan, 2007: 3–4; Somin, 2013: 8–9), rational ignorance can and is used to argue for the retraction of the state and the expansion of markets. The fact of rational ignorance has also been used to drive arguments for the geographic decentralization of government (Foldvary, 2002; Somin, 2013: ch. 5), an increase in choice-based mechanisms in government services (Taylor, 2014) and the separation of certain government functions such as the judiciary and central banks from political influence (Somin, 2013: ch. 6).

Not all rational choice theorists share this view, of course, and there have been a number of responses to arguments about rational ignorance. Before discussing these, it is worth considering what the empirical evidence of voter ignorance shows us. As we pointed out above, political scientists since the 1950s have produced a great deal of survey research which shows that voters know very little. It is easy to be shocked by such findings, but it is not quite clear how relevant they are. Voter knowledge is far from perfect, but we also know that consumers have serious gaps in their knowledge. People shop for cars and laptops all the time despite knowing very little about how cars and laptops work. IT specialists, or at least the stereotypical versions of them, scoff at the ignorance of the average computer user but despite their ignorance people manage to make reasonable choices. The theoretical argument for rational ignorance suggests that collective choices will be made on the basis of less information than individual ones, but the evidence of political ignorance does not establish this. What we would need here is comparative evidence of information acquisition in collective and individual choices which are otherwise similar. As far as we know, no such evidence exists. To treat the survey results cited above as decisive evidence for rational ignorance theory would be to commit what Harold Demsetz (1969) calls 'the nirvana fallacy' – taking the imperfection of one option as a decisive argument for its alternative and therefore implicitly assuming that the latter is perfect.

One critique of Downs's argument for rational ignorance is that it oversimplifies the preferences of voters when it comes to electoral outcomes. It may be that voters are not primarily interested in deciding the winner of an election, but in influencing the margin of victory in order to strengthen or weaken the winning party's mandate, improving a party's future electoral prospects by signalling support, or influencing candidates' perception of public opinion (Fowler and Smirnov, 2007; Mackie, 2010; Stigler, 1972). This means that a non-decisive vote is not entirely wasted, since in some small way it contributes to the vote share of the party. This could explain why people vote when voting is costly, and it may also provide some incentive to become informed in order to ensure that the contribution is on the correct side of the ledger. The existence of such non-contingent benefits will indeed increase the value of political information, but it should be noted that there will remain a large gap between the private and social benefits of political knowledge, with the non-contingent contributory benefit of a vote being every bit as external as the contingent threshold benefit. Contributory voting will mitigate the effect of rational ignorance to some extent but does not remove it altogether (Brennan and Lomasky, 1993: 70–72).

Another common complaint against rational ignorance theory, and indeed information economics in general, is its supposed conceptual incoherence. To know the value of a piece of information, we need to acquire that information and at this stage it is clearly too late to begin evaluating the information's value (Evans and Friedman, 2011). It is obviously true that we never know with certainty the precise value of information, but this does not rule out reasoned choice altogether. In everyday life we rely on vague estimates of utility in order to make decisions and this is what voters must do in deciding whether to become informed about politics. If voters know that their vote is very unlikely to make a difference and information is costly, an extremely vague estimate of the value of information may well be enough for a reasonable judgement that becoming informed is not worth the hassle.

Low-information rationality

The objections to rational ignorance mentioned above are, we think, quite weak. There is, however, a line of research in political science drawing on rational choice theory and empirical political psychology which argues that voters are able to select wisely even in the absence of very basic political information. On this account, the costs of political information and the requirements for democratic competence have been seriously overestimated. If voters come across a great deal of 'free information' or can rely on informational shortcuts, they may vote *as if* they were well informed despite making little or no effort to acquire political knowledge.

Before discussing the methods voters might be able to use in to make wise choices, it is worth pausing to explicitly consider what we mean by a 'wise' choice here. In light of the discussion above, we may be tempted to evaluate the quality of choices solely on the basis of the information at hand: A decision is wise if it is well informed and rational. For those in the low-information rationality line of research, this is a mistake. Rather than focusing on the inputs to the decision-making process – information and cognitive effort – we should focus on the output – the choices actually made. Thus, individuals who vote for the candidate they would have chosen if they had the time and inclination to make a perfectly reasoned choice are voting 'correctly' even if they do not have much information and make no effort to weigh the alternatives (Lau and Redlawsk, 1997). Just as people are quite capable of buying a decent laptop while knowing virtually nothing about how CPUs or RAM work, voters might be capable of voting wisely despite knowing virtually nothing about the constitutional structure of the polity or the platforms of the parties.

In a two-party system we would expect those choosing randomly to vote correctly 50 per cent of the time. The basic idea of low-information rationality is that voters come across various pieces of imperfectly reliable information in order to shift the proportion of correct votes closer to 100 per cent without needing to incur significant costs. If this is the case, voters may fulfil the behavioural requirements of well-functioning democracy despite low levels of political knowledge as measured by surveys which ask the questions academics deem important: voters need shortcuts rather than encyclopaedias (Lupia, 1994). Putting the same point a different way, Lupia and McCubbins insist that democracy does not require that voters have some minimum quantity of *information*; rather voters need *knowledge*, defined as 'the ability to predict the consequences of actions' (Lupia and McCubbins, 1998: 6). Information often contributes to knowledge, but information which seems relevant may sometimes be redundant and perhaps counterproductive insofar as it complicates the issue and undermines reliable prediction. In general, a piece of information is only valuable when it prevents a costly mistake (Lupia and McCubbins, 1998: ch. 2).

There are a number of shortcuts on which uninformed voters could potentially rely to make reasoned choices. As Downs (1957b: 146) recognized, voters come across a great deal of 'free' information in their everyday lives. When watching television, reading and talking to friends and family, political issues often arise and this can give otherwise ignorant voters a certain degree of political knowledge even if they were perfectly unwilling to expend any effort on becoming informed. Political knowledge will also arise as a by-product of private activity. Voters may have little incentive to think carefully about monetary policy, but in their capacity as homeowners or investors they will have a reasonable idea of whether they want interest rates to increase or decrease (Popkin, 1991).

Moreover, ignorant but rational voters can use simple cues to gain useful but imperfect information about the desirability of political candidates. Popkin provides the example of a gaffe made by President Gerald Ford while campaigning for Mexican-American votes in San Antonio, Texas. As is common in political campaigns targeting particular ethnic groups, Ford publicly indulged in a local delicacy – in this case a tamale, which he bit into without removing the corn husk which served as a wrapper and was not meant to be consumed. Unsurprisingly, much was made of this faux pas in the media, and Mexican-American voters seem to have turned away from Ford as a result. At face value, this may seem like an irrational reaction to an honest mistake, but Popkin argues that Ford's failure to shuck his tamale provided a useful cue for Mexican-American voters insofar as it showed Ford to be unfamiliar with Mexican culture. If he did not know to shuck his tamale, chances are he would be out of touch with the needs and values of Mexican-American voters more generally. Mitt Romney's widely publicized remarks at a private fundraising event in May 2012 that 'there are 47 per cent who are with him [Obama], who are dependent upon government ... who pay no income tax' and 'that [my] job is not to worry about these people' sent a more direct signal. Similarly, voters often punish politicians for extramarital affairs or other sex scandals, even though it seems that such private behaviour has little impact on one's ability to govern. If such private misconduct reveals a general untrustworthiness which makes it more likely for the individual to engage in professional misconduct, punishing private misconduct may be a reasonable (though imperfect) heuristic which increases the average trustworthiness of representatives. More common cues might come from party identification (Downs, 1957b), opinion leaders (Berelson et al., 1954) or interest groups (Lupia, 1994). In all these cases it seems at first glance that voters are being superficial and irrational, but it may be that they are simply making the best use of the limited information they have available.

Lupia and McCubbins (1998) emphasize the importance of learning from other people. If a well-informed friend or celebrity with similar values and interests is voting one way rather than another, a rational but uninformed voter might conclude that they should do likewise. As long as we have confidence in the knowledge and trustworthiness of others, we can use their judgement as a simple and reliable summary of all the information they have been exposed to. The question here becomes whom we consider knowledgeable and trustworthy. Most people will be faced with a number of friends and celebrities offering conflicting political advice while claiming to share a basic set of interests and values. To make a reasoned choice in such circumstances, the voter needs to assess the relative knowledge and trustworthiness of different people. This may be no trivial task, but it will often be much simpler than making a direct evaluation of the political alternatives.

For voting choices, we are often forced to evaluate the knowledge and trustworthiness of politicians themselves. In competitive elections, however, there are obvious incentives for deceit, and politicians are often so distant from us that competence and character are difficult to assess. In this situation, knowledgeable and trustworthy candidates have strong incentives to credibly signal these traits as long as competition is sufficiently strong. Such signalling might happen by developing a reputation for intelligence or moral behaviour or by using political parties as 'brand names' which lend credibility to individuals (Lupia, 1992; Milgrom and Roberts, 1986). This brings us back to Downs's argument regarding reliability and responsibility. As we saw in Chapter 3, Downs argued that parties will seek to assure voters that they will keep their promises by building a reputation. According to advocates of low-information rationality, the same is true of individual candidates.

If voters can use these informational shortcuts to improve their tendency to make correct electoral choices, the informational requirements of democratic competence are much lower than supposed by rational ignorance theory and not undermined by empirical findings that voters often have low levels of encyclopaedic political knowledge. Attention to various cues and some consideration of candidate reliability may be required, but such hurdles might plausibly be overcome with only a mild preference for making correct electoral decisions. This means that democracy might be performing very well indeed despite shockingly low levels of political knowledge.

Moreover, even if a large proportion of the population is uninformed and unable to vote correctly via informational shortcuts, democracy may perform well at the aggregate level. Suppose that in a large election 95 per cent of voters are completely ignorant and make no effort to think about how to vote. Instead, they simply turn up to the polls and vote randomly. The other 5 per cent take their democratic duty very seriously and make correct decisions most of the time. We might think that the 5 per cent of voters who are informed will be overwhelmed by the hoi polloi and electoral outcomes will reflect the whims of the ignorant. Surprisingly, this is not necessarily the case. If the ignorant voters really are completely ignorant there will be no pattern to their errors and in large elections they will cancel each other out. This will leave the election to be decided by the small proportion of informed voters (Page and Shapiro, 1993; Wittman, 1995). Looking at aggregate public opinion data in the United States, Page and Shapiro (1992) show that public opinion is reasonably coherent and stable at the population level despite fluctuations and widespread ignorance at the individual level. Moreover, public opinion seems to change in a broadly predictable and sensible way in response to new information. Changes in public opinion over tax and employment policies, for example, are correlated with changes in the underlying economic conditions in a broadly coherent way. Page and Shapiro's research in no way shows that voting outcomes *do* resemble those that a fully informed populace would make, but they do show despite individual-level ignorance there are reasonable interpretations of aggregate data which reveal a broadly coherent and reasonable response to changing conditions.

Rational irrationality

Donald Wittman (1989, 1995) argues that accounts of government failure grounded in rational ignorance covertly assume that voters are not simply ignorant, but *irrational*. Rational choice theory may predict that voters will have low levels of political knowledge, but as long as voters are interested in voting wisely they will employ useful but imperfect heuristics, and in any case ignorance at the individual level will tend to have no effect at the aggregate level. Unless we assume that voters are irrational, rather than simply uninformed, democratic outcomes can safely be assumed to reflect the well-informed will of the people despite the logic of rational ignorance and the empirical findings that voters are unaware of many basic political facts. This is a serious challenge to rational choice accounts of political ignorance, since it suggests that those arguing for government failure on the grounds of rational ignorance are violating the rules of rational choice theory by assuming irrationality. Wittman's point here is that economists are unwilling to conclude that markets fail simply because information is costly but they *are* willing to do so in political markets. This violates the principle of behavioural symmetry at the heart of rational choice theory.

One proponent of the government failure view who has taken Wittman's challenge very seriously is Bryan Caplan (2007), who argues that voters are indeed irrational rather than simply ignorant. Caplan offers a rational choice account of political irrationality, with the central analysis relying on basic price theory. Caplan assumes, with economists and other rational choice theorists, that individuals value their own material wealth and happiness. The pursuit of instrumental goals is mediated by individuals' beliefs about the world, with inaccurate beliefs generally leading to suboptimal decisions. An individual with a preference for wealth and a false belief that burning $100 bills as a sacrifice to the gods increases long-term prosperity will not pursue his goals as effectively as a similar individual without such a belief. As long as individuals recognize that their beliefs could be mistaken and have some means of updating them to be more in line with reality, everyday life has a built-in incentive which pushes us towards holding true beliefs.

At the same time, however, people also have intrinsic preferences over their own beliefs (Caplan, 2007: 14–16, 115–19). We have 'cherished views, valued for their own sake' (Caplan, 2007: 14), and holding such beliefs 'increases subjective well-being' (Caplan, 2007: 100). For many decisions, such preferences will be so strongly outweighed by the instrumental incentive for rationality that we can safely ignore them. You might like to believe you can fly, but your preference for not falling to your death is likely to keep any irrationality in check on this issue (Caplan, 2007: 119–22). On the other hand, some beliefs are only weakly connected to, or even entirely divorced from, real-world consequences. Our position on whether there is a teacup orbiting the sun will generally have no impact on our behaviour. In instrumental terms, inaccuracy of this belief is costless, and any preference we have over the substantive nature of the belief will dominate. Few of us have strong preferences over our beliefs in orbiting teacups, but there are other materially inconsequential issues we do feel more strongly about – the artistic merit of various genres of music, the prowess of a local sports team and, Caplan argues, questions of public policy in a democracy. On these questions, Caplan argues that beliefs will be 'rationally irrational'.

Although 'rational irrationality' sounds like a simple contradiction, it is quite easy to understand once we distinguish two ways in which 'rationality' is being used. Caplan maintains that voters are *instrumentally* rational but *epistemically* irrational. Instrumental rationality requires that individuals take those actions which best satisfy their preferences, and this will sometimes involve accepting beliefs which are unsupported by evidence and would easily be rejected if subjected to critical scrutiny. Caplan takes instrumental rationality as given but treats the level of epistemic rationality as endogenously determined by the costs of inaccuracy and the strength of intrinsic preferences over beliefs (Caplan, 2007: 122–5).

When 'deciding' whether or not to accept a belief, individuals need to consider both the instrumental and intrinsic effects of this acceptance. Instrumental effects depend on the importance of having an accurate belief when making decisions; intrinsic effects depend on emotional attachment to the issue. For voting choices, any instrumental benefit coming from having the best candidate win will need to be discounted by the probability of pivotality, which as we know is extremely small. Votes are cast based on the psychological appeal of underlying political beliefs rather than the practical desirability of policies, and the end result is political failure. Voters do not choose those policies which would best satisfy their preferences, and candidates are forced to compete on psychological appeal rather than practical superiority. For Caplan, this produces government failure. Irrational voters demand harmful policies and competing candidates are forced to pander to these misguided preferences. In the words of H. L. Mencken: 'Democracy is the theory that the common people know what they want, and deserve to get it good and hard' (quoted in Caplan, 2007: 18).

As empirical evidence for his theory, Caplan shows that American survey respondents have systematically biased beliefs about economics and policy preferences on economic matters compared to experts on economics – PhD-holding economists. On a variety of questions, Caplan shows that the errors of the uninformed public are not randomly distributed. By controlling for a variety of demographic variables, income, education and political ideology, Caplan is able to see how a PhD in economics affects political preferences, and interprets this gap as resulting from economic ignorance. For example, when asked whether excessive spending on foreign aid or welfare are major reasons for poor economic performance, non-economists will generally respond that they are and economists will generally respond that they are not (Caplan, 2007: 58–61). This seems to be because the general public radically overestimates the size of aid and welfare budgets. In a 2010 poll, the average respondent thought foreign aid constituted 25 per cent of the United States federal budget and favoured cutting aid spending to 10 per cent of the budget. In fact, aid spending is less than 1 per cent of the budget (World Public Opinion, 2010). If voters think foreign aid spending should be radically reduced to more than ten times its current level, democratic outcomes seem problematic, to say the least. Moreover, a great deal of experimental research has shown that people make political judgements in a biased way, motivated by ideology and partisan attachment rather than simply truth (Taber and Lodge, 2006; Taber et al., 2001). Although Caplan's rational irrationality model has not been directly tested experimentally, a small number of studies have recently found that incentives are able to overcome partisan differences on factual survey questions (Bullock et al., 2013; Prior and Lupia, 2008; Prior et al., 2013).

When we consider these findings in light of the low-information rationality and heuristics literature discussed above, however, it is far from obvious that such irrationality necessarily flows through to incorrect voting. Factual evaluations may well be biased by partisanship, but partisan loyalties may be formed 'correctly' in the sense that they are consistent with underlying values and interests. Much disagreement remains on the epistemic rationality of voter choice, and a great deal more theoretical and empirical work will be required before such disagreements are resolved.

Expressive voting

A related view of political behaviour is the 'expressive voting' hypothesis – the idea that voters cast their ballots in order to express their values and preferences. Unlike rational ignorance and rational irrationality, the claim here is not that the insignificance of a single voter leads to false beliefs, but that people vote in order to express their values and preferences. This idea was originally formulated as a possible solution to the paradox of not voting discussed above. If it is irrational to vote in order to influence election outcomes and yet otherwise rational people vote in large numbers, it must be that that they are voting for some other reason. Riker and Ordeshook (1968) point out that the paradox arises because the benefits of voting (i.e. better policy outcomes) are contingent on a vote being pivotal whereas the costs of voting (i.e. time and effort) are not. For voting to make any sense in large elections, it must be that there is some non-contingent benefit from voting. For Riker and Ordeshook, these non-contingent benefits include, among other things, the chance to affirm partisan preference. On this view, a voter casts a ballot not to get the better candidate into office, but simply to 'stand up and be counted for the candidate he supports' (Riker and Ordeshook, 1968: 28).

Expressive voting as a solution to the paradox of not voting has proved popular among rational choice theorists (e.g. Grofman, 1993; Goldfarb and Sigelman, 2010; Knack, 1992), though it has also been criticized for removing any empirical content from rational choice accounts of voting (Barry, 1978; Green and Shapiro, 1994). The most interesting recent extension of the idea of expressive voting has sought to put empirical content back into rational choice by asking how expressive preferences affect the decision of *how* to vote. Morris Fiorina (1976) extends the work of Riker and Ordeshook by arguing that voters derive utility not just from the act of voting, but from voting one way rather than another. If expressive value varies across choices like this, expressive preferences will have an effect on how voters decide and consequently on how candidates compete for votes. This line of argument has been pursed most fully by Geoff Brennan along with co-authors including James Buchanan (Brennan and Buchanan, 1984), Loren Lomasky (Brennan and Lomasky, 1993) and Alan Hamlin (Brennan and Hamlin, 1998, 2000).

According to Brennan, individuals have both instrumental and expressive preferences. Instrumental preferences are over outcomes and their satisfaction depends on the state of the world independent of the agent's own choice. This is what economists normally mean by preferences: instrumentally rational agents judge alternatives on the basis of their real-world effects. Instrumental preferences may be self-regarding, other-regarding or social in some more vague sense. An egoist's preference for wealth maximization is instrumental, as is the humanitarian's preference for the welfare of the least well-off and the bigot's preference for racial segregation. The objects of such preferences are choice-independent states of the world – they are satisfied by outcomes rather than the processes by which they are brought about. In Amartya Sen's (1997) terminology, they are over 'culmination outcomes' rather than 'comprehensive outcomes' – it is the end state which matters, not how we get there.

Yet people often seem to care about the processes through which culmination outcomes emerge, and rational choice theory ought to consider such preferences (Frey et al., 2004). The idea of expressive voting is premised on the notion that people have preferences over their own actions. Choice can be seen not simply as an instrumental way of getting things done, but as a means of showing ourselves and others what sort of person we are. When we buy fair trade coffee, our goal is not only to dose ourselves up on caffeine and give money to poor coffee farmers; it is also to say something – to ourselves or to others – about the sort of person we are and the sort of society we think appropriate. We satisfy our expressive preferences for fair trade coffee simply by making a choice. Our expressive preference would remain satisfied if it had no net effect on the welfare of coffee farmers (though if we knew this it might alter expressive payoffs) or if we spilled the coffee before taking a sip. Conversely, our expressive preference would *not* be fulfilled by a regular coffee and a sudden windfall to poor coffee farmers. Expressive preferences are over behaviour *per se*, not the expected outcomes of such behaviour.

All choices potentially have instrumental and expressive aspects. Suppose you are shopping for a new car. If you have an expressive preference for choosing luxury products, you might be inclined to buy a Rolls Royce. The price tag of such a car has a large instrumental cost, however, and many who could afford a new Rolls Royce will instead opt for a used Toyota. For most people, the expressive value of buying a Rolls Royce is not worth the tens of thousands of dollars in lost instrumental value. For many economic decisions, expressive preferences are overwhelmed by instrumental ones. This will not always be the case, however. Many people do buy expensive cars, and for lower-cost purchases such as clothing and food it may be more common to favour the expressive over the instrumental.

In the context of voter choice, the relative strength of expressive and instrumental preferences is, according to expressive voting theory, determined mostly by the chance of pivotality. An individual voter decides electoral outcomes only with some probability, and instrumental preferences over political outcomes need to be discounted by this probability for the purposes of voting choices. Since expressive preferences need not be discounted in this way, expressive preference will be given greater weight in collective rather than individual decisions. In any real-world election the chance of pivotality will be tiny and instrumental preferences will be more-or-less completely irrelevant. This allows expressive preferences to dominate.

The expressive voting hypothesis is simple, and its potential implications for rational choice political theory – and political analysis more generally – are enormous. If voters' choices are based on opaque social and psychological factors rather than their genuine preferences over the material conditions of life, predictive modelling of democratic processes and normative reasoning from voter choice become extremely complicated. Voters cannot be assumed to vote for whichever option they truly prefer all things considered. Expressive and instrumental preference may often be in alignment, but expressive preferences are virtually guaranteed of winning any conflict which does arise in the voting booth.

Assessment

The knowledge and rationality of voters is another area of rational choice theory which has generated a great deal of controversy. This controversy has come in two primary forms – rational choice theorists themselves arguing over the normative implications of voter behaviour for evaluations of democracy and the market, and rational choice theorists arguing with other political scientists over the degree to which rational choice theory can accommodate the complications wrought by the various collective action problems involved in collective decision-making. For now we focus on the normative issue, since we return to the methodological one in the next chapter.

Rational ignorance and rational irrationality are quite obviously potential problems for democracy, though it is unclear just how serious these problems are. Every variant of democratic theory holds that voters ought to know something about what government should do and what the current government is doing. If we think public policy should reflect the informed will of the people, the informational requirements will be high; if we think voters need only be willing to punish misconduct, the requirements will be lower but possibly still beyond the capacity of rationally ignorant voters. Although it may be that citizens feel a democratic duty to become informed and that voters are able to use various informational shortcuts in order to vote correctly, it is implausible that such factors will completely overcome the logic of rational ignorance. As Downs insists, this means that large-scale democracy will never be perfectly efficient in giving people what they want. This is in an obvious sense an argument for limiting democracy and expanding the market, but it must be emphasized once again that the existence of a government failure does not show the market to be superior. If the policy issue at hand entered the political agenda as an attempt to solve some market failure, an evaluation of this market failure in comparison to the political failures caused by rational ignorance will be required before any plausible policy implications can be derived. Rational ignorance, to the extent that it is a real empirical problem, is always a point against democracy and for the market, but not necessarily a decisive one.

The normative implications of expressive voting are more ambiguous. On the one hand, the fact that people can vote for options they do not really want means that we could end up with very bad policy outcomes (Hillman, 2010). In extreme cases, we could see unanimous support for alternatives everybody would reject given the decisive choice (Brennan and Lomasky, 1984). Expressive voting will be particularly troubling when people have bigoted preferences. Gary Becker (1957) has argued that 'taste-based' preferences for discrimination are less likely to be expressed in action when the individual costs of such expression are high. Consider a racist business owner evaluating job applicants. He would presumably prefer not to hire those of a different race, but if the best candidate for the job is of a different race and he wants his business to do well, there is a trade-off between his racial preferences and his financial preferences. Especially when we consider competitive pressure, there may well be little actual discrimination in the labour market despite strongly discriminatory preferences among employers. Jennifer Roback (1986) argues that the case of segregated streetcars in the American south in the Jim Crow era is an example of this logic at work. Despite complaints from some vocal white customers, privately operated streetcar companies refused to impose segregation due to the cost, both in terms of alienating black customers and reducing capacity. Segregation was imposed when the issue was put to a vote, however. Roback argues that this was because voters failed to consider the cost of their action in terms of higher streetcar fares and instead focused on their expressive preference for supporting segregation.

On the other hand, expressive voting also allows for a more impartial decision. Like John Rawls's (1971) veil of ignorance, the voting booth produces a 'veil of insignificance' (Kliemt, 1986) which encourages voters to ignore their own material welfare and make choices based on moral values. People generally like to see themselves as good, decent and reasonable people; they have a moral vision of how people ought to behave and try to follow this vision in their daily lives. Moral values and material interests often come into conflict, however, and material interests often win out. Even those who place a high value on honesty may stretch the truth at a job interview, and those who consider it a moral imperative to give as much as possible to the poor may spend money on a personal luxury when they know it could be used to save a starving child. People no doubt act on a moral basis, but not perfectly. In the voting booth, however, individual material interests can for the most part be ignored, freeing voters to follow their conscience. Thus, people will be more generous, impartial and reasonable than they would be if making individual decisions (Brennan and Lomasky,

1985; Goodin and Roberts, 1975; Kliemt, 1986; Tullock, 1971). One important implication of this can be seen in climate change policy. Due to a serious collective action problem (see Chapter 6), global solutions to the problem of climate change would be unlikely to emerge if each national government faithfully represented the best interests of its citizens. Climate change might be a serious problem which can be solved by reducing greenhouse gas emissions, but countries refusing to comply with abatement efforts cannot be excluded from the global public good of reduced climate change. In industrialized democracies, however, there seems to be a widespread expressive preference for action on climate change. If national governments respond to expressive rather than instrumental preferences, it may well be that the collective action problem can be solved by national governments' 'irrational' willingness to cooperate (Brennan, 2009).

This veil of insignificance only works by making voters focus on their good intentions, however, and we all know that the road to hell is paved with those. If expressive voting coexists with rational ignorance and rational irrationality, the chances of misguided altruism seem high, and this may be much more troubling than merely selfish voting. Rational and selfish voting may produce levels of welfare protection we deem less than desirable, but irrational public-spirited voters could support all manner of dangerous policies if they are framed in the right way by a sufficiently charismatic leader. On balance, it seems to us that rational ignorance, rational irrationality and expressive voting should be somewhat troubling to democratic theorists. It may however be that there are ways of mitigating the effects of rational ignorance. Civic education is an obvious possibility, though it is unclear whether this could be effective without being excessively intrusive for liberal tastes. Increasing choice through political decentralization or the reform of public services may be another option (Foldvary, 2002; Taylor, 2014).

Though we think the theoretical case for the insignificance of a single vote being a problem is a strong one, the empirical case for it being a *significant* problem is far weaker. Those positing a civic duty to become informed and informational heuristics make powerful points, but the central comparative conclusion that collective choice is *less* informed, *less* rational and *more* expressive than individual choice remains. There is a great deal of empirical research which sheds light on various specific questions, but compelling evidence of just how general and important the collective action problems discussed in this chapter are have yet to arrive.

Chapter 9

Rational Choice Explanation

Overview: Rational choice theory seeks to explain political actions, events and outcomes. But what does explanation require? This chapter identifies two general accounts of explanation drawn from the philosophy of social science. The first, positivism, equates explanation with the identification of general laws and equates explanation with prediction. The second, scientific realism, equates explanation with the identification of causal mechanisms and is more sceptical about the possibility of successful prediction. In the opening chapter we noted that the development of rational choice theory in the 1970s and 1980s was threatened by Green and Shapiro's (1994) argument that rational choice had a poor empirical record. If rational choice theory is tied to a positivist account of explanation then Green and Shapiro's argument is potentially devastating. If, on the other hand, we associate rational choice with the search for causal mechanisms, this same criticism is less damning. A mechanism-based approach to explanation suggests that rational choice theory can be combined with other perspectives in order to provide a rich understanding of political processes.

Introduction

Rational choice theorists do not simply try to describe political actions and events. They seek to explain them. That is they try to show not only what happened in some particular case but *why* it happened and, in doing so, to make something which had previously appeared puzzling seem entirely explicable. Rational choice theory can be used to explain why parties frequently converge upon the centre ground (Chapter 3); why minority governments can survive for long periods (Chapter 4); why groups which share a common interest do not always mobilize to advance that interest (Chapter 6); and why the rent-seeking industry is relatively small (Chapter 7). Does rational choice theory offer good explanations? This is an important but difficult question. It is important because, ultimately, criticisms of rational choice theory amount to a claim that it does *not* offer good explanations. It is a difficult question because there is no agreement within the social sciences upon what a good explanation requires.

In this concluding chapter we tie a general discussion of rational choice theory to debates about explanation. We outline two basic accounts of what good explanation requires. The first and positivist answer is that explanation involves showing how it is that something which happened could have been expected to happen in virtue of the existence of some law or set of laws. The second answer, now most closely associated with scientific realism, is that explanation involves showing how something happened as a result of the operation of some causal mechanism or mechanisms.

Rational choice theory has usually been understood, by its proponents and critics alike, in positivist terms as attempting to formulate a 'science of politics' grounded upon the discovery of empirical laws. During the period in which rational choice theory first emerged, in the late 1950s and 1960s, positivism was the methodological orthodoxy within the social sciences and this association between rational choice theory and positivism hugely benefited rational choice. Yet the association with positivism ultimately risks casting rational choice in an unfavourable light because it conceptually ties explanation to prediction. Green and Shapiro (1994) ruthlessly exploited this weakness by showing how rational choice theorists had sidestepped arguments about the realism of their assumptions by suggesting that theories ought to be judged in terms of their predictive success (Box 1.2) when, in fact, their predictive record was very poor. There is however no reason why rational choice theory must be associated with positivism. In the second part of this chapter we argue that rational choice theory might be better understood (and defended) as involving the search for causal mechanisms.

Positivism and explanation through laws

The single most influential account of what constitutes a good explanation in both the natural and social sciences is provided by the German-born philosopher Carl Hempel (1905–1997) (1942, 1962, 1965). Hempel suggests that a good explanation of some outcome or event is a causal explanation, that causal explanations depend upon and are derived from laws and that laws are empirical regularities taking the form 'whenever X, then Y'. Consider the following examples. Newton's law of universal gravitation states that two bodies attract each other with equal and opposite forces; that the magnitude of this force is proportional to the product of their two masses and is also proportional to the inverse square of the distance between the centres of the two bodies. Brewster's law states that the extent of the polarization of light reflected from a transparent surface is a maximum when the reflected ray is at right angles to the refracted ray. Boyle's law states that the product of the pressure and volume of an ideal gas at constant temperature is a constant.

Hempel argues that a scientific explanation of some outcome or event can be derived from (1) a set of 'initial' or 'boundary' conditions, and (2) a set of laws.

> As an illustration, let the event to be explained consist in the cracking of an automobile radiator during a cold night. The sentences of group (1) may state the following initial and boundary conditions: the car was left in the street all night. Its radiator, which consists of iron, was completely filled with water, and the lid was screwed on tightly. The temperature during the night dropped from 39° F. in the evening to 25° F. in the morning; the air pressure was normal. The bursting pressure of the radiator material is so and so much. Group (2) would contain empirical laws such as the following: Below 32° F., under normal atmospheric pressure, water freezes. Below 39.2° F., the pressure of a mass of water increases with decreasing temperature, if the volume remains constant or decreases; when the water freezes, the pressure again increases....*from statements of these two kinds, the conclusion that the radiator cracked during the night can be deduced by logical reasoning; an explanation of the considered event has been established.* (Hempel, 1942 [1996: 44], emphasis added)

The first point to make about this explanation is that it is entirely deterministic. Given the temperature at night, the radiator had to crack. Explanations derived from laws explain not simply by showing why something happened but why it *had* to happen. However, on this issue Hempel eventually changed his position. Whilst continuing to argue that explanations must always rest upon the identification of one or more causal laws, Hempel accepted that it is possible to derive explanations from probabilistic laws taking the form 'whenever X, then *usually* Y'. Suppose we want to know why someone died of lung cancer and we know that they smoked 40 cigarettes a day. We can explain their death in terms of a law linking smoking and cancer and we can do so even though some people who smoke do not get cancer and some people get cancers who do not smoke. Although the relationship between smoking and cancer is not deterministic, it does hold with a 'high [degree of] statistical probability' (Hempel, 1962 [1996: 22]) and this is enough for the purposes of explanation.

One second and crucial feature of deductive-nomological explanations is that they establish a clear logical relationship between prediction and explanation. Positivists commit themselves to what is known as the 'symmetry thesis'; the claim that the information needed to provide explanations can also be used to make predictions (Ruben, 1990: 123–5). Why did the water in the radiator freeze? Because it was left overnight in the cold and 'whenever X (water is cooled to below 32 F.) then Y (it freezes)'. When *will* the water freeze? The answer is that it will do so when the evening temperature drops below 32 degrees. The symmetry thesis is an important one because if explanation and prediction are simply different sides of the same coin, explanations can be assessed in terms of the accuracy of their predictions.

The examples of laws cited so far are drawn from the natural sciences. The obvious question to address here is whether social science explanations (including rational choice explanations) can and should take the same basic form. Hempel argues not only that they *should* take the same basic form but that they *do*, in practice, take the same form. This is a surprising answer. After all, social scientists do not generally cite the existence of laws in their explanations. With the exception of Duverger's law which we encountered in Chapter 3 (pp. 57–60), we have not invoked the use of laws in this text. So on what basis can rational choice theory be understood as explaining via laws?

Hempel argues that whilst social scientists do not appear to invoke or rely upon laws, such appearances are deceptive. Whether they appreciate it or not, social scientists, and even historians, invariably ground their explanations upon the existence of purported laws and, in particular, upon a claim that people are rational and that their actions are for this reason predictable. As one example Hempel cites the claim that dust bowl farmers migrated to California in the 1930s because continual drought and sandstorms in the Midwest had made their existence increasingly precarious, and because California promised better living conditions. No mention of any empirical laws can be found here. But this explanation rests upon and is, Hempel argues, derived from an implicit but presumably probabilistic law that 'populations tend to migrate to regions which offer better living conditions' (Hempel, 1942 [1996: 47]). What, then, of rational choice theory? Whether it is described in terms of a law or not, rational choice theory rests upon the assumption that people are instrumentally rational and that their actions can be explained and predicted on this basis. The argument that political parties will converge upon the centre ground, that individuals will not usually contribute to the provision of a collective good, that voters will be uninformed, and so on, are all built upon this foundation.

The important point to make about Hempel's argument is that it reduces the explanatory gap between rational choice theory and the rest of political and social science. Rational choice theory assumes instrumental rationality but in Hempel's view so does the rest of social science. Rational choice theory only differs to the extent that it explicitly catalogues its assumptions so exposing them to critical scrutiny and then uses these assumptions to construct models which can be used to identify equilibrium outcomes making it possible, in turn, to generate quite precise predictions about behaviour and outcomes. On this reading, the key difference between rational choice theory and other parts of political science is its formalism. It is worth briefly stating one objection to this argument. In Chapter 1 we argued that rational choice theory does not simply assume that people are rational in the sense that their actions are related to their beliefs and desires but that they are *optimally* related and that their desires are reflective of their self-interest (but see Box 1.3). Rational choice is, in this respect, different. The basic point Hempel is making however, still stands. Rational choice is committed to the same basic explanatory exercise as other parts of political science. It just goes about it in a different and more transparent manner.

All other things being equal: tendency laws and the inexact (social) sciences

Let us accept for the moment the positivist's argument that explanation rests upon the identification of causal laws and that prediction and explanation are different sides of the same coin. Let us also accept that rational choice can be understood in positivist terms. The question now is about how successful rational choice explanations have been. One answer to this question has already been encountered in Chapter 1. In *Pathologies of Rational Choice Theory*, Green and Shapiro (1994: 6) argued that 'a large proportion of the theoretical conjectures of rational choice theorists have not been tested empirically' and that 'those tests that have been undertaken have either failed on their own terms or garnered theoretical support for propositions that ... can only be characterised as banal'.

One rejoinder to be offered on rational choice's behalf here is Shepsle's first law of wing-walking (p. 19). Don't let go until you have something else to hold on to. Rational choice may have a poor empirical record but so do other branches of political science. A second response might be to say that rational choice theorists have raised their game in response to Green and Shapiro's argument. Sanchez-Cuenca (2008: 363) argues that the 'last ten years or so' have 'witnessed an impressive integration of formal modelling and empirical testing' within rational choice theory.

Yet it would be difficult to argue that rational choice theory can now claim for itself a predictive record which matches or surpasses the natural sciences. Why not? The easy answer available to a critic would be to argue that rational choice fails because it rests upon a foundation of unrealistic assumptions and that bad assumptions lead inexorably to poor predictions. An alternative argument which we will explore here is that rational choice's poor predictive record tells us more about the challenges involved in the social sciences *per se* than it does about rational choice theory in particular. The deductive-nomological account maintains that natural and social science explanations can and should take the same basic form. This may be a laudable statement of principle but it also serves to obscure some important epistemic differences.

Suppose we want to explain why a match lit when it was struck. It is not difficult to imagine formulating a law that 'whenever A (a match is struck), then B (the match will light)'. This is not the stuff of which Nobel Prizes are made but it will do for illustrative purposes. But whilst striking a match may be necessary for it to light, it is not sufficient. The match will not light *if* C (it is wet), D (there is a strong wind), E (it is struck against the wrong material), F (there is no oxygen) and so on. The important lesson to be drawn here is that *all* laws are conditional and only hold when all other things are equal or *ceteris paribus*. This is as true of natural science laws as it is of social sciences ones (Cartwright, 1983, Hausman, 1992: 132–42). Newton's law of universal gravitation only holds in the absence of any magnetic forces. But for two reasons, the conditional nature of laws makes life much harder for social scientists than it sometimes does for natural scientists.

(1) Laws only hold all other things being equal. But in many of the cases where natural scientists are interested in predicting outcomes

and events, it just so happens that other things are equal or at least sufficiently equal. Consider, for example, predictions about tide times. Given some fairly basic information about gravitational laws and the position of the moon and sun, meteorologists can predict tide times in different parts of the country. But tide times in any one place also depend upon local conditions. Whether a beach shelves gently or sharply makes a difference to tide times. Furthermore, the action of the tide can, over a period of time, affect whether a beach shelves gently or sharply. So the prediction that if A (the moon and sun are in a certain position) then B (high tide will be at a certain time) only holds *if* C (the beach does not shelve too sharply). But it just so happens that in most cases the difference C makes to tide times can be measured in minutes rather than hours. This means that meteorologists who know nothing about the slope of a particular beach can nevertheless make reasonably accurate predictions.

The problem social scientists face is that other things are rarely equal. Suppose that we are interested in predicting whether there will be a leadership challenge within an incumbent governing party in a prime ministerial system. Suppose our initial hypothesis is that leadership contests are often triggered by the resignation of a senior member of the government following a policy disagreement (rather than personal scandal). The relationship between resignations and leadership contests will however only hold all other things being equal. So we might say that if N (a senior minister resigns) then O (a leadership contests will occur) *if* P (the country is not at war), Q (the party is already behind in the opinion polls), R (there is a credible challenger), S (the party is already divided on ideological lines) and T (the minister challenges the prime minister's personal competence in his or her resignation speech). In this respect, there is no difference between the social and natural sciences. All laws only hold all other things being equal. But in this case the presence or absence of each of these things (P–T) may make a great deal of difference to whether a resignation leads to a leadership contest. The slope of a beach does not usually make that great a difference to tide times. The presence or absence of a credible leadership challenger is likely to make a significant difference to the chances of a resignation leading to a leadership contest. So if they are to predict whether and when ministerial resignations will lead to leadership contests, political scientists will need to know what difference the presence or absence each of these factors makes.

(2) The social scientist is at a further disadvantage here. All laws are conditional and only hold all other things being equal. We have

argued that 'things' are sometimes equal in the natural sciences. But even when they are not 'naturally' equal, natural scientists can often *make* things equal through the careful design of laboratory experiments. The claim that a match will light when struck so long as there is no wind can be tested by first striking matches in a sealed room and by then striking them in front of a powerful fan. Social scientists are not powerless here. First, they can use large-scale data-sets on voting behaviour, the outbreak of war, the contents of the policy agenda, political participation and a range of other subjects to test specific predictions. Here, the social scientist can either wait to see whether the predictions they make now are vindicated in the future or whether the predictions they make are consistent with existing data (this process of making predictions about the past has been given the rather unlovely name of retrodiction). Second, and increasingly, political scientists have constructed field experiments resting upon randomized control trials to test predictions and uncover causal relationships (Druckman et al., 2011). One particularly productive line of research has been electoral participation. Through carefully designed experiments, researchers have been able to measure how much more likely people are to vote when they are phoned and reminded about the election, sent mailshots or given 'startling facts' about turnout and whether people who are 'nudged' to vote in one election are then more likely to vote in subsequent elections (see Green and Gerber, 2008 and John, 2013 for reviews). Yet social scientists are still at a relative disadvantage here in so far as the number of databases they can use and field experiments they can draw upon is much lower than those available to natural scientists.

Social scientists have long been aware of the problems posed by *ceteris paribus* conditions (see Hausman, 1992: 131–42 for a detailed discussion). In his *Essays on Some Unsettled Questions of Political Economy*, John Stuart Mill (1806–1873) (1844, [1948: 54]) argues that because things are rarely equal, the social sciences are an 'inexact' science in which there are only 'tendency laws' from which it is only possible to derive 'tendency predictions'. The relevant passage is worth quoting at some length.

Doubtless a man often asserts of an entire class what is only true of a part of it; but his error generally consists not in making too wide an assertion, but in making the wrong *kind* of assertion; he predicted an actual result, when he should only have predicted a tendency to that result – a power acting with a certain intensity in that direction ... thus if it were stated to be a law of nature, that all heavy bodies fall to the ground, it would probably be said that the resistance of the atmosphere, which prevents a balloon from falling, constitutes the balloon an exception to that pretended law of nature. But the real law is, that all heavy bodies *tend* to fall; and to this there is no exception, not even the sun and the moon.

Tendency laws should not be confused with probabilistic laws. Recall Hempel's argument that we can explain and predict outcomes and events using probabilistic laws in which the relationship between factors holds with a 'high [degree of] statistical probability'. This argument is ambiguous because Hempel provides no indication of what constitutes a 'high' degree of probability. But for the reasons outlined previously, it is unlikely that the relationships social scientists find will usually satisfy even a relatively loose definition of what counts as a 'high' probability. The most the social scientist may be able to claim is the existence of a tendency law linking the two.

How does this apply to rational choice theory? Clearly the kind of causal relationships rational choice theorists are interested in only hold all other things being equal. Political parties will only converge upon the position of the median voter *if* there is one ideological dimension. Political parties will only form a minimal winning coalition *if* coalitions control their membership. People will not contribute to the provision of a collective good *unless* there are selective incentives. In the models rational choice theorists formulate, these other things are specified in terms of a precise list of assumptions. But in the world to which these models are meant to be applied, things will not always be equal and these assumptions will not always hold. In such cases, the most rational choice theorists might be able to achieve is the formulation of tendency predictions. So, on this basis, it might be argued that political parties have a tendency to converge upon the position of the median voter, that political parties have a tendency to formulate minimal winning coalitions, that people will not tend to contribute to the provision of collective goods unless the 'number of individuals is quite small, or there is coercion' and that bureaucrats have a tendency to try and maximize the size of their budget.

Of what explanatory value are such tendency predictions? The obvious answer here is that they are better than nothing. Yet there is a potentially significant problem here. In a classic statement of the positivist philosophy, Karl Popper (1902–1994) argues that scientific theories can be distinguished from non-scientific ones in terms of the predictions they make. Theories are scientific if they can be used to make predictions which can be falsified. Theories, and here Popper has his sights on Marxism and Freudian psychoanalysis, are unscientific if they do not make any predictions, or, and this amounts to the same thing, their predictions cannot be falsified. Philosophers of science have emphasized that it is actually almost impossible to formulate 'critical' tests that can be used to falsify theories. For no matter what happens in some experiment, scientists can always save their theory by proclaiming it to be unsuitable for direct empirical testing or by adding auxiliary hypotheses to account for particular and otherwise uncomforting pieces of evidence. For this reason, Popper is now often dismissed as a 'naive falsificationist' (see Blaug, 1992: 17–21). Yet Popper, whose classic work *The Logic of Scientific Discovery* is, like most classic works, cited more frequently than it is read, recognizes this problem. He argues that it is precisely because scientists can be expected to adopt what he calls 'immunizing stratagems', that auxiliary assumptions should only be accepted if they 'do not diminish the degree of falsifiability or testability of the [theory] in question' (Popper, 1959: 83).

Why does this matter? If, following Popper, it is the capacity to make falsifiable predictions which distinguishes scientific and non-scientific theories, then, if rational choice theory can only make tendency predictions, it may be that it ought not to be counted as a positivist science. In the case of economic theory this was precisely the point made, several decades ago, by Terrence Hutchinson in *The Significance and Basic Postulates of Economic Theory*. Drawing on Popper's work, Hutchinson argued that the tendency laws formulated by classical economists were essentially meaningless and that economists ought to devote themselves to the specification of precise and falsifiable predictions. Yet the problem not only for economics but for rational choice theory is that such predictions have proven extremely difficult to formulate so leaving it exceptionally vulnerable to the kind of criticisms levelled by Green and Shapiro.

Scientific realism and the search for mechanisms

When the 'moral' sciences were first being consciously fashioned in the late eighteenth century, the Marquis de Condorcet (1743–1794) – whose work on voting we touched upon in Chapter 5 – suggested that the sole foundation for belief in the natural sciences is this idea, that the general laws dictating the phenomena of the universe are necessary and constant. Why should this principle be any the less true for the development of the intellectual and moral facilities of man than for the operations of nature?

Scientific realists like Tony Lawson (1997, 2003 and Fulbrook, 2008), whose work we will concentrate on in this section, argue that social science laws have not been discovered for the very simple reason that they do not exist. His argument is directed specifically at economics but can be applied equally well to rational choice theory. In the subjects studied by social scientists there just happen to be very few, if any, probabilistic let alone deterministic laws. There are often 'demi-regularities'; imperfect but nevertheless discernible relationships between two or more 'things' (Lawson, 1997: 204). But, Lawson adds, such relationships usually only hold in and for particular times and places. At a first glance, this argument seems quite similar to the one considered in the previous section. There does not appear to be a great deal of difference between arguing that causal laws only hold all other things being equal and that they rarely are equal and arguing that empirical relationships are neither strong nor enduring. There is however an important difference between positivists and scientific realists at this point. Positivists regard the problems confronting social scientists as epistemological ones. Positivists believe that empirical laws exist but that they are, for the reasons previously discussed, very difficult to identify. The problem rational choice theorists face is an epistemological one relating to their knowledge and this is a problem which can, potentially at least, be overcome if and when more databases are constructed to test empirical predictions and more field experiments conducted. Scientific realists, on the other hand, regard the problem social scientists face as an ontological one; that is as relating to what exists. They believe that there are no empirical laws out there.

So what should economists (and rational choice theorists) do? Clearly they should not launch themselves into wild goose chases for non-existent laws. Instead, Lawson argues, they should try to explain why 'demi-regularities' which hold at certain times and places do not hold at other apparently similar times and places. To return to the previous example, rational choice theorists should not, in other words, be asking whether ministerial resignations cause leadership contests. This is a question to which there is no meaningful answer. They should instead be asking why resignations sometimes lead to such contests and why at other times they do not. Similarly, rather than trying to predict whether parties will converge upon the position of the median voter, rational choice theorists should be asking why parties do sometimes converge whilst at other times maintaining distinct policy profiles. Rather than seek to predict the construction of minimum winning coalitions, rational choice theorists should be asking why minority governments are sometimes able to survive in office for long periods of time and why, on other occasions, grand coalitions are formed. Rather than offer predictions about group mobilization, rational choice theorists should be looking to explain why it is that collective action sometimes occurs when, at other times, groups do not act to advance their shared interests. This is the kind of 'puzzle-driven' research which Shapiro (2005) argues that political scientists ought to be routinely engaged in.

So how can we go about explaining the existence of demi-regularities? Lawson argues that we need to identify the mechanisms causing things to happen (or not happen).

> A mechanism is basically a way of acting or working of a structured thing. Bicycles and rockets work in certain ways. Of course they cannot work or act in the ways they do without possessing the power to do so. Mechanisms then exist as causal powers of things ... the world is composed not only of such 'surface phenomena' as skin spots, puppies turning into dogs, and relatively slow productivity growth in the UK, but also of underlying and governing structures or mechanisms such as are entailed in the workings of, respectively, viruses, genetic codes and the British system of industrial relations. (Lawson, 1997: 21–2)

Mechanisms cause things to happen in particular ways. But particular mechanisms only cause things to happen in predictable ways when left to operate in isolation. In the social sciences prediction is extremely difficult because most outcomes are the results of the operation of a number of mechanisms. As a result, Lawson (1997: 23) suggests that social scientists can only say that mechanisms have a 'tendency' to cause things to happen. Does this matter? We have just seen why, for the positivist, it matters a great deal. Under the terms of the symmetry thesis, a theory's failure to predict casts into doubt its explanatory value. But scientific realists regard the inability to predict as being less significant. They argue that it is perfectly possible to predict without being able to explain and to explain without being able to predict.

As an example of prediction without explanation assume that the declaration of war on a country is *always* preceded by the withdrawal of the ambassador from that country. The withdrawal of the ambassador can then be used to predict the declaration of war but does not help explain it. As an example of explanation without prediction, consider evolutionary theory. Evolution explains how particular and highly specialized animals (including *Homo sapiens*) developed from a succession of less specialized ones by way of a mechanism, natural selection, which results in the survival of the fittest. Yet it is a 'cliché among philosophers and historians of science' (McCloskey, 1986: 36) that evolutionary theory cannot be used to predict how species might adapt and evolve in the future (although see Rosenberg, 1992: 44–7 and Sober, 1984: 136–47).

John Gerring (2007: 161) suggests that there has been a 'widespread turn' toward mechanism-centred explanation in the social sciences in recent years. Rational choice theory might also be understood as invoking the existence of causal mechanisms in its explanations (MacDonald, 2003; Chong, 2006). What are these mechanisms? One such set of mechanisms is optimizing rationality and self-interest. In trying to explain why something occurred we can cite rationality and self-interest as a part – perhaps sometimes the key part – of our explanation. Conversely, we might sometimes use the fact that actors did not act in a rational manner to, on other occasions, explain why events occurred. The fact that bank traders were accumulating staggering quantities of securitized assets on their own balance sheets in 2005–2006 might, for example, be explained by pointing to the fact that their bonuses were linked to the profits they were able to 'book' from such apparently low-risk trades (Treasury Committee, 2009). Conversely, we might also invoke bounded rationality and the effects of 'herding' and 'irrational optimism' to explain why most bank executives did not recognize that assets were being over-priced until it was too late and the market had collapsed (Bell and Hindmoor, 2015: ch. 2). The point to note here is that rationality and self-interest are attractive candidates for explanatory mechanisms because 'rational action is its own explanation' (Hollis, 1977: 26). In so far as we can account for somebody's actions instrumentally in terms of their interests, then we have gone a long way toward explaining why something happened.

> The rational actions of individuals have a unique attractiveness as the basis for social theory. If an institution or a social process can be accounted for in terms of the rational actions of individuals, then

and only then can we say that it has been 'explained' ... and need ask no more questions. (Coleman, 1986: 1)

Rationality and self-interest are not however the only explanatory mechanisms we can associate with rational choice theory. We can explain why particular political parties or candidates sometimes converge upon the political centre and adopt similar policies in terms of the median voter theorem. Conversely, we can explain why they sometimes do not in terms of the presence of multiple parties, multiple issue dimensions, the need to maintain a reputation for reliability or responsibility or the threat of voter abstention. We can explain the survival of minority governments using the portfolio-allocation model in terms of ministerial discretion and the presence of 'strong' parties (p. 94). We can explain instances of collective action in terms of the privileged status of a group (p. 150), the presence of selective incentives (pp. 152–3) or the evolution of norms of cooperation over a period of time (pp. 41–4).

The important point to note here is that the veracity of rational choice explanation does not stand or fall upon the plausibility of its core assumptions. The causal mechanisms identified by rational choice theorists include but are not exhausted by optimizing rationality and self-interest. Indeed John Ferejohn (2002: 226) has argued that 'the standard way' in which rational choice theory is used within political science is as a form of structural explanation in which it is variations in the constraints on actors' choice sets and not variations in their motives and decision-making capacities which carries the explanatory burden.

Consider the example of a rational choice theorist who wants to explain historic variations in fertility rates. Ferejohn argues that the theorist will want to start by assuming that agents are rational and that they seek to maximize their wealth. These assumptions do not however themselves explain anything. Their role is instead to provide a fixed backdrop against which it can be more clearly seen how parametric shifts in constraints – presumably including such things as changes in inheritance laws and the introduction of labour-saving technologies – affect behaviour.

In analysing the operation of structural, that is aggregative, mechanisms like free-riding, sorting, structure-induced equilibrium, cycling and agenda-setting, rational choice theorists need not argue that people really *are* perfectly rational and exclusively self-interested. They can simply argue that they are practicing a division of labour and 'sealing-off' the influence of these other factors. As an example of the issues at stake here consider Thomas Schelling's (1978) famous 'chequerboard' explanation of racial discrimination. Assume that a city is like a 'grid' composed of a series of squares. Each square (with the exception of those on the borders) will be in contact with eight other neighbouring squares. Assume that there are two sets of inhabitants, noughts and crosses. Assume that these two groups are randomly allocated to spaces and, once this allocation has been completed, that there are still a number of empty squares. Assume *nobody* wants to live in a square in which their only neighbours are members of the same group. Assume finally that everyone wants to live in a square in which at least one third of their neighbours belong to the same group and that they will move to an empty square if this condition is not satisfied. Schelling then shows that for almost every possible initial distribution: (1) at least one person will want to move; (2) that each such move is likely to lead someone else to want to move; and (3) that the result of this process is likely to be segregation.

To see the dynamics at work here, consider the situation indicated in Figure 9.1. There are five rows (A–E), five columns (1–5) and, in total, 25 squares. Of these, 13 squares are occupied. Consider first the position of the X occupying D4. They have six neighbours of whom two (C3 and E5) are also Xs. They will therefore not want to move. The X occupying C3 has seven neighbours, two of whom (D2 and D4) are Xs. Because less than one-third of their neighbours are from the same

Figure 9.1   *The dynamics of segregation*

	1	2	3	4	5
A	–	–	–	X	X
B	–	O	O	–	–
C	–	O	X	O	–
D	–	X	O	X	O
E	X	–	O	–	X

group they will therefore want to move. Say they move to the vacant square at A3. The X occupying D4 now has five neighbours, only one of whom (E5) belongs to the same group. So they will now move. Played-out on a larger scale, it is not hard to see how this process might, over time, lead to complete segregation.

Schelling's argument has rightly been lauded as a classic example of mechanistic explanation (Cowen, 1998). Yet it clearly makes a number of unrealistic assumptions including optimizing rationality, homogeneity of preferences, costless moving and the absence of any income differences. Yet the use of these unrealistic assumptions might be defended on the grounds that they allow Schelling to 'seal-off' his model from the effects of other mechanisms in order to show how, when left undisturbed, the sorting mechanism operates. In this way Schelling's model can be said to provide a 'credible' (Sugden, 2000) account of racial discrimination even though it employs unrealistic assumptions.

None of the rational choice models we have discussed in this book offer a completely accurate representation of the phenomena they attempt to explain. There is an obvious sense in which this is a shortcoming of these models – if Schelling's model is an attempt to explain segregation, wouldn't it be better if it took other factors into account? Perhaps, but the problem with this line of reasoning is captured by Jorge Luis Borges's 1948 short story *On Exactitude in Science*, which imagines such advances in the art of cartography that the map of a province came to occupy the space of an entire city. Even these maps left out a lot of detail, however, and eventually cartographers managed to create a 1:1 map of the entire empire. This map was useless, of course, and a model which completely described some political process would be similarly useless. If the point of modelling is to bring certain aspects of a situation in focus, greater realism may simply get in the way. As Dowding (2001: 95) puts it: 'Without oxygen on this planet there would be no policy process, but I have never seen oxygen mentioned in an explanation of any policy outcome.'

The place of rational choice theory in political science

In the opening chapter of this book, we likened rational choice theory's 'difficult decade' (1994–2004) to a mid-life crisis and asked whether its transition to maturity has been a graceful one. Have rational choice theorists adequately responded to accusations of unrealism and irrelevance, or should we impatiently predict the demise of the economic approach to politics? Before giving our answer to this question, it is worth noting each co-author's position on this and clarifying the status of our answer. In the preface we described ourselves as a 'sympathetic sceptic' (Hindmoor) and a 'guarded believer' (Taylor) in rational choice theory. As such, our opinions differ on specific issues, but the position advocated here represents an 'overlapping consensus' we both endorse.

Writing just prior to the beginning of the difficult decade, Dennis Mueller (1993) described three possible scenarios for public choice over the following 25 years: (1) formal rational choice models making the conventional assumptions of selfishness of hyper-rationality will completely dominate political science and eclipse other approaches; (2) a bifurcation in political science between rational choice theory and other approaches, with little interaction between approaches; and (3) rational choice theorists broaden their horizons by integrating the insights of the other social sciences such as psychology and sociology into their models. Mueller considered scenario (1) the most likely but scenario (3) the most desirable.

Given the intensity of the disputes between rational choice theorists and their opponents, it might seem that it is scenario (2) which has come to pass. In recent years, however, scenario (3) has emerged as a real possibility as the methodological horizons of economics have expanded and public choice theorists have begun to take psychological and sociological insights more seriously. Mueller's conclusion that scenario (1) was the most probable was based on the historical development of economics from a pluralistic discipline to one dominated by the neo-classical approach and the use of abstract mathematical models. It is therefore important to note that criticism of the unrealistic assumptions and abstract nature of rational choice theory has mirrored earlier methodological disputes between neo-classical economists and other now heterodox approaches to the study of economics. The reason for thinking that rational choice would win out in political science (i.e. that scenario (1) would come to pass) is that the neo-classical approach appeared to have vanquished all rivals in economics and that the lesson to draw from that was that 'inductive theorizing invariably loses out to deductive reasoning; less formal modelling loses out to more formal modelling' (Mueller, 1993: 146).

Yet there are signs that the battle within economics may not actually be over. Although neo-classical economics remains dominant among academic economists, various heterodox approaches such as behavioural economics (Pesendorfer, 2006), complexity theory (Arthur, 2010) and evolutionary economics (Hodgson, 2012) have been gaining traction in recent years, and criticism of the mainstream approach has accelerated since the global financial crisis of 2008, with critics claiming that the scientific hubris of neo-classical economists contributed to the crisis (Lawson, 2009; Colander et al., 2009). Rational choice theorists have been somewhat slower than economists to embrace heterodox approaches, but, as we have shown in this book, there have been developments in this direction which are suggestive of scenario (3).

Perhaps the best example of rational choice theorists making use of other social sciences is the work of Elinor Ostrom (see Chapter 6), whose distinction between first-generation and second-generation models of rationality also provides a useful way of thinking about the movement in rational choice theory towards greater behavioural realism. First-generation models of rationality are based on narrow self-interest and calculative rationality, whereas second-generation models allow for bounded rationality, learning and norm-following behaviour (Ostrom, 1998). Geoff Brennan and Alan Hamlin (2008) make a similar distinction between mainstream and 'revisionist' public choice theory, with the latter emphasizing the motivating force of morality, esteem and self-expression.

This expansion of rational choice theory has often been criticized as an *ad hoc* attempt to evade falsification which reduces the theory's empirical content. The introduction of an intrinsic preference for voting as a solution to the paradox of not voting, for example, has been criticized by both defenders (e.g. Mueller, 2003: 306) and critics (e.g. Green and Shapiro, 1994: ch. 4) of rational choice theory on these grounds. The validity of such critiques depends on what we think rational choice theory is and what we think it ought to achieve. Are we dealing with a falsifiable theory which makes specific predictions or with a broader 'approach' (Eriksson, 2011: 8–9) or 'organising perspective' (Dowding, forthcoming: ch. 2) which provides a way of looking at the social world?

Rational choice as an organizing perspective does not require that we assume epistemic rationality or selfishness, but simply that we can in some way make sense of preferences in a way consistent with the axiomatic approach introduced in Box 1.3. In organizing our enquiry in this way we gain access to the methods of rational choice theory – game theory, price theory, social choice and so on – but we are quite entitled to incorporate preferences which are altruistic (Margolis, 1982), reciprocal, (Rabin, 1993), meddlesome (Sen, 1970b) or envious (Kolm,

1995). On the axiomatic account, it is the structure rather than the content of preferences which determine rationality, meaning that there is no single model of rational choice, but rather myriad competing models based on different assumptions and making different predictions (Eriksson, 2011: 24–7). Rational choice theory understood in this way is not (and should not be) falsifiable. As an organizing perspective it may be useless or misleading, but it cannot be false.

In the preceding chapters we have introduced some of the major contributions to political science made by rational choice theorists. Although many of the specific predictions made by these theorists are not supported by reality – party platforms do not usually converge and large groups often engage in collective action without coercion or material selective incentives – we maintain first, that each has provided a valuable contribution to our understanding of politics and second, that these contributions were made possible by the use of rational choice theory as an organizing perspective. Although many had noticed the centripetal tendencies of democratic competition, it required the formalism of Duncan Black and Anthony Downs to provide a simple mechanistic explanation of why parties who spend much of their time criticizing each other's approaches nevertheless routinely adopt similar (although not identical) policy positions on many issues. Their explanations provided us not only with a more systemic 'nuts and bolts' (Elster, 1989a, 2007) understanding of the mechanics of elections, but, as we argued in Chapter 4, also makes clear the conditions under which we should expect divergence from the centre.

Rational choice theory is a useful lens through which we can view politics, but it is not the only one. Simple 'first-generation' rational choice models based on narrow self-interest have produced a number of important insights, and for many questions in political science such assumptions remain appropriate. Economics excels at explaining the behaviour of firms in competitive markets because any firm which does not roughly conform to the assumption of profit-maximization will soon find itself out of business (Alchian, 1950). Similarly, we might think that competitive elections act as a screening mechanism to ensure vote-maximizing behaviour among serious candidates. Thus, first-generation rational choice models may do a good job of predicting behaviour for high-stakes decisions with regular feedback (e.g. candidates in competitive elections) but not low-stakes decisions without regular feedback (e.g. voters in those elections). First-generation models are also useful in drawing out those aspects of political processes driven by self-interest. Although Olson's collective action theory does not offer anything close to a complete explanation of group behaviour, it does focus attention squarely on an important aspect of group behaviour (Chapter 6).

For other questions, rational choice as an organizing perspective can provide a useful way of structuring argument and generating hypotheses while allowing for non-material motivation. We have already seen how Ostrom introduced norms into collective action theory (Chapter 6) and how Brennan and Lomasky considered the expressive aspects of political choice (Chapter 8). Other examples of 'second-generation' or 'revisionist' rational choice theory include Dennis Chong's (2000) work on symbolic politics and Eli Berman's (2009) work on terrorism. Each of these theorists has considered the non-material factors which motivate human beings while continuing to use economic methods and see their work in rational choice terms.

This is what makes polarizing debates regarding the value of public choice theory so problematic and the recent reduction in hostilities discussed in Chapter 1 so encouraging. Although it is reasonable for some to specialize in the use of rational choice theory, we believe that the approach is at its best when combined with other empirical and theoretical methods. We have already discussed Elinor Ostrom's methodological pluralism as an example. Others include the 'analytic narratives' approach of combining simple formal modelling with qualitative historical analysis (Bates et al., 1998) and the use of experimental methods to test rational choice models (Plott, 2014).

The 'horses for courses' (or partial universalism, p. 16), approach we advocate here also defuses some of the tension between various understandings of what rational choice theory is and what it can achieve. It is sometimes appropriate to assume pure self-interest and perfect information and sometimes it isn't. Whether we ought to restrict the label 'rational choice' to first-generation models is a purely semantic one without an interesting answer. The work surveyed in this book shows that rational choice narrowly construed offers some important insights and that the tools of rational choice theory can usefully be modified to incorporate epistemic limitations and non-selfish preferences. We think it also shows that rational choice, even when understood broadly, does not lend itself to answering every important question in political science.

Bibliography

Abramowitz, A. I. & Saunders, K. L. (2008). Is Polarization a Myth? *The Journal of Politics*, 70(2), 542–55.

Agrawal, A. (2010). Local Institutions and Adaptation to Climate Change. In R. Mearns & A. Norton (eds), *Social Dimensions of Climate Change: Equity and Vulnerability in a Warming World* (pp. 173–98). Washington, DC: World Bank.

Ahmed, S. & Greene, K. (2000). Is the Median Voter a Clear-Cut Winner? Comparing the Median Voter Theory and Competing Theories in Explaining Local Government Spending, *Public Choice*, 105, 207–30.

Akerlof, G. 1970. The Market for Lemons: Quantitative Uncertainty and the Market Mechanism, *Quarterly Journal of Economics*, 84, 388–400.

Albright, J. J. (2010). The Multidimensional Nature of Party Competition, *Party Politics*, 16(6), 699–719. doi:10.1177/1354068809345856.

Alchian, A. (1950). Uncertainty, Evolution, and Economic Theory, *The Journal of Political Economy*, 58(3), 211–21.

Aleskerov, F., Avci, G., Iakouba, V. & Türem, U. (2002). European Union Enlargement: Power Distribution Implications of the New Institutional Arrangements, *European Journal of Political Research*, 41, 379–94.

Algaba, E., Bilbao, J. & Fernandez, J. (2007). The Distribution of Power in the European Constitution, *European Journal of Operational Research*, 176, 1752–66.

Almond, G. (1996). History of the Discipline, in R. Goodin & H. Klingemann (eds), *A New Handbook of Political Science* (pp. 5–96). Oxford: Oxford University Press.

Amadae, S. M. & Bueno de Mesquita, B. (1999). *The Rochester School*: The Origins of Positive Political Theory, *Annual Review of Political Science*, 2(1), 269–95. doi:10.1146/annurev.polisci.2.1.269.

Anderson, T. L. & Hill, P. J. (1975). The Evolution of Property Rights: A Study of the American West, *Journal of Law and Economics*, 18, 163–79.

Anderson, T. L & Hill, P. J. (2004). *The Not So Wild, Wild West: Property Rights on the Frontier*. Stanford: Stanford University Press.

Ansolabehere, S., De Figueiredo, J. M. & Snyder Jr, J. M. (2003). Why is There So Little Money in US Politics? *Journal of Economic Perspectives*, 17(1), 105–30.

Armingeon, K. (2002). The Effects of Negotiation Democracy: A Comparative Analysis, *European Journal of Political Research*, 41, 81–105.

Arrow, K. (1950). A Difficulty in the Concept of Social Welfare, *Journal of Political Economy*, 58, 328–46, reprinted in Arrow, (1984). *Social Choice and Justice*. Oxford: Basil Blackwell.

Arrow, K. (1951). *Social Choice and Individual Values*. New York: Wiley.

Arrow, K. (1967). Values and Collective Decision Making, in P. Laslett & W. Runciman (eds), *Philosophy, Politics and Society* (pp. 215–32). Oxford: Basil Blackwell.

Arrow, K. & Debreu, G. (1954). Existence of an Equilibrium for a Competitive Economy, *Econometrica*, 22, 265–90.

Arthur, W. B. (2010). Complexity, the Santa Fe Approach, and Non-equilibrium Economics, *History of Economic Ideas*, 18(2), 149–66.

Ashworth, S. (2012). Electoral Accountability: Recent Theoretical and Empirical Work. *Annual Review of Political Science*, 15(1), 183–201. doi:10.1146/annurev-polisci-031710-103823.

Axelrod, R. M. (1970). *Conflict of Interest*. Chicago: Markham.

Axelrod, R. M. (1984). *The Evolution of Cooperation*. New York: Basic Books.

Back, H. (2003). Explaining and Predicting Coalition Outcomes: Conclusions from Studying Data on Local Coalitions, *European Journal of Political Research*, 42, 441–72.

Bachrach, P. & Baratz, M. (1970). *Power and Poverty*. Oxford: Oxford University Press.

Baggott, R. (1995). *Pressure Groups Today*. Manchester: Manchester University Press.

Bakker, R., Jolly, S. & Polk, J. (2012). Complexity in the European Party Space: Exploring Dimensionality with Experts. *European Union Politics*, 13(2), 219–45. doi:10.1177/1465116512436995.

Balliet, D. (2010). Communication and Cooperation in Social Dilemmas: A Meta-analytic Review, *Journal of Conflict Resolution*, 54(1), 39–57.

Barber, B. R. (1993). Education for Democracy, *The Good Society*, 7, 21–39.

Barrett, C. R., Pattanaik, P. K. & Salles, M. (1986). On the Structure of Fuzzy Social Welfare Functions, *Fuzzy Sets and Systems*, 19(1), 1–10.

Barry, B. (1978). *Sociologists, Economists, and Democracy*. Chicago: University of Chicago Press.

Barry, B. (1980). Review Article: The Limits of Liberty, *Theory and Decision*, 12(1), 95–114.

Barry, B. (1989). The Continuing Relevance of Socialism, in R. Skidelsky (ed.), *Thatcherism* (pp. 143–58). Oxford: Basil Blackwell.

Bates, R., Greif, A., Levi, M., Rosenthal, J. L. & Weingast, B. R. (1998). *Analytic Narratives*. Princeton: Princeton University Press.

Baumol, W. J. (1959). *Business Behaviour, Value and Growth*. London: Palgrave Macmillan.

Baumol, W. J. (2004). Red-Queen Games: Arms Races, Rule of Law and Market Economies, *Journal of Evolutionary Economics*, 14(2), 237–47. doi:10.1007/s00191-004-0207-y.

Becker, G. S. (1957). *The Economics of Discrimination*. Chicago: University of Chicago Press.

Beck, N. (1975). A Note on the Probability of a Tied Election, *Public Choice*, 23(1), 75–9.

Beetham, D. (1987). *Max Weber and the Theory of Modern Politics*. Cambridge: Polity Press.

Bell. S. (2002). The Limits of Rational Choice: New Institutionalism in the Test Bed of Central Banking Politics in Australia, *Political Studies*, 50(3), 477–96.

Bell. S. (2011). Do We Really Need a New Constructivist Institutionalism to Explain Institutional Change? *British Journal of Political Science*, 41(4), 883–906.

Bell, S. & Hindmoor. A. (2015). *Masters of the Universe But Slaves of the Market: Bankers and the Great Financial Meltdown ... and How Some Bankers Avoided the Carnage*. Cambridge, MA: Harvard University Press.

Bendor, J., Diermeier, D. & Ting, M. (2003). A Behavioural Model of Turnout, *American Political Science Review*, 97(2), 261–80.

Benhabib, J. (1996). On the Political Economy of Immigration, *European Economic Review*, 40(9), 1737–43.

Benoit, K. & Laver, M. (2006). *Party Policy in Modern Democracies*. London: Routledge.

Benoit, K. (2006). Duverger's Law and the Study of Electoral Systems, *French Politics*, 4(1), 69–83.

Benson, B. L. (1990). *The Enterprise of Law: Justice without the State*. San Francisco: Pacific Research Institute for Public Policy.

Berelson, B., Lazarsfeld, P. F. & McPhee, W. N. (1954). *Voting: A Study of Opinion Formation in a Presidential Campaign*. Chicago: University of Chicago Press.

Bergson, A. (1938). A Reformulation of Certain Aspects of Welfare Economics, *The Quarterly Journal of Economics*, 52(2), 310–34.

Berman, E. (2009). *Radical, Religious, and Violent: The New Economics of Terrorism*. Cambridge: MIT Press.

Berman, H. J. (1983). *Law and Revolution: The Formation of the Western Legal Tradition*. Cambridge: Harvard University Press.

Bernstein, L. (2000). Private Commercial Law in the Cotton Industry: Creating Cooperation Through Rules, Norms, and Institutions, *Michigan Law Review*, 99, 1724–90.

Besley, T. (2005). Political Selection, *The Journal of Economic Perspectives*, 19(3), 43–60.

Besley, T. (2006). *Principled Agents?: The Political Economy of Good Government*. Oxford: Oxford University Press.

Besley, T. & Smart, M. (2007). Fiscal Restraints and Voter Welfare, *Journal of Public Economics*, 91(3), 755–73.

Bianco, W. T., Jeliazkov, I. & Sened, I. (2004). The Uncovered Set and the Limits of Legislative Action, *Political Analysis*, 12(3), 256–76. doi:10.1093/pan/mph018.

Bianco, W. T., Lynch, M. S., Miller, G. J. & Sened, I. (2008). The Constrained Instability of Majority Rule: Experiments on the Robustness of the Uncovered Set, *Political Analysis*, 16(2), 115–37. doi:10.1093/pan/mpm024.

Bish, R. L. & Ostrom, V. (1973). Understanding Urban Government: Metropolitan Reform Reconsidered. American Enterprise Institute for Public Policy Research Washington, DC.

Black, D. (1948). On the Rationale of Group Decision-making, *The Journal of Political Economy*, 56(1), 23–34.

Black, D. (1958). *The Theory of Committees and Elections*. Cambridge: Cambridge University Press.

Blau, A. (2004). Fairness and Electoral Reform, *British Journal of Politics and International Relations*, 6, 165–81.

Blaug, M. (1992). *The Methodology of Economics* (2nd edition). Cambridge: Cambridge University Press.

Block, F. (1977). The Ruling Class Does not Rule, *Socialist Revolution*, 33, 6–28.

Bobbio, N. (1996). *Left and Right: The Significance of a Political Distinction*. Cambridge: Polity Press.

Boettke, P. J., Coyne, C. J. & Leeson, P. T. (2011). Quasimarket Failure, *Public Choice*, 149(1–2), 209–24.

Bogdanor, V. (1984). *What is Proportional Representation? A Guide to the Issues*. Oxford: Martin Robertson.

Booth, K. & Wheeler, N. J. (2008). *The Security Dilemma: Fear, Cooperation and Trust in World Politics*. Basingstoke: Palgrave Macmillan.

Bowles, S. (1998). Endogenous Preferences: The Cultural Consequences of Markets and Other Economic Institutions, *Journal of Economic Literature*, 36(1), 75–111.

Bormann, N. & Golder, M. (2013). Democratic Electoral Systems around the world, 1946–2011, *Electoral Studies*, 32, 360–9.

Boudreaux, D. J. & Holcombe, R. G. (1989). Government By Contract, *Public Finance Review*, 17(3), 264–80.

Brekke, K. A. & Johansson-Stenman, O. (2008). The Behavioural Economics of Climate Change, *Oxford Review of Economic Policy*, 24(2), 280–97.

Braendle, T. (2013). *Do Institutions Affect Citizens Selection into Politics?* (No. 2013/04). Basel: Universität Basel.

Brand, R. (5 November 2013). We Deserve More from Our Democratic System. *The Guardian: Comment is Free*. Retrieved from http://www.theguardian.com/commentisfree/2013/nov/05/russell-brand-democratic-system-newsnight.

Brennan, G. (2009). Climate Change: A Rational Choice Politics View, *Australian Journal of Agricultural and Resource Economics*, 53(3), 309–26. doi:10.1111/j.1467-8489.2009.00457.x.

Brennan, G. & Buchanan, J. M. (1980). *The Power to Tax: Analytical Foundations of a Fiscal Constitution*. Cambridge: Cambridge University Press.

Brennan, G. & Buchanan, J. M. (1984). Voter Choice: Evaluating Political Alternatives, *American Behavioral Scientist*, 28(2), 185–201.

Brennan, G. & Buchanan, J. M. (2000). *The Reason of Rules: Constitutional Political Economy*. Indianapolis: Liberty Fund.

Brennan, G., Eriksson, L., Goodin, R. E. & Southwood, N. (2013). *Explaining Norms*. Oxford: Oxford University Press.

Brennan, G. & Hamlin, A. (1998). Expressive Voting and Electoral Equilibrium, *Public Choice*, 95(1), 149–75.

Brennan, G. & Hamlin, A. (2000). *Democratic Devices and Desires*. New York: Cambridge University Press.

Brennan, G. & Hamlin, A. (2002). Expressive Constitutionalism, *Constitutional Political Economy*, 13(4), 299–311.

Brennan, G. & Hamlin, A. (2008). Revisionist Public Choice Theory, *New Political Economy*, 13(1), 77–88.

Brennan, G. & Hamlin, A. (2009). Positive Constraints on Normative Political Theory, in G. Brennan & G. Eusepi (eds), *The Economics of Ethics and the Ethics of Economics: Values, Markets and the State* (pp. 106–28). Cheltenham: Edward Elgar.

Brennan, G. & Lomasky, L. E. (1984). Inefficient Unanimity, *Journal of Applied Philosophy*, 1(1), 151–63.

Brennan, G. & Lomasky, L. E. (1985). The Impartial Spectator goes to Washington: Toward a Smithian Theory of Electoral Behavior, *Economics and Philosophy*, 1(2), 189–211.

Brennan, G. & Lomasky, L. E. (1993). *Democracy and Decision: The Pure Theory of Electoral Preference*. Cambridge: Cambridge University Press.

Brennan, G. & Pettit, P. (2004). *The Economy of Esteem: An Essay on Civil and Political Society*. Oxford: Oxford University Press.

Buchanan, J. M. (1949). The Pure Theory of Government Finance: A Suggested Approach, *The Journal of Political Economy*, 57(6), 496–505.

Buchanan, J. M. (1954). Social Choice, Democracy, and Free Markets, *The Journal of Political Economy*, 62(2), 114–23.

Buchanan, J. M. (1959). Positive Economics, Welfare Economics, and Political Economy, *Journal of Law & Economics*, 2, 124.

Buchanan, J. M. (1975). *The Limits of Liberty: Between Anarchy and Leviathan*. Chicago: University of Chicago Press.

Buchanan, J. M. (1979). Politics Without Romance: A Sketch of Positive Public Choice Theory and its Normative Implications, Inaugural lecture, Institute for Advanced Studies, Vienna, Austria.

Buchanan, J. M. (1980). Rent Seeking and Profit Seeking, chap. 1 in Buchanan, J., Tollison, R. & Tullock, G. (eds) *Toward a Theory of the Rent-Seeking Society*, College Station: Texas A & M University Press.

Buchanan, J. M. (1985). The Moral Dimension of Debt Financing, *Economic Inquiry*, 23(1), 1–6. doi:10.1111/j.1465-7295.1985.tb01748.x.

Buchanan, J. M. (1995a). Federalism as an Ideal Political Order and an Objective for Constitutional Reform, *Publius*, 25(2), 19–27. doi:10.2307/3330825.

Buchanan, J. M. (1995b). Clarifying Confusion about the Balanced Budget Amendment, *National Tax Journal*, 48, 347–47.

Buchanan, J. M. (2004). The Status of the Status Quo, *Constitutional Political Economy*, 15(2), 133–44.

Buchanan, J. M. (2008). Same Players, Different Game: How Better Rules Make Better Politics, *Constitutional Political Economy*, 19(3), 171–79.

Buchanan, J. M. (2013). Better than Ploughing, *PSL Quarterly Review*, 66(264), 59–76.

Buchanan, J. M. & Congleton, R. D. (1998). *Politics by Principle, Not Interest: Towards Nondiscriminatory Democracy*. Cambridge: Cambridge University Press.

Buchanan, J. M. & Tullock, G. (1962). *The Calculus of Consent: Logical Foundations of Constitutional Democracy*. Ann Arbor: University of Michigan Press.

Buchanan, J. M. & Wagner, R. (1977). *Democracy in Deficit: The Political Legacy of Lord Keynes*. New York: Academic Press.

Buchanan, J. M. & Yoon, Y. J. (2014). The Costs of Collectivization, per se, *Public Choice*, 159(3–4), 321–26.

Budge, I. (1999). Party Policy and Ideology: Reversing the 1950?, in G. Evans and P. Norris (eds), *Critical Elections: British Parties and Voters in Long-Term Perspective* (pp. 1–21). London: Sage.

Budge, I. & Laver, M. (1992). *Party Policy and Government Coalitions*. London: Palgrave Macmillan.

Bull, H. (1981). Hobbes and the International Anarchy, *Social Research*, 48, 717–38.

Bullock, J. G., Gerber, A. S., Hill, S. J. & Huber, G. A. (2013). Partisan Bias in Factual Beliefs About Politics, Working Paper No. 19080. National Bureau of Economic Research.

Burnham, T. C. & Hare, B. (2007). Engineering Human Cooperation: Does Involuntary Neural Activation Increase Public Goods Contributions? *Human Nature*, 18(2), 88–108. doi:10.1007/s12110-007-9012-2.

Butler, D. & Stokes, D. (1969). *Political Change in Britain*. London: Palgrave Macmillan.

Cain, M. (2001). Social Choice Theory, in W. Shughart & L. Razzolini (eds), *The Elgar Companion to Public Choice* (pp. 83–114). Cheltenham: Edward Elgar.

Cameron. D. (2006). Modern Conservatism, *The Guardian*, 30th January.

Campbell, A., Converse, P. E., Miller, W. E. & Stokes, D. E. (1960). *The American Voter*. New York: Wiley.

Campbell, A., Gurin, G. & Miller, W. (1954). *The Voter Decides*. Evanston: Peterson.

Campbell, J. (2011). The US Financial Crisis: Lessons for Theories of Institutional Complementarity, *Socio-Economic Review*, 9(2): 211–34.

Caplan, B. (2007). *The Myth of the Rational Voter*. Princeton: Princeton University Press.

Carling, A. (1992). *Social Division*. London: Verso.

Cartwright, N. (1983). *How the Laws of Physics Lie*. Oxford: Clarendon.

Chappell, H. & Keech, W. (1986). Party Differences in Macroeconomic Policies and Outcomes, *American Economic Review*, 76, 71–4.

Chomsky, N. (1965). *Aspects of the Theory of Syntax*. Cambridge, MA: MIT Press.

Chong, D. (1991). *Collective Action and the Civil Rights Movement*. Chicago: University of Chicago Press.

Chong, D. (2000). *Rational Lives: Norms and Values in Politics and Society*. Chicago: University of Chicago Press.

Chong, D. (2006). Rational Choice Theory's Mysterious Rivals, in J. Friedman (ed.) *The Rational Choice Controversy* (pp. 37–58). New Haven, CT: Yale University Press.

Christiano, T. (2004). Is Normative Rational Choice Theory Self-Defeating? *Ethics*, 115, 122–41.

Coase, R. (1960). The Problem of Social Cost, *Journal of Law and Economics*, 3, 1–44.

Cockett, R. (1995). *Thinking the Unthinkable: Think-Tanks and the Economic Counter-Revolution*. London: Fontana.

Colander, D., Föllmer, H., Haas, A., Goldberg, M., Juselius, K., Kirman, A., Lux, T. & Sloth, B. (2009). The Financial Crisis and the Systemic Failure of the Economics Profession, *Critical Review*, 21 (2–3), 249–67.

Cole, G. D. H. (1936). *Money: Its Present and Future*. London: Cassell & Co.

Coleman, J. (1986). *Individual Interests and Collective Action: Selected Essays*. Cambridge: Cambridge University Press.

Colomer, J. (2005). It's Parties that Choose Electoral Systems (or Duverger's Law Upside Down), *Political Studies*, 53, 1–23.

Comanor, W. S. (1976). The Median Voter Rule and the Theory of Political Choice, *Journal of Public Economics*, 5(1), 169–77.

Congleton, R. (1980). Competitive Process, Competitive Waste, and Institutions, in J. M. Buchanan, R. D. Tollison & G. Tullock (eds), *Toward a Theory of the Rent-seeking Society* (pp. 153–79). College Station, TX: Texas A & M University Press.

Converse, P. E. (1964). The Nature of Belief Systems in Mass Publics, in D. E. Apter (ed.), *Ideology and Discontent* (pp. 206–61). New York: Free Press.

Cowen, T. (1998). Do Economists Use Social Mechanisms to Explain?, in P. Hedstrom & R. Swedberg (eds), *Social Mechanisms: An Analytical Approach to Social Theory*. Cambridge: Cambridge University Press.

Cox. G. (1997). *Making Votes Count*. Cambridge: Cambridge University Press.

Culpepper, P. (2011). *Quiet Politics and Business Power: Corporate Control in Europe and Japan*. Cambridge: Cambridge University Press.

Dahl, R. A. (1956). *A Preface to Democratic Theory*. Chicago: University of Chicago Press.

Dahl, R. A. (1989). *Democracy and its Critics*. New Haven, CT: Yale University Press.

Davidson, D. (1980). *Essays on Actions and Events*. Oxford: Clarendon Press.

Debus, M. (2011). Portfolio Allocation and Policy Compromises: How and Why the Conservatives and the Liberal Democrats Formed a Coalition Government, *The Political Quarterly*, 82(2), 293–304. doi:10.1111/j.1467-923X.2011.02191.x.

Deemen, A. V. (2014). On the Empirical Relevance of Condorcet's Paradox, *Public Choice*, 158(3–4), 311–30. doi:10.1007/s11127-013-0133-3.

De Jasay, A. (1989). Is Limited Government Possible? *Critical Review*, 3(2), 283–309.

Del Rosal, I. (2011). The Empirical Measurement of Rent-Seeking Costs, *Journal of Economic Surveys*, 25(2), 298–325. doi:10.1111/j.1467-6419. 2009.00621.x.

Delli Carpini, M. X. & Keeter, S. (1996). What Americans Know About Politics and Why it Matters. New Haven, CT: Yale University Press.

Demsetz, H. (1969). Information and Efficiency: Another Viewpoint, *Journal of Law and Economics*, 12(1), 1–22.

Dennett, D. (2002). *The Intentional Stance*. Cambridge: MIT Press.

Diermeier, D. (2006a). Coalition Government, *The Oxford Handbook of Political Economy*, 162–79.

Diermeier, D. (2006b) Rational Choice and the Role of Theory in Political Science, in Jeffrey Friedman (ed.) (2006), *The Rational Choice Controversy* (pp. 59–60). New Haven, CT: Yale University Press.

De Swaan, A. (1973), *Coalition Theory and Government Formations*. Amsterdam: Elsevier.

Dowding, K. (1991). *Rational Choice and Political Power*. Aldershot: Edward Elgar.

Dowding, K. (forthcoming). *Philosophy and Methods of Political Science*. London: Palgrave Macmillan.

Dowding, K. (2001). There Must Be End to Confusion: Policy Networks, Intellectual Fatigue, and the Need for Political Science Methods Courses in British Universities, *Political Studies*, 49(1), 89–105.

Dowding, K. & Hindmoor, A. (1997). The Usual Suspects: Rational Choice Theory, Socialism and Political Theory, *New Political Economy*, 2, 51–66.

Downs, A. (1957a). *An Economic Theory of Democracy*. New York: Harper.

Downs, A. (1957b). An Economic Theory of Political Action in a Democracy, *The Journal of Political Economy*, 65(2), 135–50.

Downs, A. (1995). The Origins of an Economic Theory of Democracy, in Bernard Grofman (ed.), *Information, Participation and Choice: An Economic Theory of Democracy in Perspective* (pp. 197–200). Ann Arbor: University of Michigan Press.

Druckman, J. N., Donald P. G., James H. K. & Arthur L. (eds) (2011). *Cambridge Handbook of Experimental Political Science*. New York: Cambridge University Press.

Dryzek, J. S. (2010). *Foundations and Frontiers of Deliberative Governance*. Oxford: Oxford University Press.

Dryzek, J. S. & List, C. (2003). Social Choice Theory and Deliberative Democracy: A Reconciliation, *British Journal of Political Science*, 33(1), 1–28.

Dryzek, J. S. & Niemeyer, S. (2006). Reconciling Pluralism and Consensus as Political Ideals. *American Journal of Political Science*, 50(3), 634–49. doi:10.1111/j.1540-5907.2006.00206.x.

Dummett, M. (1998), The Borda Count and Agenda Manipulation, *Social Choice and Welfare*, 15, 287–96.

Dunleavy, P. (1985). Bureaucrats, Budgets and the Growth of the State: Reconstructing an Instrumental Model, *British Journal of Political Science*, 15, 299–328.

Dunleavy, P. (1991). *Democracy, Bureaucracy and Public Choice*. Basingstoke: Palgrave Macmillan.

Dunleavy, P. & Gilson, C. (2010). Is the UK Electorate Disengaged?, *LSE British Politics and Policy Blog*. Retrieved from http://blogs.lse.ac.uk/politicsandpolicy/is-the-uk-electorate-disengaged/.

Dunleavy, P. & O'Leary, B. (1987). *Theories of the State*. Basingstoke: Palgrave Macmillan.

Dupuis-Deri, F. (2004). The Political Power of Words: The Birth of Pro-Democratic Discourse in the Nineteenth Century in the United States and France, *Political Studies*, 52, 118–34.

Duverger, M. (1951). *Political Parties*. London: Methuen.

Eagles, M. (2008). *Politics: An Introduction to Modern Democratic Government*. Peterborough: Broadview Press.

Egan, P. J. (2014). Do Something Politics and Double-Peaked Policy Preferences, *The Journal of Politics*, 76(2), 333–49. doi:10.1017/S0022381613001527.

Elster, J. (1985). *Making Sense of Marx*. Cambridge: Cambridge University Press.

Elster, J. (1986). Introduction, in J. Elster (ed.), *Rational Choice* (pp. 1–33). Oxford: Blackwells.

Elster, J. (1989a). *Nuts and Bolts for the Social Sciences*. Cambridge: Cambridge University Press.

Elster, J. (1989b). *The Cement of Society: A Survey of Social Order*. Cambridge: Cambridge University Press.

Elster, J. (1998). *Deliberative democracy*. Cambridge: Cambridge University Press.

Elster, J. (2007). *Explaining Social Behaviour: More Nuts and Bolts for the Social Sciences*. Cambridge: Cambridge University Press.

Elster, J. & Roemer, J. (eds) (1991). *Interpersonal Comparisons of Wellbeing*. Cambridge: Cambridge University Press.

Enelow, J. & Hinich, M. (1982), Nonspatial Candidate Characteristics and Electoral Competition, *Journal of Politics*, 44, 28–55.

Enelow, J. & Hinich, M. (1989). A General Probabilistic Spatial Theory of Elections, *Public Choice*, 61, 101–13.

Eriksson, L. (2011). *Rational Choice Theory: Potential and Limits*. Basingstoke: Palgrave Macmillan.

Estlund, D. M. (2009). *Democratic Authority: A Philosophical Framework*. Princeton: Princeton University Press.

Evans, A. J. & Friedman, J. (2011). 'search' Vs. 'browse': A Theory of Error Grounded in Radical (Not Rational) Ignorance, *Critical Review*, 23(1–2), 73–104. doi:10.1080/08913811.2011.574471.

Falcó-Gimeno, A. (2012). The Use of Control Mechanisms in Coalition Governments: The Role of Preference Tangentiality and Repeated Interactions, *Party Politics*, 1354068811436052. doi:10.1177/1354068811436052.

Farrant, A. (2004). Robust Institutions: The Logic of Levy? *The Review of Austrian Economics*, 17(4), 447–51.

Farrar, C., Fishkin, J., Green, D., List, C., Luskin, R. (2003). Experimenting with Deliberative Democracy: Effects on Policy Preferences and Social Choice, ECPR Conference, Marburg. Retrieved from http://cdd.stanford.edu/research/papers/2003/experimenting.pdf.

Farrell, D. (2001). *Comparing Electoral Systems: A Comparative Introduction*. Basingstoke: Palgrave Macmillan.

Fearon, J. D. (1999). Electoral Accountability and the Control of Politicians: Selecting Good Types Versus Sanctioning Poor Performance, in A. Przeworski, S. C. Stokes & B. Manin (eds), *Democracy, Accountability, and Representation* (pp. 55–97). New York: Cambridge University Press.

Fehr, E. & Fischbacher, U. (2002). Why Social Preferences Matter – the Impact of Non-Selfish Motives on Competition, Cooperation and Incentives, *The Economic Journal*, 112(478), C1–C33.

Feiock, R. C. & Scholz, J. T. (2009). *Self-Organizing Federalism: Collaborative Mechanisms to Mitigate Institutional Collective Action Dilemmas*. Cambridge: Cambridge University Press.

Feld, S. L., Grofman, B. & Miller, N. (1988). Centripetal Forces in Spatial Voting: On the Size of the Yolk, *Public Choice*, 59(1), 37–50.

Ferejohn, J. A. (1990). Information and the Electoral Process, in J. A. Ferejohn & J. H. Kuklinski (eds), *Information and Democratic Processes* (pp. 3–19). Urbana: University of Illinois Press.

Ferejohn, J. (2002). Rational Choice Theory and Social Explanation, *Economics and Philosophy*, 18, 211–34.

Ferejohn, J. & Fiorina, M. P. (1974). The Paradox of Not Voting: A Decision Theoretic Analysis, *The American Political Science Review*, 68(2), 525–36.

Ferejohn, J. & Satz, D. (1995). Unification, Universalism, and Rational Choice Theory, *Critical Review*, 9(1–2), 71–84.

Fiorina, M. P. (1976). The Voting Decision: Instrumental and Expressive Aspects, *Journal of Politics*, 38(2), 390–413.

Fiorina, M. P. (1990). Information and Rationality in Elections, in J. A. Ferejohn & J. H. Kuklinski (eds), *Information and Democratic Processes* (pp. 329–42). Urbana: University of Illinois Press.

Fiorina, M. P., Abrams, S. J. & Pope, J. C. (2005). *Culture War? The Myth of a Polarized America*. New York: Longman Publishing Group.

Fischer, J., Dowding, K. & Dumont, P. (2012). The Duration and Durability of Cabinet Ministers, *International Political Science Review*, 33(5), 505–19.

Foldvary, F. E. (2002). Small-Group, Multi-Level Democracy: Implications of Austrian Public Choice for Governance Structure, *The Review of Austrian Economics*, 15(2–3), 161–74.

Fowler, J. H. & Smirnov, O. (2007). *Mandates, Parties, and Voters: How Elections Shape the Future*. Philadelphia: Temple University Press.

Francey, D. & Bergmüller, R. (2012). Images of Eyes Enhance Investments in a Real-life Public Good, *PloS one*, 7(5), e37397.

Frank, R. (1988). *Passions Within Reason: The Strategic Roles of the Emotions*. New York: W. H. Norton.

Frey, B. S., Benz, M. & Stutzer, A. (2004). Introducing Procedural Utility: Not Only What, But Also How Matters, *Journal of Institutional and Theoretical Economics JITE*, 160(3), 377–401.

Friedman, M. (1953). The Methodology of Positive Economics, in Friedman, J. (ed.) *Essays on Positive Economics* (pp. 3–13). Chicago: University of Chicago Press.

Friedman, J. (ed.) (2006). *The Rational Choice Controversy*. New Haven, CT: Yale University Press.

Fulbrook, E. (2008). *Ontology and Economics: Tony Lawson and his Critics*. London: Routledge.

Gaertner, W. (2001). *Domain Conditions in Social Choice Theory*. Cambridge: Cambridge University Press.

Gailmard, S. & Patty, J. W. (2012). Formal Models of Bureaucracy, *Annual Review of Political Science*, 15(1), 353–77. doi:10.1146/annurev-polisci-031710-103314.

Galbraith, J. K. (1953). *American Capitalism*. Harmondsworth: Penguin Press.

Galbraith, J. K. (1972). *The New Industrial State*. London: Deutsche.

Galston, W. A. (2001). Political Knowledge, Political Engagement, and Civic Education, *Annual Review of Political Science*, 4(1), 217–34.

Gambetta, D. (1993). *The Sicilian Mafia: The Business of Private Protection*. Cambridge: Harvard Business Press.

Gaus, G. (2010). *The Order of Public Reason: A Theory of Freedom and Morality in a Diverse and Bounded World*. Cambridge: Cambridge University Press.

Gauthier, D. P. (1969). *The Logic of Leviathan: The Moral and Political Theory of Thomas Hobbes*. Oxford: Clarendon Press.

Gehrlein, W. V. (2004). Consistency in Measures of Social Homogeneity: A Connection with Proximity to Single Peaked Preferences. *Quality and Quantity*, 38(2), 147–71.

Gehrlein, W. V. (2005). Probabilities of Election Outcomes with Two Parameters: The Relative Impact of Unifying and Polarizing Candidates, *Review of Economic Design*, 9(4), 317–36.

Gelman, A. (2009). *Red State, Blue State, Rich State, Poor State: Why Americans Vote the Way They Do* (Expanded Edition). Princeton: Princeton University Press.

Gelman, A., Silver, N. & Edlin, A. (2009). What Is the Probability Your Vote Will Make a Difference? *Economic Inquiry*, 50(2), 321–26. doi:10.1111/j.1465-7295.2010.00272.x.

Gerber, A. S., Green, D. P. & Larimer, C. W. (2008). Social Pressure and Vote Turnout: Evidence from a Large-scale Field Experiment, *American Political Science Review*, 102(1), 33.

Gerring, J. (2007). The Mechanismic Worldview: Thinking Inside the Box, *British Journal of Political Science*, 38, 161–79.

Gibbard, A. (1973). Manipulation of Voting Schemes: A General Result, *Econometrica*, 41, 587–601.

Gibilisco, M. B., Gowen, A. M., Albert, K. E., Mordeson, J. N., Wierman, M. J. & Clark, T. D. (2014). *Fuzzy Social Choice Theory*. Cham: Springer.

Giddens, A. (1994). *Beyond Left and Right: the Future of Radical Politics*. Cambridge: Cambridge University Press.

Gilabert, P. & Lawford-Smith, H. (2012). Political Feasibility: A Conceptual Exploration. *Political Studies*, 60 (4), 809–25.

Goldfarb, R. S. & Sigelman, L. (2010). Does 'Civic Duty' 'Solve' The Rational Choice Voter Turnout Puzzle? *Journal of Theoretical Politics*, 22(3), 275–300. doi:10.1177/0951629810365798.

Goodin, R. E. & Roberts, K. W. (1975). The Ethical Voter, *The American Political Science Review*, 69(3), 926–28.

Grafstein, R. (1992). Rational Choice Inside and Out. *The Journal of Politics*, 54, 259–68.

Green, D. & Gerber, A (2008). *Get Out the Vote: How to Increase Voter Turnout* (2nd edition). Washington, DC: Brookings Institution Press.

Green, D. P. & Shapiro, I. (1994). *Pathologies of Rational Choice Theory: A Critique of Applications in Political Science*. Cambridge: Cambridge University Press.

Green, D. P. & Shapiro, I. (2006). Pathologies Revisited: Reflections on our Critics, in Friedman, J. (ed.), *The Rational Choice Controversy*. New Haven, CT: Yale University Press.

Greif, A. (2006). Institutions and the Path to the Modern Economy: Lessons from Medieval Trade. Cambridge: Cambridge University Press.

Grofman, B. (1993). Is Turnout the Paradox that Ate Rational Choice Theory, in B. Grofman (ed.), *Information, Participation, and Choice: An Economic Theory of Democracy in Perspective* (pp. 93–103). Ann Arbor: University of Michigan Press.

Grofman, B., Blais, A. & Bowler, S. (eds) (2009). *Duverger's Law of Plurality Voting*. New York: Springer.

Grossman, G. M. & Helpman, E. (2002). *Special Interest Politics*. Cambridge, MA: MIT Press.

Gsottbauer, E. & Van den Bergh, J. C. (2011). Environmental Policy Theory Given Bounded Rationality and Other-regarding Preferences, *Environmental and Resource Economics*, 49(2), 263–304.

Gulick, L. (1957). Metropolitan Organization, *The ANNALS of the American Academy of Political and Social Science*, 314(1), 57–65.

Gutmann, A. & Thompson, D. (2009). *Why Deliberative Democracy?* Princeton: Princeton University Press.

Hall, R. L. & Deardorff, A. V. (2006). Lobbying as Legislative Subsidy, *American Political Science Review*, 100(1), 69–84.

Hampsher-Monk, I. & Hindmoor, A. (2010). Rational Choice and Interpretive Evidence: Caught Between a Rock and a Hard Place? *Political Studies*, 58 (1), 47–65.

Hampton, J. (1986). *Hobbes and the Social Contract Tradition*. Cambridge: Cambridge University Press.

Harberger, A. (1954). Monopoly and Resource Allocation, *American Economic Review*, 44, 77–87.

Hardin, G. (1968). The Tragedy of the Commons, *Science*, 162(3859), 1243–48.

Hardin, R. (1982). *Collective Action*. Baltimore: The Johns Hopkins University Press.

Hardin, R. (1989). Why a Constitution?, in B. Grofman & D. Wittman (eds), *The Federalist Papers and the New Institutionalism* (pp. 100–20). New York: Agathon Press.

Hardin, R. (1995). *One for All: The Logic of Group Conflict*. Princeton: Princeton University Press.

Hardin, R. (1999). *Liberalism, Constitutionalism, and Democracy*. Oxford: Oxford University Press.

Hardin, R. (2009). *How Do You Know?: The Economics of Ordinary Knowledge*. Princeton: Princeton University Press.

Hargreaves-Heap, S. & Varoufakis, Y. (1995). *Game Theory: A Critical Introduction*. London: Routledge.

Hausman, D. (1992). *The Inexact and Separate Science of Economics*. Cambridge: Cambridge University Press.

Hay, C. (2007). *Why We Hate Politics*. Cambridge: Polity Press.

Hay, C. & Rosamond, B. (2002). Globalisation, European Integration and the Discursive Construction of Economic Imperatives, *Journal of European Public Policy*, 9, 147–67.

Hayek, F. A. (1944). *The Road to Serfdom*. London: Routledge.

Held, D. (2006). *Models of Democracy* (3rd edition). Cambridge: Polity Press.

Held, D. & Fane-Hervey, A. (2011). Democracy, Climate Change and Global Governance: Democratic Agency and the Policy Menu Ahead, in D. Held, A. Fane-Hervey & M. Theros (eds), *The Governance of Climate Change* (pp. 89–110). Cambridge: Polity Press.

Helm, D. (2010). Government Failure, Rent-seeking, and Capture: The Design of Climate Change Policy, *Oxford Review of Economic Policy*, 26(2), 182–96.

Hempel, C. (1942). The Function of General Laws in History, *Journal of Philosophy*, 39, 209–27, reprinted (1996) Martin & McIntyre, *Readings in the Philosophy of Social Science*.

Hempel, C. (1962). Explanation in Science and History, in R. Colodny (ed.), *Frontiers of Science and Philosophy* (pp. 7–34). London: Allen & Unwin, reprinted in Ruben, D. (ed.) (1993). *Explanation*. Oxford: Oxford University Press.

Hempel, C. (1965). *Aspects of Scientific Explanation*. New York: Free Press.

Hennessy, P. (2010). David Cameron: I will never Shift from the Centre Ground, *The Daily Telegraph*, 2nd October.

Hermens, F. (1951). *Europe Between Democracy and Anarchy*. Notre Dame: University of Notre Dame Press.

Herne, K. & Setala, M. (2004). A Response to the Critique of Rational Choice Theory: Lakatos' and Laudan's Conceptions Applied, *Inquiry*, 47, 67–85.

Higgs, R. (1988). Can the Constitution Protect Private Rights During National Emergencies?, in J. D. Gwartney & R. E. Wagner (eds), *Public Choice and Constitutional Economics* (pp. 369–86). New York: JAI Press.

Hillman, A. L. (2010). Expressive Behavior in Economics and Politics, *European Journal of Political Economy*, 26(4), 403–18. doi:16/j.ejpoleco.2010.06.004.

Hillman, A. L. & Katz, E. (1984). Risk-averse Rent Seekers and the Social Cost of Monopoly Power, *Economic Journal*, 94(373), 104–10.

Hillman, A. L. & Riley, J. G. (1989). Politically Contestable Rents and Transfers, *Economics & Politics*, 1(1), 17–39.

Hillman, A. L. & Samet, D. (1987). Dissipation of Contestable Rents by Small Numbers of Contenders. *Public Choice*, 54(1), 63–82.

Hindess, B. (1988). *Choice, Rationality and Social Theory*. London: Unwin Hyman.

Hindmoor, A. (1998). The Importance of Being Trusted: Transaction Costs and Policy Network Theory, *Public Administration*, 76, 25–43.

Hindmoor, A. (1999). Rent Seeking Evaluated, *Journal of Political Philosophy*, 7(4), 434–52.

Hindmoor, A. (2004). *New Labour at the Centre: Constructing Political Space.* Oxford: Oxford University Press.

Hindmoor, A. (2005a). Public Choice Theory, in Colin Hay, Michael Lister & Dave Marsh Cambridge, Mass: (eds), *The State: Theories and Issues* (pp. 79–97). Palgrave Macmillan.

Hindmoor, A. (2005b). *New Labour at the Centre: Constructing Political Space.* Oxford: Oxford University Press.

Hindmoor, A. (2010). Major Combat Operations have Ended? Arguing About Rational Choice, *British Journal of Political Science*, 41, 191–210.

Hindriks, F. (2008). False Models as Explanatory Engines, *Philosophy of the Social Sciences*, 38, 334–60.

Hinich, M. & Munger, M. (1996). *Ideology and the Theory of Political Choice.* Cambridge: Cambridge University Press.

Hinich, M. & Munger, M. (1997). *Analytical Politics.* Cambridge: Cambridge University Press.

Hodgson, G. M. (2012). *From Pleasure Machines to Moral Communities: An Evolutionary Economics without Homo Economicus.* Chicago: University of Chicago Press.

Hollis, M. (1977). *Models of Man: Philosophical Thoughts on Social Action.* Cambridge: Cambridge University Press.

Horn, M. (1995). *The Political Economy of Public Administration.* Cambridge: Cambridge University Press.

Hotelling, H. (1929). Stability in Competition, *Economic Journal*, 39, 41–57.

Hummel, P. (2010). Flip-flopping from Primaries to General Elections, *Journal of Public Economics*, 94(11–12), 1020–27. doi:10.1016/j.jpubeco.2010.08.006.

Iannaccone, L. R. (1994). Why Strict Churches are Strong, *American Journal of Sociology*, 99(5), 1180–211.

IPCC. (2013). *Climate Change 2013: The Physical Science Basis.* Cambridge: Cambridge University Press.

Jacobsen, K. (2001). Political Scientists Have Turned Guerrillas, *The Guardian*, 3rd April, p. 14.

Jacobsen, K. (2005). Perestroika in American Political Science, *Post-Autistic Economics Review*, 32, Article 6.

John, P. (2013). Field Experiments in Political Science. University College of London Working Paper. Retrieved from http://ssrn.com/abstract=2207877.

Johnson, H. (1958). The Gains from Freer Trade with Europe: An Estimate, *Manchester School of Economic and Social Studies*, 26, 247–55.

Johnston, L. (2011). *Politics: An Introduction to the Modern Democratic State.* North York: University of Toronto Press.

Kahneman, D. (2011). *Thinking, Fast and Slow.* London: Allen Lane.

Kahneman, D. & Frederick, S. (2002). Representativeness Revisited: Attribute Substitution in Intuitive Judgment, in T. Gilovich, D. Griffin & D. Kahneman (eds), *Heuristics and Biases: The Psychology of Intuitive Judgment* (pp. 49–81). Cambridge: Cambridge University Press.

Kalt, J. P. & Zupan, M. A. (1990). The Apparent Ideological Behavior of Legislators: Testing for Principal-Agent Slack in Political Institutions, *Journal of Law and Economics*, 33(1), 103–31.

Karp, J. A. & Bowler, S. (2001). Coalition Government and Satisfaction with Democracy: An Analysis of New Zealand's Reaction to Proportional Representation, *European Journal of Political Research*, 40(1), 57–79.

Kau, J. B. & Rubin, P. H. (1979). Self-interest, Ideology, and Logrolling in Congressional Voting, *JL & Econ.*, 22, 365.

Kau, J. B. & Rubin, P. H. (1993). Ideology, Voting, and Shirking, *Public Choice*, 76(1–2), 151–72.

Kavka, G. S. (1983). Hobbes's War of all Against all, *Ethics*, 93, 291–310.

Keohane. R. (1984). *After Hegemony: Co-operation and Discord in the World Political Economy*. Princeton: Princeton University Press.

Khalil, E. L. (1997). The Red Queen Paradox: A Proper Name for a Popular Game-Note, *Journal of Institutional and Theoretical Economics*, 153(2), 411–15.

Kindleberger, C. (1981). Dominance and Leadership in the International Economy: Exploitation, Public Goods and Free Rides, *International Studies Quarterly*, 25, 242–54.

King, D. (1987). *The New Right: Politics, Markets and Citizenship*. Basingstoke: Palgrave Macmillan.

King, G., Alt, J., Burns, N. & Laver, M. (1990). A Unified Model of Cabinet Dissolution in Parliamentary Democracies, *American Journal of Political Science*, 34, 846–71.

Kliemt, H. (1986). The Veil of Insignificance, *European Journal of Political Economy*, 2(3), 333–44.

Knack, S. (1992). Civic Norms, Social Sanctions, and Voter Turnout, *Rationality and Society*, 4(2), 133–56.

Kolm, S.-C. (1995). The Economics of Social Sentiments: The Case of Envy, *Japanese Economic Review*, 46(1), 63–87.

Kostelnik, J. & Skarbek, D. (2012). The Governance Institutions of a Drug Trafficking Organization, *Public Choice*, 156, 1–9.

Kunicova, J. & Rose-Ackerman, S. (2005). Electoral Rules and Constitutional Structures as Constraints on Corruption, *British Journal of Political Science*, 35(4), 573.

Laband, D. & Sophocleus, J. (1988). The Social Cost of Rent Seeking: First Estimates, *Public Choice*, 58, 269–75.

Lalman, D., Oppenheimer, J. & Swistak, P. (1993). Formal Rational Choice Theory: A Cumulative Science of Politics, in A. Finifter (ed.), *Political Science: The State of the Discipline II* (pp. 77–104). Washington, DC: APSA.

Landemore, H. (2013). *Democratic Reason: Politics, Collective Intelligence, and the Rule of the Many*. Princeton: Princeton University Press.

Lane, R. (2006). What Rational Choice Explains, in J. Friedman (ed.), *The Rational Choice Controversy* (pp. 107–26). New Haven, CT: Yale University Press.

Lau, R. R. & Redlawsk, D. P. (1997). Voting Correctly, *The American Political Science Review*, 91(3), 585–98. doi:10.2307/2952076.

Laver, M. & Hunt, B. (1992). *Policy and Party Competition*. New York: Routledge.

Laver, M. & Schofield, N. (1990). *Multiparty Government: The Politics of Coalition in Europe*. Oxford: Oxford University Press.

Laver, M. & Shepsle, K. (1996). *Making and Breaking Governments: Cabinets and Legislatures in Parliamentary Democracies*. Cambridge: Cambridge University Press.

Laver, M. & Shepsle, K. (1998). Events Equlibria and Government Survival, *American Journal of Political Science*, 42, 28–54.

Laver, M. & Shepsle, K. (1999). Understanding Government Survival: Empirical Exploration or Analytical Models?, *British Journal of Political Science*, 29, 395–415.

Lawson, T. (1997). *Economics and Reality*. London: Routledge.

Lawson, T. (2003). *Reorientating Economics*. London: Routledge.

Lawson. T. (2009). The Current Economic Crisis: Its Nature and the Course of Academic Economics, *Cambridge Journal of Economics*, 33(4), 759–77.

Leeson, P. T. (2009). *The Invisible Hook: The Hidden Economics of Pirates*. Princeton: Princeton University Press.

Leeson, P. T. & Skarbek, D. B. (2010). Criminal Constitutions, *Global Crime*, 11(3), 279–98.

Lemennicier, B., Lescieux-Katir, H. & Grofman, B. (2010). The 2007 French Presidential Election, *Canadian Journal of Political Science*, 43(01), 137–61.

Lemieux, P. (2005). The Public Choice Revolution, *Regulation*, 27(3), 22–9.

Levi, M. (1997). *Consent, Dissent and Patriotism*. Cambridge: Cambridge University Press.

Lijphart, A. (2012). *Patterns of Democracy: Government Forms and Performance in Thirty-Six Countries* (2nd edition). New Haven, CT: Yale University Press.

Lindblom, C. (1977). *Politics and Markets: The World's Political Economic Systems*. New York: Basic Books.

Lipset, S. & Rokkan, S. (1967). 'Cleavage Structures, Party Systems and Voter Alignments: An Introduction' in S. Lipset & S. Rokkan (eds), *Party Systems and Voter Alignments: Cross-National Perspectives* (pp. 1–64). New York: The Free Press.

Lipsmeyer, C. S. & Pierce, H. N. (2011). The Eyes that Bind: Junior Ministers as Oversight Mechanisms in Coalition Governments, *The Journal of Politics*, 73(04), 1152–64. doi:10.1017/S0022381611000879.

List, C., Luskin, R. C., Fishkin, J. S. & McLean, I. (2013). Deliberation, Single-Peakedness, and the Possibility of Meaningful Democracy: Evidence from Deliberative Polls, *Journal of Politics*, 75(1), 80–95.

Lloyd, G. (1962). Left and Right in Greek Philosophy *Journal of Hellenic Studies*, 82, 56–66.

Lodge, M. & Taber, C. S. (2013). *The Rationalizing Voter.* Cambridge: Cambridge University Press.

Lomborg, B. (2007). *Cool it: The Skeptical Environmentalist's Guide to Global Warming.* New York: Alfred Knopf.

Lopez, R. & Pagoulatos, E. (1994). Rent Seeking and the Welfare Cost of Trade Barriers, *Public Choice,* 79, 149–60.

Lovett, F. (2006). Rational Choice Theory and Explanation, *Rationality and Society,* 18, 237–72.

Lowndes, V (2010). The Institutionalist Approach, in D. Marsh & G. Stoker (eds), *Theory and Methods in Political Science* (pp. 60–79). London: Palgrave Macmillan.

Luce, R. & Raiffa, H. (1957). *Games and Decisions.* New York: Wiley.

Lukes, S. (1974). *Power: A Radical View.* London: Palgrave Macmillan.

Lupia, A. (1992). Busy Voters, Agenda Control, and the Power of Information, *The American Political Science Review,* 86(2), 390–403. doi:10.2307/1964228.

Lupia, A. (1994). Shortcuts Versus Encyclopedias: Information and Voting Behavior in California Insurance Reform Elections, *American Political Science Review,* 88(1), 63–76.

Lupia, A. & McCubbins, M. D. (1998). *The Democratic Dilemma: Can Citizens Learn What They Need to Know?* Cambridge: Cambridge University Press.

MacDonald, P. (2003). Useful Fiction or Miracle Maker: The Competing Epistemological Foundations of Rational Choice Theory, *American Political Science Review,* 97, 551–65.

Mackie, G. (2003). *Democracy Defended.* Cambridge: Cambridge University Press.

Mackie, G. (2010). *Why It's Rational to Vote.* San Diego: University of California.

Maki, U. (2002). Symposium on Explanations and Social Ontology: Explanatory Ecumenism and Economic Imperialism, *Economics and Philosophy,* 18, 235–57.

Mankiw, N. G. (2014). *Principles of Economics* (7th edition). Stamford, CT: Cengage Learning.

Manin, B. (1997). *The Principles of Representative Government.* Cambridge: Cambridge University Press.

Marglin, S. (2008). *The Dismal Science: How Thinking Like an Economist Undermines Community.* Cambridge: Harvard University Press.

Margolis, H. (1982). *Selfishness, Altruism, and Rationality: A Theory of Social Choice.* Cambridge: Cambridge University Press.

Marx, K. (1867) [1932]. *Capital: A Critique of Political Economy.* London: Dent.

Maskin, E. & Sen, A. (2014). *The Arrow Impossibility Theorem.* New York: Columbia University Press.

Mayer, F. (2014). *Narrative Politics: Stories and Collective Action.* Oxford: Oxford University Press.

May, J. (1973). Opinion Structure of Political Parties: The Special Law of Curvilinear Disparity, *Political Studies*, 21, 135–51.

May, K. O. (1952). A Set of Independent Necessary and Sufficient Conditions for Simple Majority Decision, *Econometrica: Journal of the Econometric Society*, 20, 680–84.

Mayr, K. (2007). Immigration and Income Redistribution: A Political Economy Analysis,*PublicChoice*,131(1–2),101–16.doi:10.1007/s11127-006-9107-z.

McCloskey, D. (1986). *The Rhetoric of Economics.* Brighton: Wheatsheaf.

McGann, A. (2013). Fairness and Bias in Electoral Systems, in J. H. Nagel & R. M. Smith (eds), *Representation: Elections and Beyond* (pp. 90–113). Philadelphia: University of Pennsylvania Press.

McKelvey, R. D. (1976). Intransitivities in Multidimensional Voting Models and Some Implications for Agenda Control, *Journal of Economic Theory*, 12(3), 472–82.

McKelvey, R. D. (1979). General Conditions for Global Intransitivities in Formal Voting Models, *Econometrica: Journal of the Econometric Society*, 47(5), 1085–112.

McKelvey, R. D. (1986). Covering, Dominance, and Institution-free Properties of Social Choice, *American Journal of Political Science*, 30, 283–314.

McLean, I. (1987). *Public Choice.* Oxford: Blackwells.

McLean, I. & Urken, A. (1995). *Classics of Social Choice Theory.* Michigan: University of Michigan Press.

Meehl, P. E. (1977). The Selfish Voter Paradox and the Thrown-Away Vote Argument, *The American Political Science Review*, 71(1), 11–30. doi:10.2307/1956951.

Mershon, C. (1996). The Costs of Coalition: Coalition Theories and Italian Governments, *American Political Science Review*, 990, 534–54.

Mesquita, B. B. de. (2009). *Predictioneer: One Who Uses Maths, Science and the Logic of Brazen Self-interest to See and Shape the Future.* New York: Random House.

Mesquita, B. B. de & Smith, A. (2011). *The Dictator's Handbook: Why Bad Behavior Is Almost Always Good Politics.* New York: Public Affairs.

Migue, J. & Belanger, G. (1974). Towards a General Theory of Managerial Discretion, *Public Choice*, 17, 27–43.

Milgrom, P. & Roberts, J. (1986). Relying on the Information of Interested Parties, *The Rand Journal of Economics*, 17, 18–32.

Milgrom, P. & J. Roberts (1990). Bargaining Costs, Influence Costs and the Organization of Economic Activity, in J. Alt & K. Shepsle (eds), *Perspectives on Positive Political Economy* (pp. 57–89). Cambridge: Cambridge University Press.

Mill, J. S. (1844). *Elements of Political Economy.* London: Baldwin.

Mill, J. S. (1863) [1891]. *Utilitarianism.* London: Longmans.

Miller, D. (1992). Deliberative Democracy and Social Choice, *Political Studies*, 40(s1), 54–67.

Miller, N. (1980). A New Solution Set for Tournaments and Majority Voting: Further Graph-Theoretical Approaches to the Theory of Voting, *American Journal of Political Science*, 24(1), 68–96.

Miller, N. (2007). In Search of the Uncovered Set. *Political Analysis*, 15(1), 21–45.

Miller, N. R. (2014). The Spatial Model of Social Choice and Voting, in J. C. Heckelman & N. R. Miller (eds), Elgar Handbook of Social Choice and Voting. Northampton, MA: Edward Elgar.

Mitzen J. (2006). Ontological Security in World Politics: State Identity and the Security Dilemma, *European Journal of International Relations*, 12, (3), 341–42.

Mohammad, S. & Whalley, J. (1984). Rent Seeking in India: Its Costs and Significance, *Kyklos*, 37, 387–413.

Monroe, K. (1991). The Theory of Rational Action, in W. Crotty (ed.), *Political Science: Looking to the Future*. Evanston, IL: Northwestern University Press.

Moon, W. (2004). Party Activists, Campaign Resources and Candidate Position Taking: Theory, Tests and Applications, *British Journal of Political Science*, 34(04), 611–33. doi:10.1017/S0007123404000213.

Morgan, J., Steiglitz, K. & Reis, G. (2003). The Spite Motive and Equilibrium Behavior in Auctions. *Contributions in Economic Analysis & Policy*, 2(1), 1102–27.

Morgenstern, O. and Neumann, J. (1944), *Theory of Games and Economic Behaviour*. Princeton: Princeton University Press.

Mueller, D. (1993). The Future of Public Choice, *Public Choice*, 77, 145–50.

Mueller, D. C. (2003). *Public Choice III*. New York: Cambridge University Press.

Mueller, W. & Strøm, K. (2005), 'Coalition Agreements and Models of Coalition Governance', in Strøm, K. Muller, W. & Bergman, T. (eds), *Coalition Governance in Parliamentary Democracies*. Oxford: Oxford University Press.

Mulholland, S. E. (2010). Hate Fuel: On the Relationship Between Local Government Policy and Hate Group Activity, *Eastern Economic Journal*, 36(4), 480–99.

Mulligan, C. B. & Hunter, C. G. (2003). The Empirical Frequency of a Pivotal Vote, *Public Choice*, 116(1–2), 31–54. doi:10.1023/A:1024244329828.

Nelson, R. H. (2005). *Private Neighborhoods and the Transformation of Local Government*. Washington, DC: Urban Institute Press.

Niemi, R. G. (1969). Majority Decision-making with Partial Unidimensionality, *The American Political Science Review*, 488–97.

Niskanen, W. (1971). *Bureaucracy and Representative Government*. Chicago: Aldine Atherton.

Niskanen, W. (1991), A Reflection on Bureaucracy and Representative Government, in Blais, A. & Dion, S. (eds) *The Budget-Maximizing Bureaucrat* (pp. 13–33). Pittsburgh: University of Pittsburgh Press.

Niskanen, W. A. (2012). Gordon Tullock's Contribution to Bureaucracy, *Public Choice*, 152(1–2), 97–101.

Nordhaus, W. D. (1994). *Managing the Global Commons: The Economics of Climate Change.* Cambridge: MIT Press.

North, D. (1990). *Institutions, Institutional Change and Economic Performance.* Cambridge: Cambridge University Press.

Nyblade, B. (2013). Government Formation in Parliamentary Democracies, in W. C. Müller & H. M. Narud (eds), *Party Governance and Party Democracy* (pp. 13–31). New York: Springer. Retrieved from http://link.springer.com/chapter/10.1007/978-1-4614-6588-1_2.

Oates, W. E. (1972). *Fiscal Federalism.* New York: Harcourt Brace Jovanovich.

Olson, M. (1965). The Logic of Collective Action: Public Goods and the Theory of Groups (2nd edition). Cambridge: Harvard University Press.

Olson, M. (1982). *The Rise and Decline of Nations: Economic Growth, Stagflation, and Social Rigidities.* New Haven, CT: Yale University Press.

Olson, M. (1990). *How Bright are the Northern Lights?: Some Questions About Sweden.* Lund: Institute of Economic Research.

Olson, M. (1993). Dictatorship, Democracy, and Development, *American Political Science Review*, 87(3), 567–76.

Ordeshook, P. & Shvetsova, O. (1994). Ethnic Heterogeneity, District Magnitude and the Number of Parties, *American Journal of Political Science*, 38, 100–23.

Ostrom, E. (1990). *Governing the Commons: The Evolution of Institutions for Collective Action.* Cambridge: Cambridge University Press.

Ostrom, E. (1998). A Behavioral Approach to the Rational Choice Theory of Collective Action, *The American Political Science Review*, 92(1), 1–22.

Ostrom, E. (2000). Collective Action and the Evolution of Social Norms, *The Journal of Economic Perspectives*, 14(3), 137–58.

Ostrom, E. (2005). *Understanding Institutional Diversity.* Princeton: Princeton University Press.

Ostrom, E. (2010a). Beyond Markets and States: Polycentric Governance of Complex Economic Systems, *The American Economic Review*, 100(3), 641–72.

Ostrom, E. (2010b). Polycentric systems for coping with collective action and global environmental change, *Global Environmental Change*, 20(4), 550–57.

Ostrom, E. (2012). Nested Externalities and Polycentric Institutions: Must We Wait for Global Solutions to Change Before Taking Actions at Other Scales? *Economic Theory*, 49(2), 353–69.

Ostrom, E. & Cox, M. (2010). Moving Beyond Panaceas: A Multi-tiered Diagnostic Approach for Social-ecological Analysis, *Environmental Conservation*, 37(4), 451–63.

Ostrom, V., Tiebout, C. M. & Warren, R. (1961). The Organization of Government in Metropolitan Areas: A Theoretical Inquiry, *The American Political Science Review*, 55(4), 831–42.

Overbye, E. (1995). Making a Case for the Rational, Self-regarding, 'ethical' Voter … and Solving the 'Paradox of not voting' in the Process, *European Journal of Political Research*, 27(3), 369–96.

Page, B. I. & Shapiro, R. Y. (1992). *The Rational Public: Fifty Years of Trends in Americans' Policy Preferences*. Chicago: University of Chicago Press.

Page, B. & Shapiro, R. Y. (1993). The Rational Public and Democracy, in G. E. Marcus & R. L. Hanson (eds), *Reconsidering the Democratic Public* (pp. 35–64). University Park: Pennsylvania State University Press.

Pareto, V. (1909). *Manual of Political Economy*. Paris: Girad.

Pennington, M. (2010). Democracy and the Deliberative Conceit, *Critical Review*, 22(2–3), 159–84.

Persson, T., Tabellini, G. & Trebbi, F. (2003). Electoral Rules and Corruption, *Journal of the European Economic Association*, 1(4), 958–89.

Pesendorfer, W. (2006). Behavioral Economics Comes of Age: A Review Essay on Advances in Behavioral Economics, *Journal of Economic Literature*, 44(3), 712–21.

Pincione, G. & Tesón, F. R. (2006). *Rational Choice and Democratic Deliberation: A Theory of Discourse Failure*. Cambridge: Cambridge University Press.

Pinker, S. (1994). *The Language Instinct: How the Mind Creates Language*. New York: W. Morrow.

Pitkin, H. (1967). *The Concept of Representation*. Berkeley: University of California Press.

Plott, C. R. (1967). A Notion of Equilibrium and its Possibility Under Majority Rule, *The American Economic Review*, 57(4), 787–806.

Plott, C. R. (2014). Public Choice and the Development of Modern Laboratory Experimental Methods in Economics and Political Science. California Institute of Technology Working Paper No. 1383.

Popkin, S. (1979). *The Rational Peasant*. Berkeley: University of California Press.

Popkin, S. L. (1991). *The Reasoning Voter: Communication and Persuasion in Presidential Campaigns*. Chicago: University of Chicago Press.

Popper, K. (1959). *The Logic of Scientific Discovery*. London: Hutchinson.

Popper, K. (1960). *The Poverty of Historicism*. London: Routledge & Keegan Paul.

Posner, R. (1975). The Social Costs of Monopoly and Regulation, *Journal of Political Economy*, 83, 807–27.

Poteete, A. R., Janssen, M. A. & Ostrom, E. (2010). *Working Together: Collective Action, the Commons, and Multiple Methods in Practice.* Princeton: Princeton University Press.

Powell, B. & Stringham, E. P. (2009). Public Choice and the Economic Analysis of Anarchy: A Survey, *Public Choice*, 140(3/4), 503–38.

Prior, M. & Lupia, A. (2008). Money, Time, and Political Knowledge: Distinguishing Quick Recall and Political Learning Skills, *American Journal of Political Science*, 52(1), 169–83. doi:10.1111/j.1540-5907.2007.00306.x.

Prior, M., Sood, G. & Khanna, K. (2013). You Cannot be Serious: Do Partisans Believe What They Say? Princeton University. Retrieved from http://www.vanderbilt.edu/csdi/events/MPrior.pdf.

Quackenbush, S. (2004). The Rationality of Rational Choice Theory, *International Interactions*, 30, 87–107.

Rabin, M. (1993). Incorporating Fairness into Game Theory and Economics, *The American Economic Review*, 83(5), 1281–302.

Rawls, J. (1971). *A Theory of Justice.* Cambridge: Harvard University Press.

Reynolds, A., Reilly, B. & Ellis, A. (2005). Electoral System Design: The New International IDEA Handbook. Stockholm: International Institute for Democracy and Electoral Assistance. Retrieved from https://saylor.long-sight.com/handle/1/12708.

Ricardo, D. (1817) [1912] *The Principles of Political Economy and Taxation.* London: Dent.

Riker, W. H. (1957). Events and Situations, *Journal of Philosophy*, 54, 57–70.

Riker, W. H. (1961). Voting and the Summation of Preferences: An Interpretive Bibliographic Overview of Selected Developments, *American Political Science Review*, 55, 900–11.

Riker, W. H. (1962). *The Theory of Political Coalitions.* New Haven, CT: Yale University Press.

Riker, W. H. (1965). Arrow's Theorem and Some Examples of the Paradox of Voting, in J. Claunch (ed.), *Mathematical Applications in Political Science* (pp. 41–60). Dallas: The Arnold Foundation.

Riker, W. H. (1980). Implications from the Disequilibrium of Majority Rule for the Study of Institutions. The American Political Science Review, 74(2), 432–46. doi:10.2307/1960638.

Riker, W. H. (1982a). *Liberalism Against Populism: A Confrontation Between the Theory of Theory of Democracy and the Theory of Social Choice.* San Francisco: W. H. Freeman.

Riker, W. H. (1982b). The Two-Party System and Duverger's Law: An Essay on the History of Political Science, *American Political Science Review*, 76, 753–66.

Riker, W. H. (1984). The Heresthetics of Constitution-Making: The Presidency in 1787, *American Political Science Review*, 78, 96–111.

Riker, W. H. (1986). *The Art of Political Manipulation.* New Haven, CT: Yale University Press.

Riker, W. H. (1990). Political Science and Rational Choice, in J. Alt & K. Shepsle (eds), *Perspectives on Positive Political Economy* (pp. 163–91). Cambridge: Cambridge University Press.

Riker, W. H. (1996). *The Strategy of Rhetoric: Campaigning for the American Constitution.* New Haven, CT: Yale University Press.

Riker, W. H. & Ordeshook, P. C. (1968). A Theory of the Calculus of Voting. *The American Political Science Review,* 62(1), 25–42.

Riker, W. H. & Weingast, B. (1988). Constitutional Regulation of Legislative Choice: The Political Consequences of Judicial Deference to Legislatures, *Virginia Law Review,* 74, 373–402.

Roback, J. (1986). The Political Economy of Segregation: The Case of Segregated Streetcars, *Journal of Economic History,* 46(4), 893–917.

Robbins, L. (1932). *An Essay on the Nature and Significance of Economic Science.* London: Palgrave Macmillan.

Robbins, L. (1971). *Autobiography of an Economist.* London: Macmillan.

Rosenberg, A. (1992). *Economics – Mathematical Politics or Science of Diminishing Returns.* Chicago: University of Chicago Press.

Rosenberg, A. (2000). *Philosophy of Science.* London: Routledge.

Rothstein, B. (2005). *Social Traps and the Problem of Trust.* Cambridge: Cambridge University Press.

Ruben, D. (1990). *Explaining Explanation.* London: Routledge.

Rubinstein, A. (2012). *Economic Fables.* Cambridge: Open Book Publishers.

Runciman, W. (1963). *Social Science and Political Theory.* Cambridge: Cambridge University Press.

Saari, D. G. (2000), Mathematical Structure of Voting Paradoxes: Positional Voting, *Economic Theory,* 15, 55–102.

Saari, D. G. (2008). *Disposing Dictators, Demystifying Voting Paradoxes.* Cambridge: Cambridge University Press.

Samuelson, P. A. (1947). *Foundations of Economic Analysis.* Cambridge: Harvard University Press.

Sánchez-Cuenca, I. (2008). A Preference for Selfish Preferences: The Problem of Motivations in Rational Choice Political Science, *Philosophy of the Social Sciences,* 38, 361–78.

Sanders, D., Clarke, H. D., Stewart, M. C. & Whiteley, P. (2008). The Endogeneity of Preferences in Spatial Models: Evidence from the 2005 British Election Study, *Journal of Elections, Public Opinion & Parties,* 18(4), 413–31. doi:10.1080/17457280802305235.

Sandler, T. (2004). *Global Collective Action.* Cambridge: Cambridge University Press.

Sartori, G. (1976). *Parties and Party Systems: A Framework for Analysis.* Cambridge: Cambridge University Press.

Satterthwaite, M. (1975). Strategy-Proofness and Arrow's Conditions, *Journal of Economic Theory,* 10, 187–217.

Satz, D. & Ferejohn, J. (1994). Rational Choice and Social Theory. *Journal of Philosophy,* 91, 71–87.

Schelling, T. (1978). *Micromotives and Macrobehaviour.* New York: W. H. Norton.

Schofield, N. (1993). Political Competition and Multiparty Coalition Governments, *European Journal of Political Research,* 23, 1–33.

Schotter, A. (2006). Strong and Wrong: The Use of Rational Choice Theory in Experimental Economics, *Journal of Theoretical Politics,* 18, 498–511.

Schumpeter, J. A. (1942). *Capitalism, Socialism and Democracy.* New York: Harper & Row.

Schwarzman, D. (1960). The Burden of Monopoly, *Journal of Political Economy,* 68, 727–29.

Searle, J. (2001). *Rationality in Action.* Cambridge: MIT Press.

Self, P. (1993). *Government by the Market.* Basingstoke: Palgrave Macmillan.

Sen, A. K. (1970a). Interpersonal Aggregation and Partial Comparability, *Econometrica,* 38(3), 393–409. doi:10.2307/1909546.

Sen, A. K. (1970b). The Impossibility of a Paretian Liberal, *Journal of Political Economy,* 78(1), 152–57.

Sen, A. K. (1977). Rational Fools: A Critique of the Behavioural Foundations of Economic Theory, *Philosophy and Public Affairs,* 6, 317–44.

Sen, A. K. (1997). Maximization and the Act of Choice, *Econometrica,* 65(4), 745–79. doi:10.2307/2171939.

Sen, A. K. (1999). The Possibility of Social Choice, *American Economic Review,* 89(3), 349–78.

Sen, A. K. (2002). *Rationality and Freedom.* Cambridge, Mass.: Harvard University Press.

Sen, A. K. & Pattanaik, P. K. (1969). Necessary and Sufficient Conditions for Rational Choice Under Majority Decision, *Journal of Economic Theory,* 1(2), 178–202.

Shapiro, I. (2005). *The Flight from Reality in the Human Sciences.* Princeton: Princeton University Press.

Shapiro, I. (2009). *The State of Democratic Theory.* Princeton: Princeton University Press.

Shapley, L. & Shubik, M. (1954). A Method of Evaluating the Distribution of Power in a Committee System, *American Political Science Review,* 48, 787–92.

Shepsle, K. (1996b). Political Deals in Institutional Settings, in R. Goodin (ed.), *The Theory of Institutional Design* (pp. 227–39). Cambridge: Cambridge University Press.

Shepsle, K. (2006). Statistical Political Philosophy and Positive Political Theory, in Jeffrey Friedman (ed.), The *Rational Choice Controversy* (pp. 213–23). New Haven, CT: Yale University Press.

Shubik, M. (1971). The Dollar Auction Game: A Paradox in Noncooperative Behavior and Escalation, *Journal of Conflict Resolution,* 15(1), 109–11.

Simmons, R. T. (2011). *Beyond Politics: The Roots of Government Failure.* Oakland: Independent Institute.

Simon, H. (1957), *Models of Man*. New York: Wiley.

Simon, H. (1983). *Reason in Human Affairs*. Oxford: Basil Blackwells.

Singer, D. (1963). Inter-Nation Influence: A Formal Model, *American Political Science Review*, 57, 420–30.

Singh, S. P. (2010). Contextual Influences on the Decision Calculus: A Cross-national Examination of Proximity Voting, *Electoral Studies*, 29(3), 425–34. doi:10.1016/j.electstud.2010.03.014.

Skarbek, D. (2011). Governance and Prison Gangs, *American Political Science Review*, 105(4), 702–16.

Skarbek, D. (2014). *The Social Order of the Underworld: How Prison Gangs Govern the American Penal System*. New York: Oxford University Press.

Smart, M. & Sturm, D. M. (2013). Term Limits and Electoral Accountability, *Journal of Public Economics*, 107, 93–102. doi:10.1016/j.jpubeco.2013.08.011.

Smith, A. (1776) [1970], *The Wealth of Nations*. Harmondsworth: Penguin.

Smith, A. M. (1999). Public Opinion, Elections and Representation within a Market Economy: Does the Structural Power of Business Undermine Popular Sovereignty, *American Journal of Political Science*, 43, 842–63.

Smith, V. L. (2008). *Rationality in Economics: Constructivist and Ecological Forms*. Cambridge: Cambridge University Press.

Sober, E. (1984). *The Nature of Selection: Evolutionary Theory in Philosophical Focus*. Chicago: University of Chicago Press.

Somin, I. (2013). *Democracy and Political Ignorance: Why Smaller Government is Smarter*. Stanford: Stanford University Press.

Starr, R. M. (2008). Arrow, Kenneth Joseph (born 1921), in L. Blume & S. Durlauf (eds), The New Palgrave Dictionary of Economics Online. London: Palgrave Macmillan. Retrieved from http://www.dictionaryofeconomics.com/article?id=pde2008_K000067.

Steinmo, S. (2008). What is Historical Institutionalism?, in D. Della Porta & M. Keating (eds), *Approaches in the Social Sciences* (pp. 118–38). Cambridge: Cambridge University Press.

Stern, N. (2007). *The Economics of Climate Change: The Stern Review*. Cambridge University Press.

Stigler, G. J. (1961). The Economics of Information, *The Journal of Political Economy*, 69(3), 213–25.

Stigler, G. J. (1972). Economic Competition and Political Competition, *Public Choice*, 13(1), 91–106.

Stratmann, T. (2005). Some Talk: Money in Politics. A (Partial) Review of the Literature, *Public Choice*, 124(1), 135–56.

Stretton, H. & Orchard, L. (1994). *Public Goods, Public Enterprise, Public Choice*. Basingstoke: Palgrave Macmillan.

Strøm, K. (1990). *Minority Government and Majority Rule*. Cambridge: Cambridge University Press.

Strøm, K., Müller, W. C. & Smith, D. M. (2010). Parliamentary Control of Coalition Governments, *Annual Review of Political Science*, 13(1), 517–35. doi:10.1146/annurev.polisci.10.071105.104340.

Stubager, R. (2003). Preference-Shaping: An Empirical Test, *Political Studies*, 51, 241–61.

Sugden, R. (2000). Credible Worlds: the Status of Theoretical Models in Economics, *Journal of Economic Methodology*, 7, 1–31.

Sunstein, C. R. (2007). On the Divergent American Reactions to Terrorism and Climate Change, *Columbia Law Review*, 107(2), 503–57.

Swan, De. A. (1973). *Coalition Theory and Government Formations.* Amsterdam: Elsevier.

Taagepera, R. & Shugart, M. (1989). *Seats and Votes: The Effects and Determinants of Electoral Systems.* New Haven, CT: Yale University Press.

Taber, C. S. & Lodge, M. (2006). Motivated Skepticism in the Evaluation of Political Beliefs, *American Journal of Political Science*, 50(3), 755–69.

Taber, C. S., Lodge, M. & Glathar, J. (2001). The Motivated Construction of Political Judgments, in J. H. Kuklinski (ed.), *Citizens and Politics: Perspectives from Political Psychology* (pp. 198–226). London: Cambridge University Press.

Taylor, B. R. (2014). Exit and the Epistemic Quality of Voice. Working Paper, Australian National University.

Taylor, M. (1982). *Community, Anarchy and Liberty.* Cambridge: Cambridge University Press.

Taylor, M. (1987). *The Possibility of Cooperation.* London: Wiley.

Taylor, M. (2006). *Rationality and the Ideology of Disconnection.* Cambridge: Cambridge University Press.

Taylor, M. & Ward, H. (1982). Chickens, Whales and Lumpy Goods: Alternative Models of Public Good Provision, *Political Studies*, 30, 350–70.

Thelen, K. (1999). Historical Institutionalism in Comparative Politics, *Annual Review of Political Science*, 2, 369–404.

Thelen, K. (2004). *How Institutions Evolve: The Political Economy of Skills in Germany, Britain, the United States and Japan.* Cambridge: Cambridge University Press.

Thies, M. (2001). Keeping Tabs on Partners: The Logic of Delegation in Coalition Governments, *American Journal of Political Science*, 45, 580–98.

Thomson, W. (2001). On the Axiomatic Method and its Recent Applications to Game Theory and Resource Allocation, *Social Choice and Welfare*, 18(2), 327–86.

Tiebout, C. M. (1956). A Pure Theory of Local Expenditures, *The Journal of Political Economy*, 64(5), 416–24.

Tilly, C. (1985). War Making and State Making as Organized Crime, in P. B. Evans, D. Rueschemeyer & T. Skocpol (eds), *Bringing the State Back in* (pp. 169–91). Cambridge: Cambridge University Press.

Treasury Committee [House of Commons]. 2009. *Banking Crisis: Reforming Corporate Governance and Pay in the City,* HC 519, Ninth Report of Session 2008–2009.

Truman, D. (1951). *The Governmental Process.* New York: Alfred & Knopf.

Trumbull, G. (2012). *Strength in Numbers: The Political Power of Weak Interests.* Cambridge: Harvard University Press.

Tullock, G. (1965). *The Politics of Bureaucracy.* Boston: University Press of America.

Tullock, G. (1966). *The Politics of Bureaucracy.* Washington D.C.: Public Affairs Press.

Tullock, G. (1967). The General Irrelevance of the General Impossibility Theorem, *The Quarterly Journal of Economics,* 81(2), 256–70. doi:10.2307/1879585.

Tullock, G. (1971). The Charity of the Uncharitable, *Western Economic Journal,* 9(4), 379–92.

Tullock, G. (1980). Efficient Rent Seeking, in J. Buchanan, R. Tollison & G. Tullock (eds), *Toward a Theory of the Rent-Seeking Society.* College Station: Texas A & M.

Tullock, G. (1987). The Calculus: Postscript After 25 Years, *Cato Journal,* 7(2), 313–21.

Tullock, G. (1989). *The Economics of Special Privilege and Rent Seeking.* Boston: Kluwer Academic.

Tullock, G. (1990). *The Economics of Special Privilege,* in J. Alt & K. Shepsle (eds), *Perspectives on Positive Political Economy* (pp. 195–211). Cambridge: Cambridge University Press.

Tullock, G. (1993). Rent Seeking, in C. Rowley (ed.), *Property Rights and the Limits of Democracy.* Aldershot: Edward Elgar.

Tullock, G., Brady, G. & Seldon, A. (2002). People Are People: The Elements of Public Choice, in *Government Failure: A Primer in Public Choice* (pp. 3–16). Washington, DC: Cato Institute.

Tullock, G. (2006). *The Vote Motive.* London: Institute of Economic Affairs.

Turnovec, F. (2008). Duality of Power in the European Parliament. Institute of Economic Studies, Working Paper, 6/200, Charles University, Prague.

Tversky, A. & Kahneman, D. (1974). Judgment Under Uncertainty: Heuristics and Biases, *Science,* 185(4157), 1124–131.

Vanberg, V. (2008). On the Economics of Moral Preferences, *American Journal of Economics and Sociology,* 67, 605–28.

Van Parijs, P. (2004). Basic Income: A Simple and Powerful Idea for the Twenty-first Century, *Politics & Society,* 32(1), 7–39.

Voigt, S. (1999). Implicit Constitutional Change: Changing the Meaning of the Constitution Without Changing the Text of the Document, *European Journal of Law and Economics,* 7(3), 197–224.

Warwick, P. (1999). Ministerial Autonomy or Ministerial Accommodation? Contested Bases of Government Survival in Parliamentary Democracies, *British Journal of Political Science,* 29, 369–94.

Weale, A. (1999). *Democracy.* Manchester: Manchester University Press.

Weingast, B. R. (2005). Persuasion, Preference Change, and Critical Junctures: The Microfoundations of a Macroscopic Concept, in I. Katznelson & B. R. Weingast (eds), *Preferences and Situations: Points of Intersection Between Historical and Rational Choice Institutionalism* (pp. 161–84). New York: The Russell Sage Foundation.

Weingest, B. & Marshall, W. (1988). The Industrial Organization of Congress: Or, Why, Legislatures, like Firms, are not Organized as Markets, *Journal of Political Economy*, 96, 132–64.

Williamson, O. (1975). *Markets and Hierarchies.* New York: Free Press.

Witt, U. & Schubert, C. (2008). Constitutional Interests in the Face of Innovations: How Much Do We Need to Know About Risk Preferences? *Constitutional Political Economy*, 19(3), 203–25. doi:10.1007/s10602-008-9044-6.

Wittman, D. (1977). Candidates with Policy Preferences: A Dynamic Model, *Journal of Economic Theory*, 14, 180–89.

Wittman, D. (1989). Why Democracies Produce Efficient Results, *The Journal of Political Economy*, 97(6), 1395–424.

Wittman, D. (1995). *The Myth of Democratic Failure: Why Political Institutions are Efficient.* Chicago: University of Chicago Press.

Wolff, R. (1970). *In Defence of Anarchism.* New York: Harper & Row.

World Public Opinion (2010). American Public Opinion on Foreign Aid, November. Retrieved from http://www.worldpublicopinion.org/pipa/pdf/nov10/ForeignAid_Nov10_quaire.pdf.

Yandle, B. (1983). Bootleggers and Baptists: The Education of a Regulatory Economist, *Regulation*, 7(3), 12–16.

Index